MIGRATIONS

a history of where
we all come from

MIGRATIONS

a history of where we all come from

Foreword by
David Olusoga

DK LONDON

Senior Editor Kathryn Hennessy
Project Editor Abigail Mitchell
Editors Polly Boyd, Anna Cheifetz, Lydia Halliday, Scarlett O'Hara, Victoria Pyke, Helen Ridge, Lucy Sienkowska, Debra Wolter
Senior Art Editor Mark Cavanagh
Managing Editor Gareth Jones
Senior Managing Art Editor Lee Griffiths
Picture Research Sarah Smithies
Senior Production Editor Andy Hilliard
Production Controller Rachel Ng
Senior Jackets Designer Surabhi Wadhwa-Gandhi
Design Development Manager Sophia M.T.T.
Associate Publishing Director Liz Wheeler
Art Director Karen Self
Publishing Director Jonathan Metcalf

DK DELHI

Project Editor Tina Jindal
Editor Aashirwad Jain
Senior Art Editors Vikas Sachdeva, Ira Sharma
Art Editors Anukriti Arora, Tanvi Sahu
Assistant Art Editor Ankita Das
Assistant Picture Researchers Meenakshi Nihlani, Vagisha Pushp
Senior Picture Researcher Surya Sankash Sarangi
Picture Research Manager Taiyaba Khatoon
Senior Cartographer Mohammad Hassan
Cartography Manager Suresh Kumar
Managing Editor Soma B. Chowdhury
Senior Managing Art Editor Arunesh Talapatra
Senior DTP Designers Harish Aggarwal, Vishal Bhatia
DTP Designer Vijay Kandwal
Pre-production Manager Balwant Singh
Production Manager Pankaj Sharma
Jackets Editorial Coordinator Priyanka Sharma
DK India Editorial Head Glenda Fernandes
DK India Design Head Malavika Talukder

First published in Great Britain in 2022 by
Dorling Kindersley Limited,
DK, One Embassy Gardens, 8 Viaduct Gardens,
London, SW11 7BW

For the curious
www.dk.com

This book was made with Forest Stewardship Council™ certified paper – one small step in DK's commitment to a sustainable future. For more information go to www.dk.com/our-green-pledge

FSC
www.fsc.org
MIX
Paper from responsible sources
FSC™ C018179

The First Migrations
Prehistory

Professor David Olusoga OBE is a British-Nigerian historian, broadcaster, and filmmaker. His TV series include *A House Through Time* (BBC2), *Black and British: A Forgotten History* (BBC2), and the BAFTA Award-winning *Britain's Forgotten Slave Owners* (BBC2). David is also the author of *Black and British: A Forgotten History*, which was awarded both the Longman-History Today Trustees' Award and the PEN Hessell-Tiltman Prize. He writes for *The Guardian*, is a columnist for *The Observer*, and is Professor of Public History at the University of Manchester.

Ancient Empires
c. 2600 BCE–375 CE

Transcontinental Contact
375–1400 CE

CONSULTANT AND CONTRIBUTOR

Philip Parker is a critically-acclaimed author, editor, and historian specializing in the classical and medieval world. He holds a diploma in international relations from Johns Hopkins University's School of Advanced International Studies.

SPECIALIST CONSULTANTS

Anoushka Alexander-Rose is a Postgraduate Researcher in English at the University of Southampton, UK, with the Parkes Institute for the Study of Jewish/non-Jewish Relations.

Dr. Vivian Delgado (Yaqui/Tiwa-Tewa) is an Assistant Professor in the Languages and Indigenous Studies department at Bemidji State University, Minnesota.

Dr. Gabriela Ramos is an Associate Professor of Latin American History at the University of Cambridge, where she is also Director of the Centre of Latin American Studies. Her work focuses particularly on the Andean region.

Frank Starling is a Diversity, Equity, and Inclusion specialist and journalist. In 2020, he was named one of the leading Black figures by the Pathways to Success leadership programme.

Colonization and Conquest
1400–1800

Mass Movement and Freedoms
1700–1900

CONTRIBUTORS

John Farndon is a poet, songwriter, and author of over 1,000 books, including many DK titles. He is also an award-winning translator of Eurasian literature and a councillor of the Eurasian People's Assembly.

Mireille Harper is an award-winning editor, writer, authenticity reader, and communications consultant. Her work has been published in *Vogue*, *Digital Spy*, *Good Housekeeping*, and more. She contributed to DK's *Timelines of Everyone* and *The Black History Book*, and is the author of *Timelines from Black History*.

Yuka Maeno is a writer and a Japanese–English literary and subtitle translator now based in Ireland. She has contributed to various publications in the UK and Japan, and is the translator of *Ground* by Tomoko Sasaki.

Shafik Meghji is an award-winning travel writer, journalist and author. Specializing in Latin America and South Asia, he writes for publications such as *BBC Travel*, *Wanderlust*, and *Lonely Planet*; has co-authored more than 40 guidebooks for *DK Eyewitness* and *Rough Guides*; and talks about travel on TV, radio, and podcasts.

Decolonization and Diasporas
1900 onwards

Chitra Ramaswamy is an award-winning freelance journalist, author, and broadcaster. Her second book, *Homelands: The History of A Friendship* tells the story of an unlikely friendship between the daughter of Indian immigrants and a Jewish Kindertransport refugee.

George Swainston studied Arabic and Persian at the University of Oxford. He is a broadcast journalist, podcast producer, and documentary filmmaker with a particular interest in the history of the Middle East and Africa, having lived and worked in both. He was a contributor to DK's *The Black History Book*.

Phillip Tang is a travel writer who grew up in Marrickville, Sydney, moved to Melbourne to study Chinese and Spanish at Monash University, and has lived in London and Mexico City. He has written for *Lonely Planet*, *Rough Guides*, *BBC Travel*, and others.

Ben White is a journalist, analyst, and author, with over 400 articles published in media outlets including *The Independent* and *Al Jazeera*. He is the author of four books on the Israeli–Palestinian conflict, and previously worked as a researcher and writer for the Journal of Palestine Studies (University of California Press).

Vietnamese refugees board the USS *Montague* from a French landing ship at Haiphong in 1954, at the beginning of the Vietnam War.

Foreword

Migration is one of the biggest stories in all of human history and a phenomenon that is set to shape the world in the 21st-century. It began over 100,000 years ago when our human ancestors first emerged in Africa, and it was through migration that humans came to occupy most of the world – with migrant communities making epic journeys across land, and dangerous voyages over the great oceans in simple wooden ships and boats.

As migration has always been part of the human story, we live in a world that has been shaped by it in multiple ways. Languages, cultures, and religions have been transmitted across the world by migration, brought by both refugees and colonizers who built empires. Many of the foods we now grow and eat became part of our diets after they were introduced by migrants. Across the world millions of people have ancestors who, at one time or another, were migrants, while millions live in nations – like the United States and Australia – that were founded by migrants, who outnumbered the Indigenous people and stripped them of their land. Migration is so old and so vast a story that it is a background reality to our world.

There are aspects of history that are not always recognized as stories of migration and yet the resettlement of people was fundamental to them. The Industrial Revolution that began in England in the 18th century marked the beginning of one of the most important forms of migration: the movement of people from the countryside to the cities. By the middle of the 1900s, Britain had become the first country in which more people lived in the cities than the countryside. In recent decades, almost 500 million people in China have made that same journey from rural villages to urban centres. Today, the majority of the world's population live in cities.

As this book reveals, not all global migrations were voluntary. The Atlantic Slave Trade, and the trades in enslaved Africans across the Sahara Desert and the Indian Ocean, were among the greatest crimes against humanity ever committed. They can also be seen as part of a wider trend of forced migration. After slavery was brought to an end, the British Empire encouraged thousands of people from India to travel huge distances to do the work once carried out by enslaved Africans, and later to build new railways lines. Chinese people also became migrant workers in the empires built by the European nations.

Many migrations have led to the displacement and then involuntary migration of Indigenous peoples. For example, the European colonists who created new settlements in North America forced the Indigenous peoples to migrate, sometimes to reservations, their original homelands given over to new settlers.

Today, many nations rely upon migrants as workers and without them their economies could not properly operate. Many of those migrants retain strong ties to their countries of origin and millions of them regularly send money back to members of their family who still live in the countries from which they migrated. These payments are called remittances. For some of the world's poorer countries remittances represent a large proportion of their national income.

In the 21st century, migrants leave their countries of origin for many of the same reasons that people have always left – to find work and build better lives for themselves and their families, or to escape from wars and conflicts. However, a new form of "climate migration" has started to change migration patterns. As the climate of the world starts to change, with sea levels rising and farmland in parts of the world becoming too dry to support crops and animals, millions of people are at risk of losing their homes and their livelihoods. Migration and climate change are becoming ever more interconnected and climate migration may well shape the future of our world.

DAVID OLUSOGA

1

The First Migrations

PREHISTORY

The First Migrations

PREHISTORY

Almost as soon as human ancestors evolved in the forest fringes of East Africa's grasslands, they began to migrate. One group, *Homo erectus,* left Africa around 2 million years ago, reaching as far as East Asia. Modern humans, *Homo sapiens,* left the continent in two waves. The first movement, around 100,000 years ago, was unsuccessful, but in the second, from 60,000 years ago, *Homo sapiens* walked into West Asia and beyond. Generation by generation they pushed further, reaching Australia around 55,000 years ago and East Asia shortly after, entering Europe by 48,000 years ago, and then, finally, crossing a land bridge from Siberia into the Americas over 20,000 years ago. These earliest migrants moved in search of better hunting grounds and prospects, sometimes driven by climate change or the hostility of other groups. They were nomadic peoples, who lived in tents or other structures that could be dismantled as they went, and travelled on foot or using simple boats.

Around 9000 BCE, more permanent settlements developed in the Middle East, as humans began to plant grain crops such as emmer (an early form of wheat), and

***Homo erectus**, the first humans to leave Africa, use tools and fire (see pp.16–19)

This First Australian rock art dates back 50,000 years (see pp.16–19)

"Our DNA does not fade like an ancient parchment... It is the traveller from an ancient land who lives within us all."

Brian Sykes, *The Seven Daughters of Eve: The Science that Reveals our Genetic Ancestry*, 2001

reared animals like goats, cattle, and sheep. These peoples established farming villages in this Middle Eastern "Fertile Crescent", while agriculture developed later, separately, in China and the Americas. With the expansion of fixed settlements, tensions arose between neighbouring groups of farmers, who now had resources to defend.

As cities and empires rose and prospered in Egypt, Mesopotamia, India, and China from 3000 BCE, clashes also erupted amid increasingly complex societies – made up of craftspeople, rulers, and warriors – and nomadic groups, who roamed around and attacked permanent settlements. Such conflicts led to the first refugees fleeing warfare, while larger groups of people were forced – often by violent means – to migrate when others moved into their territory. Now armed with the first metal weapons of bronze, and travelling with the aid of domesticated animals such as the donkey, the horse, or in the Americas, the llama, and by seaworthy boats, migrants could travel faster and further, covering in months distances their ancestors had taken generations to achieve.

Ancient migrants are depicted in San rock paintings (see pp.20–21)

The Sea Peoples battle the Egyptians under Ramesses II (see pp.26–27)

The first humans

MIGRATION OUT OF AFRICA

Our earliest ancestors (collectively known as hominins) originated in eastern Africa around 6–7 million years ago, when the hominin lineage diverged from that of chimpanzees to walk upright on two legs. The process was very gradual. Early hominins (*Sahelanthropus*, *Orrorin*, and *Ardipithecus*) were still ape-like; they lived mainly in trees, and had a grasping foot, but their skeletons show they may also have walked upright.

A 28-metre-long trail of footprints left in volcanic ash at Laetoli, Tanzania, 3.6 million years ago revealed a species that walked upright most of the time, although given its long forearms, fingers, and toes it probably did not walk far and still climbed trees. It was identified as *Australopithecus afarensis* (like the skeleton named "Lucy", found in Ethiopia).

Venturing beyond Africa

By around 1.8 million years ago, the fully terrestrial *Homo erectus* had evolved in Africa. Among the evidence for this is the fossil of "Turkana Boy", dating to 1.6 million years ago, found in Kenya. The body proportions are more like those of a modern human, with elongated legs and shorter arms, which meant this species could walk further than its ancestors. It also had a larger brain and used tools. Unlike its predecessors, *Homo erectus* travelled beyond the continent, possibly in search of food, or as environmental conditions changed. They migrated to the Middle East, reaching modern-day Jordan by 1.1 to 1.4 million years ago. From there, they moved into China and Indonesia.

Until the 1940s, archaeologists believed that *Homo erectus* evolved into our species, *Homo sapiens,* in different regions of the world at the same time. However, experts now believe that *Homo sapiens* evolved first in Africa about 300,000 years ago, and then migrated in waves, supplanting other ancestral species (the "Out of Africa" theory). The first of these migrations dates to 100,000–200,000 years ago. These early pioneers went northeast, along the coast from modern-day Israel to Syria. However, this wave appears to have died out. A second wave took place about 60,000 years ago, probably along a southern route via modern-day Yemen (see pp.16–19). Everyone outside Africa is a descendant of those who left in this second wave.

At the time of these migrations, *Homo sapiens* still shared the planet with other human species – Neanderthals, who evolved in Europe and Asia, and Denisovans, who had settled around 400,000 years ago in Siberia, and then spread south into Southeast Asia and Melanesia. Both these species interbred in due course with *Homo sapiens.*

Our common ancestor

Scientists can trace the evolution and movement of human groups from common elements in their DNA passed down through many generations. Mitochondrial DNA passed down only through the female line indicates that every human alive today shares DNA from one female ancestor who lived in southern Africa about 200,000 years ago. Nicknamed "Mitochondrial Eve", she is not our only ancestor, but she is related to us all.

▲ **Migration from Africa** by *Homo sapiens* may have followed the routes shown on this map, according to genetic and archaeological evidence.

▼ **Footprints found at Laetoli**, Tanzania, are the earliest signs that ancestral species moved through the landscape on two legs by the Plio-Pleistocene era, over 3 million years ago.

▼ **This painting** depicts *Homo erectus* by Lake Turkana, Kenya, about one million years ago. Already, they were making use of fire for warmth and cooking.

> "Mitochondrial Eve lived in Africa, so, in a very real way, we are all Africans."
>
> Desmond Tutu,
> *The Book of Forgiving*, 2014

This illustration of an early *Homo sapiens* is based on 300,000-year-old fossils, found at Jebel Irhoud in Morocco.

Peopling the globe

HOMO SAPIENS IN ASIA, EUROPE, AND OCEANIA

KEY
Time period
→ 100,000 ya
→ 50,000–35,000 ya
→ 35,000–20,000 ya
→ 20,000–10,000 ya
■ Covered by glacier
■ Approximate land area
during ice ages

Some time around 55,000 BCE, *Homo sapiens*, the first anatomically modern humans, left Africa and began a migration that would ultimately lead our species to populate almost every habitable area of Earth. A volcanic eruption near Lake Toba, now in Indonesia, that took place around 70,000 BCE, led to temporary but catastrophic climatic cooling. While this may have disrupted the human ancestral way of life – and reduced numbers to a genetic bottleneck of a few thousand individuals – conditions in East Africa were relatively benign. Bands of *Homo sapiens* clustered around sites such as the Magubike rock shelter in Tanzania, before a migration that took modern humans to continents around the world.

Across the straits

Perhaps attracted by the rich seafood resources to be found in coastal areas, *Homo sapiens* moved towards the shore and then crossed into West Asia. Some went north through the Sinai region into the Levant (*Homo sapiens* specimens have been found in Israel, at Manot Cave, dating to 54,700 BCE), though the majority probably crossed into modern-day Yemen using the Bab el Mandeb Strait – then much narrower because sea levels were lower, and traversable in small boats or rafts.

From this Middle Eastern region, progress along the coast towards South Asia was relatively rapid. Moving eastwards, *Homo sapiens* probably reached India first, then Southeast Asia, before turning northwards to China, where the earliest specimen found – unearthed in Tianyuan Cave near Zhoukoudian – dates to 40,000 BCE, and south to Indonesia, where the discovery of stone flake and chopper tools, and an adolescent male skeleton, show that early humans were living in Niah Cave on Sarawak by 38,000 BCE.

Colonizing Europe

Homo sapiens reached Europe by 42,000 BCE, crossing first into the Caucasus and Balkans, and then Central Europe, with a smaller stream possibly entering the Iberian Peninsula via the Strait of Gibraltar. They brought with them Aurignacian culture – a stone technology characterized by more sophisticated tools, such as nose-ended scrapers and blades with concave edges, and early representative art, such as the "Lion Man" ivory statuette, found in a cave in the Swabian Jura, in Germany.

These humans reached the northern European plain by 31,000 BCE, where they manufactured on a large scale beads for personal ornamentation, which were traded over hundreds of kilometres. By 29,000 years ago, they had developed more complex technologies, known as Gravettian culture, including projectile weapons, bone and antler tools, and basketry. Communities began to adopt a semi-sedentary lifestyle, with sites such as Dolní Věstonice in the modern-day Czech Republic occupied for several months a year. The discovery of some of the world's oldest known ceramics, including a "Venus" figurine (a statuette with large hips and breasts), as well as ivory carvings, indicate the artistic skill of its residents.

Homo sapiens were spreading out to settle ever more geographically remote areas, some of which took many years to colonize. In Britain, for example, the discovery of a skeleton at Kent's

◀ **This map** shows early humans' possible migration routes – eastwards out of Africa into Asia, Oceania, and Europe, as well as towards the west and south of the African continent – based on archaeological and genetic evidence.

◀ **Homo erectus** were the first humans believed to have migrated from Africa. This painting is based on remains found at the Zhoukoudian site, China. *Homo erectus* may have co-existed with *Homo sapiens* in Asia before extinction.

◀ **The "Lion Man" statuette**, found in the Hohlenstein-Stadel cave in Germany, is 35–40,000 years old. It provides the earliest evidence of religious practices by humans in the world.

▼ **This illustration of a mammoth-hunter settlement** is based on findings at the Dolní Věstonice archaeological site in the Czech Republic, which was inhabited around 26,000 years ago.

"The... Late Stone Age is as much a colonizing and dispersal phenomenon as it is a technological and social revolution."

Paul Pettitt in Chris Scarre's *The Human Past: World Prehistory and the Development of Human Societies*, 2009

▶ **A prehistoric clay statuette** of a sleeping woman, found in the Ḥal Saflieni Hypogeum, shows the skill of artists living in Malta around 2500 BCE.

Cavern in Dorset implies the first humans arrived around 42,000 BCE. Their arrival was followed, however, by the onset of a long glacial period, during which most of Britain was buried under thick layers of ice. As a result, early peoples abandoned the isles until warmer conditions enabled permanent continuous settlement to resume around 14,000 BCE.

Mediterranean islands, such as what is now Sardinia, were settled by 20,000 BCE, suggesting that people were building boats (although examples found by archaeologists are dated 12,000 years later). It took longer for humans to reach Malta, where they arrived around 5900 BCE, and 2,000 years later their descendants built huge megalithic temples, such as the Ḥal Saflieni Hypogeum, Paola.

Settling East Asia

Even more striking is the migration from mainland Southeast Asia north into what is now China, Siberia, and Japan, and south into what is now Indonesia and Australia. Stone tools with small microblades found near Lake Baikal show that *Homo sapiens* had reached Siberia by at least 38,000 BCE. By 25,000 years ago they had crossed into Japan, reaching the northern island of Hokkaido first, and then, about 5,000 years later, the main island of Honshu. There they established the Jomon culture, characterized by some of the world's earliest pottery which was decorated by pressing cords onto a wet clay surface.

Lower sea levels around 45,000 BCE meant that much of the Indonesian archipelago was joined to the mainland, forming "Sundaland", a landmass over which early humans could move unhindered by wide expanses of water. Archaeological sites in the highlands of New Guinea, including finds on

▶ **First Australian rock art** from Awunbarna (Mount Borradaile), in Australia's Northern Territory, is part of a tradition stretching back to the continent's first residents, 50,000 years ago.

the Huon Peninsula in the northeast of the island, show that early people had begun to exploit the rich resources of the jungle for hunting and gathering. Making the most of these opportunities for food and shelter, they had formed extensive settlements by 25,000 BCE.

The First Australians

From New Guinea, humans crossed into Australia. They must have done so by boat, as Australia was separated from Sundaland by a strait of at least 90 kilometres. Although sites in the Northern Territory, including the Madjedbebe rock shelter in Arnhem Land, may date from around 65,000 BCE, footprints and human remains from Lake Mungo (see box) show that ancestors of the First Australian people had reached the continent at least 42,000 years ago.

Conditions in Australia were different from those in Southeast Asia. Enormous megafauna included carnivorous kangaroos and *Meiolania*, a turtle over 2 metres in length. Humans hunted these species and learned to manage the land, using controlled fires. They also developed a symbiosis with their environment, which fed into spiritual beliefs about the Dreamtime, a time when ancestral spirits roamed and shaped the land, and which is rooted in this prehistoric migration across the sea.

With the settlement of Japan, the Mediterranean region, and Australia, almost all of the world's major landmasses had been inhabited by humans. It remained only for them to reach the Americas.

Return of Mungo Man

Australia's oldest human, "Mungo Man", was returned by hearse to Lake Mungo in southwestern New South Wales in 2017. He was accompanied by his descendants, the Tirkandi Inaburra Indigenous dancers. His remains, believed to be 42,000 years old, had been stored at the Australian National University in Canberra since their discovery by archaeologists in 1974.

The "Marching Men" were painted on rock by the San peoples of the Drakensberg mountains in Southern Africa around 3,000 years ago. The San are shown migrating eastward to the coast to hunt for food and resources during the winter.

ARCTIC
OCEAN

Bering
Land Bridge

Siberia

PACIFIC
OCEAN

NORTH
AMERICA

ATLANTIC
OCEAN

Bridge to a new world

PEOPLING THE AMERICAS

▲ **The Bering land bridge** allowed ancient peoples to cross easily from Asia to North America. Some may also have followed the coastline, arriving on the continent by boat.

◄ **This flint spear point**, made around 11,000 BCE, is of a type used by members of the Clovis culture. More than 10,000 of these points have been found in North America alone.

▼ **Giant sloths** (right) and mastodons (left) provided a food source for early humans in the Americas, but they had disappeared – possibly hunted to extinction – by 9000 BCE.

For millions of years the Americas remained unpopulated. Their geographical isolation meant our *Homo sapiens* ancestors could only settle there once they had reached eastern Siberia, where Mal'ta mammoth hunters established themselves around 25,000 years ago. At that time, the Laurentian and Cordilleran glaciers, which covered most of North America, locked up so much water that sea levels were 90 metres lower than today, creating a land bridge between Asia and North America. Known as Beringia, this bridge allowed migration across what is now a broad expanse of water. Although a bleak treeless plain, it was home to herds of large herbivores, such as mammoth, mastodon, and caribou, which attracted hunting bands eastwards.

Crossing Beringia

The date of the first crossing is unclear. A long-standing hypothesis that the first settlers belonged to the Clovis culture, named after a site in New Mexico, which thrived from 11,500 to 11,000 years ago, has been challenged by recent evidence of an earlier migration. Artefacts including biface stone-blades found at Bluefish Cave in Yukon (which dates from 12–15,000 years ago), suggest an earlier crossing of Beringia.

Radiocarbon dating of sediment from the sea floor of the Bering Strait has shown that the land bridge was open during a period of glaciation from 25,000 to 18,000 years ago. It then opened again for several thousand years during the next glacial period, from 15,000 years ago.

Once across, small bands of humans may have pushed inland through gaps in the ice sheet and along the coast, in search of shellfish and other marine resources. Their movement southwards appears to have been relatively rapid: a site at Pedra Furada in northwestern Brazil has yielded pieces of stone tools more than 12,000 years old. There is also evidence at Monte Verde II, a site in southern Chile, that humans occupied a cave as long as 14,500 years ago, where they made small fireplaces, built wooden shelters, gathered seaweed, and ate paleocamelids, an ancestor of the llama and alpaca.

The Clovis culture

By around 11,500 years ago, members of the Clovis culture were in North America. Their relationship with previous settlers is unclear, and they may represent a new wave of migration but, like their predecessors, Clovis peoples almost certainly came from East Asia. This theory is reinforced by recent research which has linked DNA haplogroups found in Siberia with those of Indigenous Americans, and by linguistic analysis showing parallels between the main Indigenous language groups in the Americas and languages spoken in Siberia. Genetics also reveals a clear link between the Clovis peoples – who adapted to extreme climate changes and the disappearance of the large mammals on which they relied for food – to Indigenous populations in North, Central, and South America today.

◀ **"La Mujer de las Palmas"**,
who lived 10–12,000 years
ago, was found in a cave
near Tulum, Mexico in 2006.
Reconstructions of her
appearance supported theories
that early migrants to America
may have come from as far
away as Asia.

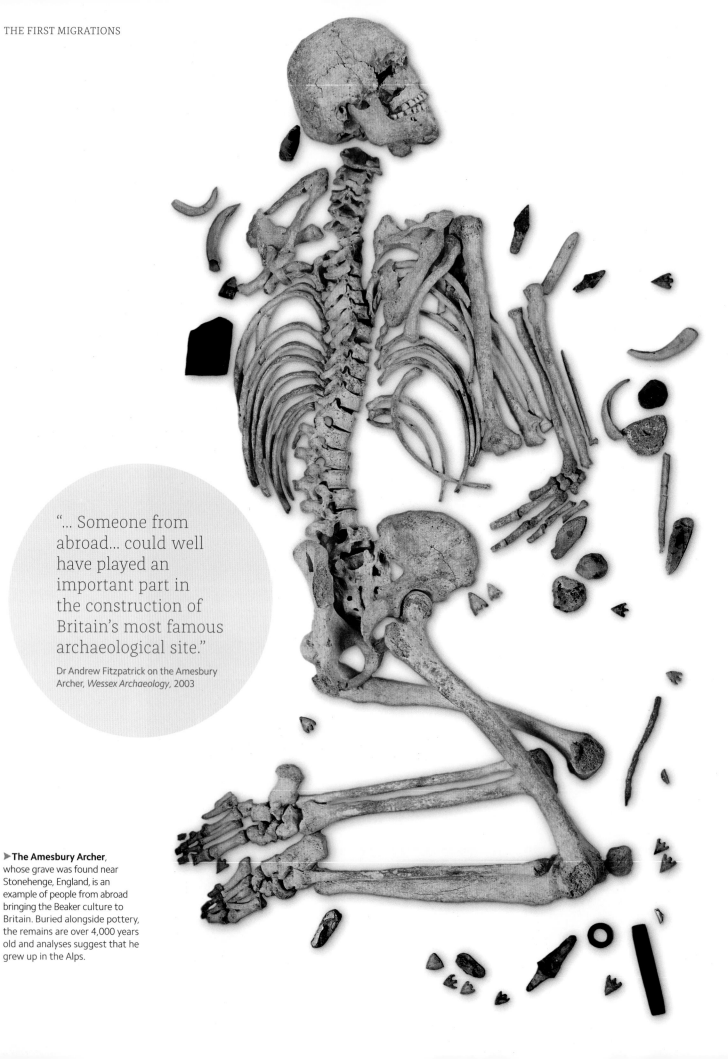

"... Someone from abroad... could well have played an important part in the construction of Britain's most famous archaeological site."

Dr Andrew Fitzpatrick on the Amesbury Archer, *Wessex Archaeology*, 2003

▶**The Amesbury Archer**, whose grave was found near Stonehenge, England, is an example of people from abroad bringing the Beaker culture to Britain. Buried alongside pottery, the remains are over 4,000 years old and analyses suggest that he grew up in the Alps.

North Sea
Baltic Sea
ATLANTIC
OCEAN
Adriatic Sea
Black Sea
Mediterranean Sea

KEY
Land bridge to the British Isles
Spread of farming communities
Agricultural diffusion, continental
Agricultural diffusion, coastal
Southeastern 7000–5500 BCE
Mediterranean 7000–4500 BCE
Central 5500–4500 BCE

Europe's first farms
THE NEOLITHIC SPREAD OF AGRICULTURE

The period from 6000 BCE brought enormous changes to Europe as a new way of life, farming, spread across the continent. New peoples – agriculturalists – moved from southwestern Asia with their flocks, displacing or absorbing Mesolithic societies that relied on hunting, and creating new villages from the Balkans to Britain.

Farming spreads across Europe
After the last Ice Age ended around 9500 BCE, warmer conditions allowed more edible plants to thrive and seafood to flourish, but the advent of agriculture was a revolution. Bringing domesticated animals such as pigs, cows, and sheep, and seed crops (as none of these were native to Europe), the early farmers probably island-hopped the Aegean, reaching Crete around 7000 BCE and mainland Greece shortly after. By 6500 BCE, they had established small villages with tells (or settlement mounds) dotting the fertile plains of Thessaly. Working their way around the Mediterranean coast, these farmers settled the Sava Valley of the northern Balkans and coastal Croatia by 5700 BCE. They then crossed into Italy and pushed through Central Europe until, by 4000 BCE, agriculture had reached Britain, Ireland, and Scandinavia.

The newcomers often settled in areas, like Thessaly, where hunter-gatherer populations were scarce. Historians once believed that agriculture spread by diffusion of ideas rather than migration and that hunter-gatherers simply took up the new way of life. However, DNA analysis has confirmed that large-scale population movements did occur, originating in southwest Asia or the southern steppes of Russia, and the presence of new cultures such as

the *Linearbandkeramik* (Linear Pottery Culture), which spread from western Hungary and Poland through Central Europe around 5500 BCE, was firmly associated with migration rather than the adoption of the characteristic pottery by pre-existing societies.

The Beaker culture, which was known for its new techniques of metalworking and bell-shaped pottery (or "beakers"), and which spread from Portugal and Spain across much of Europe from 2400 BCE, seems initially to have diffused without migration. But its onward transmission across Central Europe, and north to Britain just a century later, was brought by settlers – peoples with lighter skin, bluer eyes, and blonder hair than the Indigenous Mesolithic hunter-gatherers – who contributed as much as 90 per cent to the DNA of modern Britons.

Dangers of migration
Neolithic Europe, then, was a continent on the move, as farmers migrated north from the Mediterranean and west from Central Europe. They may have been people such as Ötzi, nicknamed "the Iceman", who died around 3300 BCE and whose corpse was found frozen in a glacier on the Italian-Austrian border in 1991. He died from an arrow to the back whilst on the move high up in the Alps. Analysis of his tooth enamel showed that he had grown up in a valley at least 64 km (40 miles) to the southeast. Neolithic migration brought not only opportunities but danger to those who undertook it.

▲ **Agriculture spread into Europe** by land and along the coast, reaching southeastern Europe and the areas around the Mediterranean, then into Central Europe.

▼ **Stonehenge in Wiltshire, UK**, is a circle of huge stones built by Neolithic peoples. It is a remarkable feat of construction and, though it clearly aligns with the sun, its purpose remains unclear.

▼ **Çatalhöyük, Turkey** was a Neolithic farming town in Anatolia. This shows a place of worship in the town, in 7000–6000 BCE. It had no doors, and people entered via an opening in the roof.

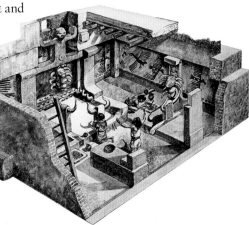

Around the Fertile Crescent

THE ANCIENT NEAR EAST

The advent of agriculture in the Near East and North Africa around 10,000 BCE encouraged people to form the first fixed settlements. As agricultural surpluses accumulated, societies became more stratified and complex, with rigid hierarchies headed by temple priests, nobles, and kings. This more sedentary lifestyle did not, however, mean people stopped moving. Instead, as villages became towns, then city-states, and finally empires, communities sought to acquire more lands, sending their peoples to settle them, often displacing those already there. In turn, the wealth of these new states attracted nomadic outsiders eager to control their resources.

Near Eastern empires

The walls of Jericho, built around 8000 BCE are a first sign of tensions between settled peoples and newcomers. Early cities in Mesopotamia (western Asia), such as Uruk, built around 4500 BCE by the Sumerians – themselves probably migrants from an unknown location – were also attractive to migrating peoples in search of somewhere to settle. In time, one group, the Akkadians, overwhelmed Sumeria in 2350 BCE, only for their leader, Sargon, to establish his own more wide-ranging empire that extended into Syria. Around 2000 BCE, Sumeria was devastated again by a new group of nomads – the Amorites, moving north from Arabia – despite the efforts of rulers such as King Shu-Sin of Ur, who built a defensive wall against them known as "the repeller of the Amorites".

Ancient Egypt – whose civilization was probably established by peoples moving east to escape the desertification of the previously fertile Sahara from around 6000 BCE – was initially successful at keeping outsiders at bay. Then, around 1650 BCE it succumbed to an invasion by the Hyksos (invaders who spoke a western Semitic language and may have originated in modern Syria or Lebanon), who conquered much of northern Egypt and ruled it for over a century.

War and deportation

When the Near East recovered from the collapse caused by the Sea Peoples (see box), the new empires that emerged from 900 BCE continued to experience waves of migration, but they also employed forced migration as a policy. The Assyrians, who built an empire based at Nineveh (near modern Mosul, Iraq) used this to brutal effect. In 689 BCE, their ruler Sargon II destroyed the ancient city of Babylon and deported its people to other Assyrian provinces.

Babylon, once rebuilt, became the new home of the Jewish people, exiled to "Babylonian Captivity" by King Nebuchadnezzar II after he destroyed Jerusalem in 597 BCE following a revolt. The Jews only returned to Jerusalem when the Persian king, Cyrus I, gave them the right to rebuild the Jewish Temple there after he took Babylon in 538 BCE. His policy of tolerance across the Achaemenid Empire's 20 provinces achieved a balance between ethnic groups which, for a time, quelled the cycle of migration and invasion that had plagued the Near East for centuries.

▼ **This frieze detail** is from the palace of Darius I at Susa, Iran. It dates to 510 BCE, during the Achaemenid Empire, which was founded by Cyrus II in 550 BCE.

The Sea Peoples

Confederations of seaborne peoples attacked the coastal states of the Mediterranean around 1300 BCE. Although the Egyptian pharaoh Ramesses II initially fought them off, the raids continued for over a century, as peoples such as the Sherden, Lukka, and Peleset destroyed cities. It caused a general collapse, pushing Egypt and Greece into centuries of political and economic chaos.

Powerful empires

The first urban settlements and organized societies gave rise to powerful empires that exerted their influence by colonizing new areas, and subjugating or deporting other populations.

KEY

- Akkadian Empire 2300 BCE
- Babylonian Empire 1750 BCE
- Egyptian Empire c. 1300 BCE
- Hittite Empire c. 1300 BCE
- Achaemenid Empire 500 BCE

Black Sea

Caspian Sea

Hattusa

Halys

Nineveh

Assur

Euphrates

Tigris

Mediterranean Sea

Akkad

Babylon

Nippur

Syrian Desert

Jerusalem

Jericho

Uruk

Ur

Susa

Avaris

Memphis

Persian Gulf

Nile

Red Sea

Thebes

▲ **This fist-shaped drinking vessel** was produced by the Hittite people – migrants to Anatolia who formed a large empire, at its peak in the mid-14th century BCE.

▲ **Nomadic visitors from Syria-Canaan** are depicted arriving in ancient Egypt on a tomb wall at Beni Hassan, Egypt, dating to around 1700 BCE.

▲ **A bronze head of Sargon**, king of Akkad between 2334 and 2279 BCE, who used forced deportations of conquered groups to maintain control in his empire.

▲ **This gold necklace**, with pendants representing deities, shows the wealth and sophistication of ancient Babylonian society by 18th–17th century BCE.

CULTURAL INFLUENCES

Hellenic hub

Alexandria became a bastion of Hellenic culture and scholarship. Greeks – many of whom travelled to the city from other parts of the Mediterranean – dominated society, but also absorbed aspects of Egyptian and Jewish cultures. This drawing shows the Greek-engineered Lighthouse of Alexandria, built in c.280 CE, one of the Seven Wonders of the Ancient World.

Jewish colony

The city's Jewish population grew during the 3rd century BCE as migrants were attracted by Alexandria's booming economy. A Jewish quarter developed, the Great Synagogue was built, key Hebrew texts were translated into Greek, and notable scholars emerged. This 1672 painting depicts a Ptolemaic ruler conversing with Jewish scholars in the Library of Alexandria.

Rome's second city

After the Romans annexed Egypt, Alexandria became the second city of the empire after Rome and a major port for exporting grain. Soldiers, traders, and administrators arrived, and an array of public buildings were built. This Roman marble sarcophagus, which was unearthed in the city, is on display in its Graeco-Roman museum.

Alexandria

THE BRIDE OF THE MEDITERRANEAN

A major seaport and industrial centre on Egypt's Mediterranean coast, Alexandria was founded in 332 BCE by Alexander the Great during his conquest of the Persian Empire. Following Alexander's death, Ptolemy I Soter became Egypt's ruler, and his Ptolemaic Dynasty turned Alexandria into a centre of Hellenic (Greek) learning and science, with a famous library and lighthouse. Cosmopolitan from the outset, it was home to Egyptians, Greeks, and Jews.

Expansion and modernization

In 30 BCE, the Romans invaded Egypt and Alexandria became part of the Roman Empire. While the city remained a key trading port, there was great persecution of Jewish and pagan communities by Christians in the 4th and 5th centuries CE. Arab armies conquered Egypt in the 7th century CE (see pp. 78–81), bringing Islam to Alexandria and leading many Greeks to flee. Under Islamic rule, the city's intellectual and commercial life thrived into the medieval era.

From the 16th century, the city's population and splendour declined due to epidemics and administrative neglect, and a brief occupation by French forces from 1798 disrupted life further. But from 1805 to 1922, during the rule of the Ottoman viceroy of Egypt and a 40-year occupation by the British, the city was modernized and became more Westernized – to the detriment of Egyptian people and culture.

The population was swelled by migrants from the countryside and settlers from Mediterranean nations such as Greece, Italy, Syria, and France who were lured by trading privileges. In the 1950s, most Egyptians of European origin emigrated when foreign-owned businesses were nationalized, but traces of their influence remain.

▲▲ **Cleopatra's Dream was a 2017 carnival** which celebrated Alexandria's history as the capital during the reign of the famed Ptolemaic Egyptian queen.

▲ **The Bibliotheca Alexandrina** is a revival of the ancient Library of Alexandria, and houses thousands of Greek, Hebrew, and Mesopotamian books.

◄ **This colourful street mosaic** features motifs – from Roman tiles to Islamic minarets to Egyptian gods – that represent the different cultures that have played a part in shaping the city over the last 2,000 years.

> "Alexandrians thronged to the festival full of enthusiasm, and shouted acclamations in Greek and Egyptian, … charmed by the lovely spectacle."
>
> Greek poet Constantine P. Cavafy (1863–1933), on the Donations of Alexandria in 34 BCE

Islamic culture

The Islamic faith arrived in Alexandria in the 7th century after the Arab invasion of Egypt. In the centuries that followed, the Arabic language and Islamic-style buildings – including Qaitbay fort's mosque, with its geometric tiled floor (shown below) – spread throughout the city. Muslim migrants also arrived from across the Middle East and North Africa.

European traders

During a century of foreign control, the city was revitalized by the creation of a new harbour and docks and a canal linking it to the Nile. European merchants constructed mansions and warehouses, building outwards from the Place des Consuls (today's Midan Tahrir). For the city's 100,000 foreigners, as well as educated Egyptians, French was the lingua franca.

Greek influences

Greek immigrants to the city founded many of Alexandria's coffee houses, patisseries, and tearooms. They were fashionable gathering places for artists, writers, and socialites. Some closed following the 1952 revolution and the rise of Egyptian nationalism, but those that remain are still popular.

2

Ancient Empires

c. 2600 BCE–375 CE

Ancient Empires

c. 2600 BCE–375 CE

The three-thousand-year period that began around 2600 BCE was one of great empires. People migrated as their heartlands expanded into vast kingdoms or moved within new territorial boundaries as their lands were taken over by conquering empires. The Babylonian and Assyrian Empires in the Middle East gathered many different peoples together under a single state, sometimes forcing groups to move to strengthen their hold on frontier lands. From 2500 BCE, the Egyptians expanded their territories into Nubia to their south; Nubians in turn moved northward into southern Egypt. For the first time, migration was motivated by trade, and peoples such as the Phoenicians established trading colonies around the Mediterranean from 1000 BCE. The Greeks followed around two centuries later, establishing cities which spread their people and culture across the continents, to North Africa, Spain, France, and Italy.

In China, the first dynasties expanded by conquest from a core around the Yellow River Basin, spreading what would later become Han culture throughout the north and central regions. Other peoples travelled in search of land,

Minoan traders depart from a coastal town (see pp.34–37)

Nubians go north to pay tribute to the Egyptian pharoah (see pp.50–51)

"I am not born for one corner of [the world] more than another; the whole of it is my native country."

Lucius Annaeus Seneca (c. 4 BCE–65 CE), Roman philosopher

often as their own territories were invaded. Groups of Bantu speakers migrated from West Africa across the continent to the east and southern coasts in a process that took over 2,000 years. From 450 BCE, the Celts moved from Central Europe into Germany and France, finally crossing into Britain and Ireland in the late 2nd century BCE.

Other migrants travelled by sea; the ancestors of the Polynesians began a prolonged journey east into the archipelagos of the Pacific. From 1300 BCE, they settled in Tonga, Fiji, Hawai'i, and eventually Rapa Nui (Easter Island),

crossing vast stretches of water in outrigger canoes, bearing the domesticated animals and crops which they cultivated in their new, island settlements.

States became more organized, and empires grew larger still, so that long-distance migration within them became possible: Roman citizens from as far as North Africa and Syria settled in northern Britain. While individuals could travel quickly, by boat or – in the Roman Empire, Persian domains, and China – by road, larger groups still moved slowly, taking many years to reach new lands.

Chang'an is influenced by Feng architecture under the Han Dynasty (see pp.58–59)

Uthina was a Roman colony in what is now Tunisia (see pp.60–63)

A Mediterranean civilization

THE ANCIENT GREEK WORLD

Migration shaped ancient Greece. Its plains and valleys were fertile but small, and broken up by mountain ranges, so as the population grew, there was not enough surplus land to feed everyone. As a result, the governments of the various states sent migrants overseas in search of new lands. Living in a country with an extensive coastline, maritime travel and trade were second nature to the Greeks.

The Minoans and Mycenaeans

From around 2000 BCE the Minoan civilization flourished on the island of Crete. It amassed enormous wealth through trade, establishing links with Greece and an eastern Mediterranean network of routes that encompassed Egypt and Phoenicia, and even extending as far west as Sicily. The Minoan civilization went into a decline after c. 1450 BCE, amid invasions by Mycenaeans from the Greek mainland. The newcomers continued the trading tradition, setting up satellite settlements in the west, near Taranto in southern Italy, and in the east along the western coastlines of Asia Minor.

Around 1100 BCE the Mycenaean civilization also collapsed. City-states such as Pylos and Mycenae fell victim to the Sea Peoples, maritime raiders of unknown origin who spread devastation

▲ **Ancient Greece was the heart** of a powerful empire around the Black Sea and Mediterranean. This map shows Greece, its colonies, and its major trading routes c. 600 CE.

▼ **This silver coin**, a dekadrachm, was issued in the Greek province of Syracuse, Sicily, in the 5th century BCE. It shows the head of Arethusa, a nymph in Greek mythology.

throughout the eastern Mediterranean. Into the vacuum, new invaders, identified by their dialect and known by later Greeks as the Dorians, arrived in central and southern Greece, most likely from the north, and conquered the last of the Mycenaean civilization. Tradition related that the invasion was led by the sons of the legendary Heracles, so the event is also known as the Return of the Heracleidae.

City-states and colonies

Around 1000 BCE a new kind of power began to emerge. The city-state (*polis*) dominated the Greek world for almost 1,000 years, the most famous examples being Athens, Sparta, and Corinth. The Proto-Geometric pottery (named for its striking geometric patterns) that the city-states produced has been found throughout the eastern Mediterranean, including Syria, an indication that Greece had reinstated trade in the region by this time. Greek settlers began to move back to areas abandoned after the Mycenaean collapse, while Cyprus and many of the eastern Aegean islands became Greek-speaking once more by 850 BCE. Important Greek settlements, such as Ephesus and Miletus, appeared along the western coastline of Asia Minor, becoming the main centres of Ionia, a region that would be home to large ethnically Greek populations until the 1920s. Small colonies further afield, such as the trading-station at Al-Mina in northern Syria, which housed Greek merchants from the island of Euboea, lived in the shadow of stronger powers such as the Assyrian Empire. But the real expansion of the Greek world was yet to come.

Beginning in the 730s BCE, the Greek city-states sent out colonists who established new cities, initially in the west – in Sicily, southern Italy, southern France, and Spain. They did so for a number of reasons: as their populations outgrew the smaller city-states, new generations of young adults had little opportunity to make an independent living; the constant state of warfare between city-states and factional strife within them drove others to seek a safer life; and the opportunities for trade provided an incentive to those in search of wealth.

◀ **This terracotta kore**, or statue of a young woman, was made in Crete c.640–625 BCE. The marked Egyptian influence of the sculpture points to the ongoing trade between Crete and the Near East.

"After leaving Pylus, the lofty city of Neleus, we came in our voyage to the long wished-for Asia and... by the will of the gods we took Aeolian Smyrna."

Greek poet Mimnermus, Fragment 9, 7th century BCE

◀ **This Minoan fresco** from Akrotiri on Thera (Santorini) depicts a naval expedition. A volcanic eruption c.1650–1550 BCE buried the settlement in ash but preserved the fresco.

"We live around the sea... like frogs around a pond."

Plato, section 109 of *Phaedo*, c.360 BCE, describing the Greek world clustered around the shores of the Mediterranean

Greek colonizers founded the coastal city of Paestum in Magna Graecia (now southern Italy), an important centre of ancient Greek civilization, and built this temple c.450 BCE.

Colonization by the Greek city-states typically began with the *metropolis* (meaning "mother city" in Greek) seeking divine sanction from an oracle for its plans, and then selecting a founder, an *oikistes*, responsible for locating the site of the new city, laying down its laws, and dividing land among the colonists. The strongest Greek city-states were not necessarily the ones that established the most or biggest colonies. Sparta, which was one of the most powerful, only ever founded Taras (modern Taranto, Italy) in 706 BCE. Meanwhile, settlers from the small town of Eretria (on the Greek island of Euboea) founded a trading post at Pithecusae, north of Naples, around 775 BCE, attracted by the rich volcanic soil and reserves of iron ore.

The largest single concentration of Greek colonies was in southern Italy and Sicily, an area so strongly permeated by Greek settlement and culture that the Romans knew it as Magna Graecia ("New Greece"). Although they had to divide Sicily with the Carthaginians, the region's Greek city-states remained independent until the Romans took Syracuse in 212 BCE. Even today, the local dialects of parts of southern Italy are influenced by Greek.

Locations and challenges

Although many local populations were integrated into the new colonies, in other places, they put up a fight. As a result, the settlers chose easily defensible coastal locations, such as the island of Ortygia in Sicily, which became the nucleus of the city of Syracuse, founded in 733 BCE. They also picked strategic locations, such as Byzantium, which dominated the Hellespont seaway leading from the Aegean into the Black Sea, or where they had access to goods for trading, such as Panticapaeum on the Crimea, which allowed for the shipments of large quantities of grain to feed mainland Greece.

The first Greek settlers usually faced a precarious existence. They were often few in number – for example, only 200 men from the city of Corinth were involved in founding the city of Apollonia Illyrica (in modern-day Albania) around 600 BCE. Other colonists faced resistance from the local inhabitants, such as the Sicels, who were native to Sicily, or they were forced to fight rival colonizing powers, such as the Phoenicians (from modern-day Lebanon). Some were unwilling colonizers: when drought hit Thera (modern-day Santorini), the island's governors conscripted people to found a new settlement, and Cyrene (in modern-day Libya)

was established in 630 BCE. Those who refused to go faced the death penalty, but they could return home after five years if the settlement was a failure.

Migration turns east

Greek migration spread west from Italy and North Africa to Massilia (now Marseille, France), where a Greek colony was founded in c. 600 BCE, and to Emporion (near Gerona, Spain), established around 575 BCE. Both became important trading posts for Greek merchants. But the growing power of the Carthaginians and Etruscans prevented further expansion. From the early 7th century, the Greek colonizing effort focused further east, with a string of new colonies established along the shores of the Black Sea.

The Greeks shaped the Mediterranean world through migration, exerting their influence on many different peoples, including the Romans. But the descendants of those migrants also influenced the culture of Greece. Archimedes, a mathematician from Syracuse, for example, achieved eminence in the 3rd century BCE, while the roots of Greek philosophy owe much to the ideas of thinkers such as Thales of Miletus, in Ionia (modern-day Turkey).

▲ **This mosaic of a *trireme*,** a type of oar-driven boat used by the ancient Greeks, is in the Notre-Dame de la Garde Basilica in Marseille, France. The Greek colony of Massilia (Marseille) was an important trading port.

◀ **This Riace Warrior,** one of a pair of full-size bronze statues, was found off the coast of Riace, southern Italy, in 1972. Cast c. 460–450 BCE, it shows how far ancient Greek culture had spread across the Mediterranean.

Across the open sea

THE AUSTRONESIAN EXPANSION

Around 3,000 years ago, the ancestors of today's Polynesians crossed the sea. They travelled vast distances in large double-hulled canoes, reaching and settling on almost all the island groups of the Pacific, even travelling across the vast ocean as far as Hawai'i, Easter Island, and New Zealand.

The Polynesians form part of a wider language group known as the Austronesians, today found in New Guinea and the westernmost Pacific islands (Melanesia), the archipelagos to the northeast (Micronesia), as well as across the bulk of the Pacific east of the Solomons (Polynesia).

Lapita exploration

The western part of the Pacific had been populated long before the main Austronesian expansion began: humans settled on the north coast of New Guinea at least 35,000 years ago and reached Buka in the Solomon Islands by 28,000 years ago.

To reach these islands they needed some form of water-craft, perhaps bamboo rafts (as bark canoes are not robust enough to cross more than a small stretch of water). However, the islands beyond the Bismarck Archipelago northeast of New Guinea remained uninhabited. Then, around 1500 BCE a new group appeared. DNA evidence and the linguistic traces along their route suggest that these people, known as Lapita, probably originated in Taiwan or coastal Southeast Asia. Once in the Bismarck islands, they developed a culture that included pottery featuring geometric designs, stone adzes, and rectangular stilt houses built along the coastline. The Lapita people began to spread eastwards, reaching Tonga by 1300 BCE, and Samoa and Fiji about 700 years later. The reasons why they travelled to these islands are unclear; there is no strong evidence of overpopulation, but younger members of kinship lineages may have been seeking a new land in which they would not be subordinate.

Setting off for new lands

Their voyages were enabled by the invention of large double-hulled canoes, with triangular lateen sails and outriggers that gave them more stability and allowed them to sail against the wind. About 30 people could travel in each canoe; whole families sailed with their livestock – the dogs, pigs, and chickens they would introduce to the islands they found (as well as the rats that came along as stowaways). They brought taro, yam, breadfruit, banana, and coconut plants, and the sacred *ti*, a plant believed to be imbued with divine power. They also carried tools and images of their ancestors – everything they would need for life in their new homes. It is probable that scouts would have been sent ahead of the main group to find suitable locations for settlements. The Lapitans did not have access to navigational devices such as the compass, but relied on observing the stars, noting the patterns of wind and waves, and spotting seabirds to indicate that new land might be near.

▼ **The face of a 3,000-year-old Lapita woman** from Fiji was reconstructed in 2002 from a well-preserved skeleton. Scientists named her "Mana", which means "truth" in the Lau dialect of the Solomon Islands.

▼ **Petroglyphs** on the Mamalahoa Trail at Waikoloa, Kohala Coast, Hawai'i, may have been a way to record births. They include human figures, animals, and canoes, as well as patterns and symbols.

Islands of the Pacific

The vast expanse of the Pacific Ocean is home to dozens of islands that form part of Polynesia. Though far apart, they are linked by common ancestors who journeyed between the island groups to settle or to trade.

KEY
- Micronesia
- Polynesia
- Melanesia
- → Migration of Austronesian peoples

TAIWAN

PHILIPPINES

Marianas

Hawai'i

Palau

Marshall Islands

Caroline Island

Bismarck Archipelago

NEW GUINEA

Solomon Islands

Marquesas

INDONESIA

Samoa

to Madagascar

Vanuatu

Fiji

Tahiti

AUSTRALIA

Tonga

New Caledonia

Easter Island

NEW ZEALAND

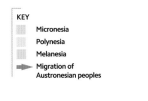

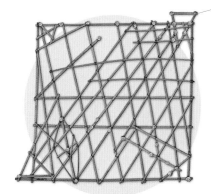

▲ **Marshall Islands stick charts**, such as this one dating from 1920, were used for navigation. They indicated currents and wave patterns between islands. The shells denote islands.

▲ **Lapita pottery** decorated with fine geometric patterns and made using sharp, toothed tools, has been found in burial areas on Vanuatu.

▲ **A Polynesian outrigger canoe** could travel short distances between bays or islands. The later, double-hulled canoe could venture much larger distances.

▲ **Tapa bark cloth** has been produced for hundreds of years. It is made using the bark of the paper mulberry, which is soaked and pounded into a cloth, and can then be dyed.

▲ A 19th-century illustration of Puynipet Island (Pohnpei) in the Caroline Islands, shows islanders travelling by outrigger canoe seeking a way through the coral reef around the island.

Once they reached Samoa, the Lapitans paused and there was a thousand-year gap in the Austronesian expansion. This may have been caused by the isolation of island groups further east. The large expanses of open ocean between them made speculative scouting expeditions perilous. By the time the migrations resumed around 300 CE, the Lapita culture had waned – in Tonga and Samoa the practice of making pottery had disappeared completely. DNA evidence and artefacts from across Eastern Polynesia, including stone adzes and fishing tackle, which show little material change over time, suggest few pioneers set out.

Settling Eastern Polynesia

Polynesians had settled the Marquesas by around 400 CE, Hawai'i by around 650 CE, and the Cook Islands and Tahiti by about 750 CE. A century or two later, they reached Easter Island off the coast of Chile. They found an abundance of native animals, though this bounty of seabirds and turtles was soon exhausted, providing some of the motivation for voyages to even further-flung islands.

On each new island that was reached, the settlers were able to exploit the riches of fish and shellfish in the ocean and shore, and build farms to cultivate their crops. They established lineage groups based on the ancestors who had travelled in the first canoes that reached an island – consequently, the names of these pioneers were remembered centuries later. While the majority of these famed travellers were men, some were women: the canoe that was said to have originally settled Pohnpei in the eastern Caroline Islands carried 16 people and nine of these were female, while women on a later canoe also brought the precious banana and yam seedlings needed to plant new crops.

Trading to survive

Polynesian peoples may have reached even beyond Easter Island, because they grew one crop that they had not brought with them: the sweet potato, a native of South America. They probably acquired it through some form of contact with South America (some historians once believed that Polynesians themselves were of South American descent).

In Polynesia, this crop supplemented a delicate island ecosystem based on trading. Some islands could not produce everything they needed, and so engaged in a system of trade to make up shortfalls. A three-way trade grew between Mangareva, Pitcairn, and the Henderson islands: oyster shells from Mangareva to Pitcairn; obsidian glass from Pitcairn to Henderson; and basalt stone for ovens from Mangareva to Henderson.

Then, around 1500 CE, the trade stopped. The populations on the Polynesian islands had grown, causing damage to the environment. On Mangareva deforestation made the soil infertile, leading to hunger and civil war. There were no more resources to continue the trade with smaller islands such as Henderson. The people there struggled on, using clam shells in place of stone for adzes, but life on the island became unsustainable, and by 1600, settlers abandoned Henderson. Islanders reacted in different ways to this loss of trade, new chieftainships arose, and on Hawai'i a highly stratified society developed, with kings, nobles, and even enslaved people. The egalitarian society of the original migrants was lost.

The art of tattooing

Polynesians used carved bone "combs" and pigment derived from soot or ash to tattoo those who had reached adulthood. In Samoa, men were tattooed from the knee to the waist and women sometimes from the knee to the top of their leg or at the back of the knee only. Designs indicated lineage and links to the community and the painful process reinforced identity and asserted maturity.

"Tahu-oi is the canoe! It is a canoe. Draw ashore Tahu-oi! Disembark the big canoe! Two hundred strong!"

Chant from Kave, Tahuata, Marquesas Islands

◄ **Great stone figures, or *moai*,** stand tall on the island Rapa Nui (Easter Island), now in Chile. Some set on *ahu* (platforms), they probably depict the living faces of the ancestors and were treated with immense respect.

The horse lords

INDO-ARYANS AND INDO-EUROPEANS

Around 3.2 billion people today speak Indo-European languages, making it the largest language group in terms of numbers of speakers and geographical dispersal. The origins of these languages lie in a small area of the Russian steppe, from where the ancestors of languages as diverse as Gaelic, German, Russian, Farsi, and Hindi began a prolonged migration some 5,000 years ago.

Language trees

Clues about the journey of these far-distant Indo-European ancestors were first revealed by researchers in the 19th century, who noticed similarities in vocabulary between certain ancient languages, such as Sanskrit and Latin, and also between modern tongues such as English and Russian. They theorized that all descended from an original language called Proto-Indo-European.

Similar words in many Indo-European languages for axle and wheel suggest that the original Indo-Europeans had wheeled vehicles and horses; other parallels indicate they were pastoralists, herding sheep and cattle on the grasslands, and had close kinship groups and chieftains. The homeland of these ancient herders probably lay on the Russian steppe, and modern genetic research analysing DNA haplogroups suggests they were members of the Yamnaya (Pit Grave) culture. These peoples dominated the area north of the Black Sea around 3000 BCE, and may have begun to move west and southwards shortly afterwards, carrying their technology and language.

A separate group, the Sintashta culture, split off from the homeland a little later, around 2200 BCE and migrated eastwards and then southwards. One

◀ **The Trundholm sun chariot**, found in Denmark, dates to c. 1400 BCE. The wheeled vehicle pulled by a horse is evidence of the spread of Indo-European culture there.

▼ **These Bronze Age grave markers** were created by the Yamnaya people in Kyrgyzstan. They migrated across parts of Europe and Asia.

group (who became known as Indo-Iranians) settled in Iran, while another (the Indo-Aryans) travelled even further south into the Indian subcontinent. Their descendants now speak such languages as Hindi, Urdu, Bengali, and Punjabi.

Culture and genetics

The origins of the Indo-Aryans have long been controversial. Many historians believe the culture described in ancient Hindu texts, the "Vedas", arrived in India with these migrants; others suggest it developed instead among Indigenous groups. However, DNA markers in the modern South Asian population linked to Indo-European ancestry reinforce the view that the Indo-Aryans travelled to India from the steppelands far to the north.

As they migrated, the Indo-Europeans displaced or replaced speakers of other languages such as Hurrian (in the Near East) and Etruscan (in Italy), leaving Basque in northern Spain as the sole survivor of the languages that preceded them. Over time their cultures also diverged, giving rise to city-states in Greece, great empires such as Rome and Persia, and chieftainships in Germany and the Celtic-speaking lands. Yet, wherever they settled, the vast numbers of Indo-Europeans and Indo-Aryans remained linked by language to their steppe-dwelling ancestors, some of whom remain as nomads in the original Indo-European homeland.

▲ **The Indo-Aryan migration** was part of the eastwards migration of Indo-European peoples, some of whom remained in Iran, developing Indo-Iranian culture.

▼ **This scene** from the ancient epic poem "Mahabharata" depicts the Hindu god Krishna and Prince Arjuna. The poem is part of an evolving religious tradition that can be traced back to Indo-Aryan migrants.

▲ **This frieze** from the palace of Assyrian king Sargon II (r. 721–705 BCE) shows Phoenician sailors towing and unloading Lebanese cedar logs.

▶ **The city of Carthage** was founded by the Phoenicians, but the Romans razed the city to the ground and built a new Carthage on the same site. This was destroyed by Arab forces in the 7th century CE.

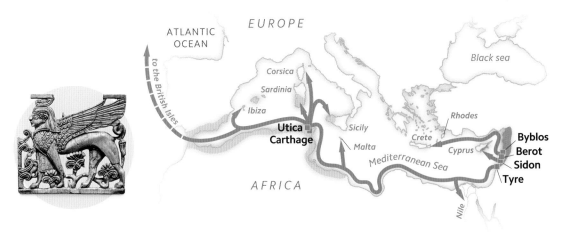

The purple people
THE PHOENICIANS AND THE MEDITERRANEAN

KEY
Phoenician homeland
Phoenician colonies
Trade route

The Phoenicians emerged as a trading people around 1500 BCE, based in coastal cities such as Byblos, Tyre, Sidon, and Berot (modern-day Beirut), in modern Lebanon. They were great seafarers and shipbuilders, and grew rich on exporting timber (notably cedar), papyrus, and luxury goods. Among these were glass beads, and their famous textiles, coloured with a purple dye extracted from sea snails.

The Phoenician expansion west

As their power diminished in their homeland following multiple raids – starting with those of the Sea Peoples around 1100 BCE (see p.26) – the Phoenicians embarked on a massive colonizing venture in the Mediterranean. On the way, they set up trading stations (*emporia*), some of which grew into great cities. Typically, their colonies were situated on an island or promontory, either along a major trade route or where mineral resources were easily accessible. By the mid-10th century BCE, they had established a colony at Kition (modern-day Larnaca) on Cyprus, and smaller settlements on the Greek islands of Rhodes and Crete.

The main arena of the Phoenicians' activities, however, was in the western Mediterranean, where competition with other powers was less fierce than in the east. Around the 8th century BCE, colonies at Utica (in Tunisia), Motya (on Sicily), and Nora (on Sardinia) emerged, the latter being near a source of silver, gold, and tin, which the Phoenicians mined for their metalworking industry and traded. Around 750 BCE, they went beyond the Strait of Gibraltar and founded Gades (modern-day Cádiz, in western Spain), to export silver and tin from the interior, and Lixus (in Morocco).

By the 6th century BCE, navigators (such as Hanno) embarked on explorations to West Africa, the Iberian Peninsula, and possibly the British Isles.

The growth of Carthage

The largest and most affluent of all Phoenician cities was Carthage (in modern Tunisia). It was founded in 814 BCE, and grew rapidly after an influx of Phoenician refugees following Alexander the Great's invasion of Tyre in 332 BCE. Unusually for a Phoenician settlement, Carthage came to dominate a large inland area of North Africa, and became an empire in its own right. The Carthaginian Empire traded with the Indigenous Berber peoples, and also recruited them to the military – mainly as cavalry, as the Berbers were renowned equestrians.

After three wars against the Roman Empire (see pp.60–63), which ended with the destruction of Carthage itself in 146 BCE, the Phoenicians lost their power base, and the days of their colonies were over. However, Phoenician merchants continued to ply their trade throughout the Mediterranean, and their art – such as their carved ivory plaques, seals, jewellery, glassware, and metal bowls – continued to be highly prized.

▲ **The Phoenicians originated** on the coast of what is now Lebanon. They travelled west on ships, building colonies around the Mediterranean to create an impressive trading network.

▼ **This ivory plaque**, which depicts a winged sphinx, is a fine example of Phoenician art (c.900–700 BCE). It was found at Fort Shalmaneser in Nimrud, once a major city (called Kalhu in ancient times), in modern Iraq.

The Phoenician alphabet

Among the Phoenicians' most enduring legacies is their writing system. Partially derived from earlier models used in Canaan and Ugarit, it comprised one of the earliest alphabetic scripts. Reaching its full form by about 1000 BCE, it was transmitted across the Mediterranean by Phoenician merchants who settled in southern Europe and North Africa. It was the foundation of the Greek alphabet and Latin scripts.

The Gundestrup Cauldron (c. 100 BCE), an ornate metal bowl made in the La Tène style, features the Celtic god Cernunnos.

"All Gaul is divided into three parts, one of which the Belgae inhabit, the Aquitani another... Gauls, the third."

Julius Caesar, *The Gallic Wars*, 58–49 BCE

Gaul

La Tène Hallstatt

Black Sea

Iberia

Mediterranean Sea

KEY
Celtic people over time
La Tène culture
Hallstatt culture
Greatest Celtic expansion by 275 BCE
Areas where Celtic languages are still spoken today

Swords and spirals
THE CELTS SPREAD THROUGH EUROPE

Celtic peoples once dominated large parts of the continent of Europe. Although they lacked political unity and were dubbed *Keltoi* and *Galli* (meaning "barbarians") by their contemporaries the Greeks and Romans, this collection of tribes shared a rich culture of warrior aristocracies, hill forts, fine metalwork, and Celtic languages.

The origins of the Celts
Archaeologists disagree over whether the Celts constituted a single group or a disparate collection of tribes linked by little save language. The roots of a shared Celtic culture – including the Proto-Celtic language, which evolved into Continental Celtic on the European mainland and Insular Celtic in the British Isles and Brittany, France – are traditionally traced to central Europe. There, the Hallstatt culture (named after an Austrian village) emerged around 1100 BCE, its graves containing long slashing swords and ornate four-wheeled wagons. Evidence suggests that around 500 BCE some Celtic peoples migrated north, resulting in the newer La Tène culture (named after a site in Switzerland), which is distinguished by metalwork often decorated with spiral motifs.

Some archaeologists believe that Celtic origins lie instead with the Beaker culture (see pp.24–25), whose bell-shaped pottery appears to have spread north and west from the Iberian Peninsula around 2800 BCE. Yet it is unclear whether or not the Beaker people themselves migrated. Others place Celtic origins with a later Celtiberian population, which settled in northeastern Spain around 1000 BCE.

DNA evidence suggests a link between populations moving westwards from the Russian steppe and the Celtic world. It is likely that the ancestral Celts intermarried with local peoples in the areas they settled, such as modern-day Spain and Portugal, some time after the mid-3rd millennium BCE.

An age of migration
Around 450 BCE the Celts began to move, possibly under pressure from Germanic-speaking groups from Scandinavia, such as the Vandals. First, the La Tène people shifted towards the Rhineland (western Germany) and the Marne area of France. Other Celtic populations moved south into the Balkans and sacked Delphi in Greece in 279 BCE. They then crossed into Asia Minor, where their descendants became known as Galatians. Celts also surged over the Alps into northern Italy, and then in 390 BCE captured Rome. Lastly, in the late 2nd century BCE, the Belgae crossed the English Channel from Gaul and settled in the British Isles.

Europe's landscape was soon dotted with hill forts and circular shrines to gods such as Cernunnos, the "lord of wild things" and the Genii Cucullati ("hooded spirits"). But though effective warriors, the Celts were unable to fight off the Romans, and soon Iberia, Gaul, and most of Britain were in Roman hands. Only northern Scotland and Ireland were unconquered, and here, traces of Celtic culture, including Celtic languages such as Irish and Gaelic, have survived to the present day.

▲ **Celtic languages and cultures** once proliferated across a vast swathe of Europe. Today, only six Celtic languages remain in use – Irish, Scottish Gaelic, Welsh, Manx, Cornish, and Breton.

▼ **This illustration** accompanies the opening words of St Mark's gospel in the medieval Irish *Book of Kells* (c.800 CE), an illuminated version of the gospels filled with intricate Celtic designs.

▼ **This Celtiberian house** in Numantia, Spain, has been reconstructed with stone walls and a wattle-and-daub roof, made by sticking mud or clay to a mesh of interwoven twigs.

Santa Tecla, a mountain in what is now Galicia, Spain, is home to the ruins of a Celtic castro – a village with circular houses and no straight roads (the Celts believed that crossroads held evil spirits). Castros were built in strategic places, often on high ground.

KEY

▢ Kingdom of Kush c. 1000 BCE

▢ Extent of Kushite territory, 8th century BCE

▢ Extent of Egyptian territory, New Kingdom period

···· Traditional boundary between Egypt and Nubia

Mediterranean Sea

Memphis

Lower Egypt

Upper Egypt

River Nile

Thebes

Aswan

Lower Nubia

Red Sea

Kerma

Napata

Meroë

Upper Nubia

Lands of the Black Pharaohs

ANCIENT EGYPT AND THE KINGDOM OF KUSH

Around 3100 BCE, large numbers of people left the Sahara – which had become increasingly arid – and settled on the fertile banks of the Nile, in Egypt and Nubia (modern-day northern Sudan and southern Egypt). A trading relationship emerged between these lands, with Nubia trading ivory and black-rimmed pottery for Egyptian grain and other goods.

Egypt invades Nubia

From 2500 BCE, Egypt (which was by then a unified country under a pharaoh) began expanding into Nubian territory, establishing forts such as the one at Buhen, in the north. Around this time, a new

group settled in Nubia – possibly pastoralists from the Western Desert of Egypt. The culture that emerged in Nubia by around 2040 BCE (the start of the Middle Kingdom period in Egypt) was known as the Kerma culture. The Kermans asserted Nubia's independence from Egypt but continued to trade with them, bartering cattle and luxury goods such as gold, which was highly prized by the Egyptians.

In the New Kingdom period (c. 1570–1069 BCE), Egypt adopted a more aggressive stance towards Nubia, spreading south to occupy more territory, and dividing the region into two administrative units. The southern part was known as Upper

▲ **This map shows** the expansion of Kushite territories from the Kingdom of Kush, which spanned a section of the Nile c. 1000 BCE, northwards into Nubia and Egypt.

▼ **This gold amulet** probably formed part of a necklace worn by one of the Kushite kings. Rams were associated with Amun – an Egyptian god also worshipped by the Nubians.

Nubia (or Kush), with its capital at Napata (in modern-day Sudan); the northern portion was called Lower Nubia (or Wawat), with its main settlement at Aswan (in modern-day Egypt).

The Kushite expansion

Around 1000 BCE, the Nubians founded the independent Kingdom of Kush. The Kushites absorbed much of Egyptian culture during this time – including using hieroglyphics in official documents and worshipping some of the Egyptian gods, notably the sun god, Amun. There are also records of marriages between the Kushite and Egyptian royal families. However, Egypt and Kush maintained distinct identities. Kushites depicted themselves wearing animal-skin cloaks, patterned fabrics, and large earrings, while in Egyptian art they were shown with darker skin and cropped hairstyles. Unlike Egyptian art, Kushite art depicted sub-Saharan animals, such as elephants and giraffes.

In the 8th century BCE, there was a power shift. A series of Kushite kings (the "Black Pharaohs") began to take over Egypt, which they subsequently ruled for a century. Taharqa (r. 690–664 BCE), who was possibly the most influential Kushite pharaoh, began major construction projects throughout Egypt and Kush, including lavish temples and monuments. It was during this period that the Nile

Valley saw the first widespread construction of pyramids (many in modern-day Sudan) since the Middle Kingdom period.

In the 7th century BCE, the Assyrian Empire drove the Kushites out of Egypt. The Kushites retreated south to Meroë, which became their new capital, and their kingdom continued to flourish until the 4th century CE. However, it no longer had any close links with Egypt. There were no more Kushite pharaohs, and the Meroites abandoned Egyptian hieroglyphics in favour of their own script.

▲ **The ancient Kushite city of Meroë**, with its pyramids built in the Egyptian style (c. 300 BCE–400 CE), shows the cultural crossover between the two rival kingdoms.

◀ **This facsimile of a wall painting** in the tomb of Huy (the Egyptian viceroy of Kush) depicts Huy presenting a tribute to the Egyptian pharaoh Tutankhamun (r. 1333–1323 BCE).

Dispersal through Africa
THE BANTU EXPANSION

◀ **This brass plaque** dates from the 16th century and features the *Oba*, or king, of Benin. The Benin Empire was comprised of Bantu-speaking peoples.

The 300 million speakers of Bantu languages make up Africa's largest linguistic group, with over 500 separate languages spread across much of the continent. Yet the original homeland of the Bantu peoples, from where these languages dispersed so widely, was a comparatively small area located in the Mambilla and Bemanda highlands between Cameroon and Nigeria.

Evidence of migration

Sometime around 2500 BCE, Bantu peoples began to migrate southwards, possibly driven by climatic changes, to find better conditions. Their progress can be traced through various evidence: the Bantu languages, characteristic pottery (with bevelling at the rims and a dimple impression at the base), iron tools, and DNA evidence, which all suggest the route and the rate at which they migrated.

The expansions, which were not continuous, halted once they reached the barrier of the Central Africa rainforest, which Bantu speakers did not penetrate until about 500 BCE. From here some groups moved slowly westwards down the coast, while others pushed eastwards towards the Great Lakes of East Africa, which Bantu peoples reached in c. 1000 BCE. By the first centuries CE, Bantu peoples in the west had reached the modern borders of South Africa, while those in the east moved towards the coast of Tanzania and then into South Africa, reaching the Limpopo in Northern Transvaal by 500 CE.

Although the Bantu peoples were not originally agriculturalists, they acquired knowledge of farming along the way, beginning to plant sorghum, ground nut, and millet (found in the Democratic Republic of Congo, dating to 200 BCE) at a time when further climate change in equatorial Central Africa made the traditional gathering of forest products more difficult. They also discovered ironworking, which seems to have begun in the Urewe region of the Great Lakes around 500 BCE, and became a skill the Bantu peoples made use of across the continent.

From village to states

The Bantu lived in small villages. Every 10 years or so they abandoned their old fields to avoid exhausting the soil, and cleared new ones in the forest as they migrated deeper into the continent. Their movements, however, displaced existing peoples such as the Khoi and the San of southern Africa, whose descendants were pushed into the Namibian desert and other less productive areas.

Once established, the Bantu peoples began to coalesce from small bands into chiefdoms and then form into larger states. Between the 11th and 15th centuries, powerful Bantu kingdoms emerged such as the Kongo in Angola, the Bunyoro Kita in the Great Lakes, and the Monomotapa, whose rulers built the imposing structures of Great Zimbabwe. Today, the Bantu languages are spoken from Cameroon to Kenya and right down to the south of the continent.

▼ **The Great Enclosure, Zimbabwe**, was home to a wealthy city from around 1100. It formed the capital of the successful trading empire of the Bantu Shona people.

Movements of the Bantu peoples

Bantu peoples spread from their homelands in the Mambilla and Bemanda highlands into the African continent. Bantu peoples in the east went as far as the Great Lakes, while those in the west reached what is now South Africa.

KEY

Bantu expansion

➤ c. 2000 BCE
➤ c. 1000 BCE–500 CE
➤ c. 500–1500 CE

Bantu homeland
Initial migration
Eastern Bantu
Western Bantu

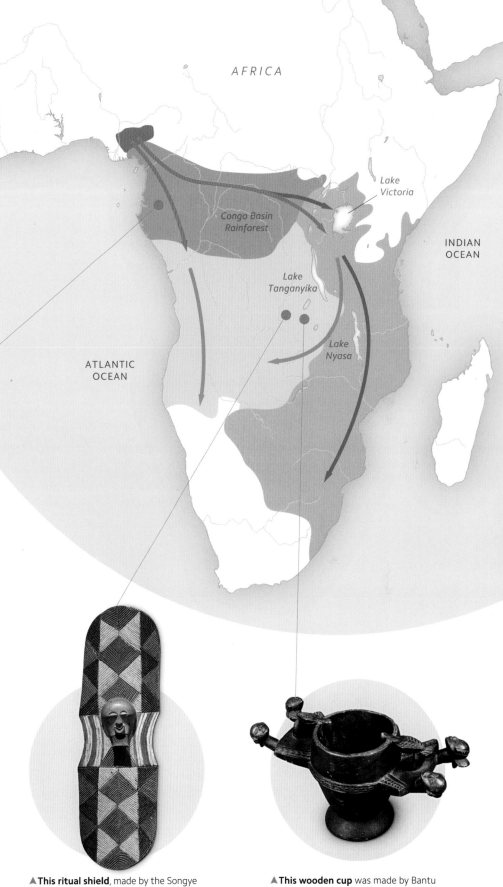

AFRICA

Lake Victoria

Congo Basin Rainforest

INDIAN OCEAN

Lake Tanganyika

ATLANTIC OCEAN

Lake Nyasa

▲ **Fine metalwork** on this stylized figure shows the skills of the Bakota (Kota) people, a Bantu-speaking ethnic group from Gabon. This reliquary guardian figure could be removed for ceremonial dances.

Ironworking

Early iron-smelting furnaces dating from at least 500 BCE have been found in Central African locations, including Urewe. They consisted of conical shafts made of clay bricks over a pit in which the iron ore was heated to high temperatures. Iron created harder and longer-lasting tools, which Bantu peoples used to clear dense undergrowth and break up soil for planting. It also allowed them to make weapons, giving them an advantage over the Indigenous peoples of the region.

▲ **This ritual shield**, made by the Songye people of the Congo, features a depiction of a Kifwebe mask. These masks were worn during key Songye ceremonies.

▲ **This wooden cup** was made by Bantu peoples in Central Africa, probably from the Congo. Its handles are carved in the shape of human heads.

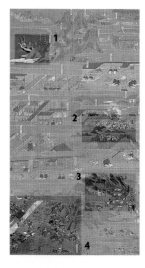

1. Prince Shōtoku sends an envoy to China. His letter contains the first reference to Japan as the "Land of the Rising Sun".

2. The young prince plays with other children, showing his own prowess.

3. The prince joins his family (the Soga clan) in defeating the rival Mononobe clan, who oppose Buddhism.

4. The vengeful soul of Mononobe no Moriya destroys the prince's great Buddhist temple, Shitennō-ji.

▶**This 14th-century scroll** depicts scenes from the life of Prince Shōtoku (574–622 CE), who was a keen proponent of Buddhism. Episodes from his life decorated temples and shrines, aiding the spread of Buddhism throughout Japan.

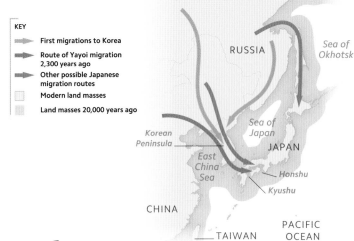

Crossing the land bridges
SETTLING JAPAN AND KOREA

The land that is now Japan remained unpopulated until about 35,000 BCE. The first people to arrive were nomadic hunter-gatherers from eastern Siberia, who probably entered Japan from the north via a land bridge that linked Japan to Asia's mainland. These early settlers became known as the Jōmon – a name that derives from their cord-marked pottery, which dates to around 13,000 BCE. The Jōmon tended to settle near the coast or rivers, in semi-subterranean pit dwellings, and they obtained their food by hunting, fishing, and gathering. Some archaeologists believe that the Ainu people – an Indigenous minority group in modern-day Japan – are descendants of these original Jōmon settlers.

The Yayoi come to Japan
Around 300 BCE, a new group – the Yayoi – arrived in Japan. They originated in Southeast Asia, and went north via what is now China and the Korean Peninsula, probably crossing into Japan via a southwestern land bridge. They introduced rice cultivation (which they had discovered in China) and metallurgy, which they used to craft bronze mirrors. The Yayoi intermingled with the Jōmon, and became the ancestors of the modern Japanese.

Yayoi Japan was open to cultural influence and incomers from neighbouring lands. The first mention of the Japanese is in the ancient Chinese text *Han Shu* (*Book of Han*) in about 111 CE. The practice of erecting dolmen tombs, with stone slabs, possibly came from Korea. The Yayoi period was followed by the Yamato period (250–710 CE), during which the peoples of Japan merged to form a centralized empire.

The creation of Korea
The modern-day Koreans are probably descended from a mix of peoples who came from Southeast Asia, eastern Siberia, Mongolia, and China around 6000 BCE. A thriving culture developed in what is known as the Chulmun period, with a tradition of pottery decorated with comb-like patterns. The Chulmun people were growing millet and rice by 3500 BCE and 1500 BCE respectively – both crops introduced by the Chinese.

In the mid-1st millennium BCE, Korea's first kingdom, Gojoseon, emerged in the north of the peninsula. It developed into a powerful state until the Chinese Han Dynasty conquered it in 108 BCE. After Gojoseon's collapse, three smaller kingdoms were formed: Silla (in the southeast), Baekje (in the southwest), and Goguryeo (in the north). It was the latter that finally drove out the Chinese in 313 CE. Silla became increasingly powerful and conquered the other kingdoms. In 668 CE, it founded the first unified state, covering most of the Korean Peninsula.

At the time of the Three Kingdoms, there were close connections with Japan. Baekje introduced Buddhism to Japan in 552 CE (the Chinese had introduced Buddhism to Goguryeo in the 4th century). After Silla's victory, refugees from the rival kingdoms fled to Japan. Many settled near Yamato Japan's imperial capital, Nara, and intermarried with Japanese noble clans.

▲ **This map shows** the possible migration routes of Japanese and Korean ancestors from Siberia and Southeast Asia, across land bridges that once linked Japan to the mainland.

▼ **The impressed rope decoration** on this neolithic earthenware vessel (made c. 3500–2500 BCE) is typical of Jōmon pottery.

▼ **This pit-house** – a shelter dug into the ground with a straw roof – is a reconstruction of a typical prehistoric house in Korea from the 1st millennium BCE.

The lands of Qin

EARLY CHINESE MIGRATION

In Neolithic times, the Han – who now make up the vast majority of China's population and are the largest ethnic group in the world – were a small ethnic group in the Yellow River valley. Over time, they grew in number and settled far beyond their central heartland. Meanwhile, waves of nomadic peoples who invaded China from the north modified their way of life and became sinicized (assimilated into Chinese culture).

The Han Chinese are descendants of the Huaxia, who lived along the Yellow River. Although the Huaxia descended from several different cultures, they saw themselves as a cohesive, civilized society united by shared values, which included a respect for central authority and the family. This idea of a single people helped Qin Shi Huangdi ("First Emperor of Qin") to defeat rival kingdoms and unite the country in 221 BCE, with the Huaxia as its largest ethnic group.

Two-way migrations

To reinforce his new empire's borders, Qin Shi Huangdi sent more than 1 million people to the northern and southern frontiers. There, protected by army garrisons, the settlers established farms and began to cultivate millet and rice. Under the Han (202 BCE–220 CE) and Tang (618–907 CE) dynasties, army garrisons were also established in Central Asia, bringing soldiers into contact with nomadic groups such as the Turks, Khitan, and Uyghur, who alternately fought and allied with Chinese armies, but did not adopt a Han Chinese way of

life. These bases, such as Dunhuang, became important staging posts on the Silk Road, along which merchants carried Chinese silk and spices in exchange for cotton, ivory, and silver from lands further west. This route was also used by travellers, such as the Buddhist monk Faxian, who brought Buddhist texts from India to China in 414 CE.

Migrants also settled in the Chinese heartlands. Some were forced to move, including the thousands of regional aristocrats the First Emperor transferred to his capital, Xianyang (near Xi'an, in Shaanxi province), to break up their power bases. Others moved for economic reasons, making Chang'an, the Tang capital, a diverse hub with over 1 million people. Northern nomads arrived, too – invading China, settling, and establishing new dynasties, such as the Jurchen Jin Dynasty (1115–1234).

Adopting Chinese culture

Migration occurred in the greatest numbers on China's fringes. Kingdoms such as Dian (in modern Yunnan province) saw more and more Han settlers – some of them peasants who had been promised land, others convicts who had been sent to the frontiers. By the 1st century CE, the Dian had adopted Chinese traditions, such as burying their dead with mirrors, coins, and crossbows, rather than the traditional drums and cowrie shells from Southeast Asia. However, the local population was not displaced. Dian, like elsewhere in China, became a mixture of newcomers and Indigenous peoples who adopted a Han Chinese way of life.

▶ **Bronze mirrors** were first made in China in the Warring States period (475–221 BCE), when different kingdoms vied for power. This mirror has animal carvings on one side.

◀ **Bronze containers** held cowrie shells, which the Dian used as currency. As contact with Han Chinese culture grew, coins supplanted shells and pots like this fell out of use.

▲ **Rice cultivation** in China expanded in the 6th and 7th centuries, after canals were built to transport crops from south to north. This wall painting is from around 650 CE.

◀ **China's borders** were in a constant state of flux during its imperial history. This map shows its borders during the Qin, Han, and Tang dynasties.

KEY

▢ Qin Empire 221–206 BCE
▢ Han Empire 206 BCE–220 CE
▢ Tang Empire 618–907 CE

CULTURAL INFLUENCES

Feng streets

Emperor Gaozu of Han founded the Han Dynasty (206 BCE–220 CE) and made Chang'an its capital. Born a peasant in the Feng district of Peixian (now in Jiangsu Province), the emperor rebuilt some of Chang'an's streets to imitate those of Feng for his homesick father, as depicted in this painting. He also relocated Feng's residents to the capital.

Silk Road travellers

The Silk Road brought a wide range of merchants and immigrants to Chang'an from the 7th to the 10th centuries. Among them were people from the Iranian civilization of Sogdia. Often multilingual, Sogdians played a key role as middlemen in the exchange of goods and ideas. As metalworkers they brought new styles to their Chinese counterparts.

Buddhist teachings

Buddhism reached China from India via the Silk Road in the 1st or 2nd centuries CE. In the 4th century, scholar-monks travelled to India to study Buddhism, returning with texts translated into Chinese. Built in 648 to house Buddhist sutras, Big Goose Pagoda in Chang'an was famously extended by Wu Zetian in 704.

Xi'an

CITY OF MANY FAITHS

For a millennium of China's history, Xi'an (formerly Chang'an), now in the central Shaanxi Province, was a commercial and cultural crossroads home to people with a multitude of ethnic identities and belief systems. Along with Luoyang, Nanjing, and Beijing, Chang'an was one of the principal capital cities of ancient and imperial China (in this era, the ruling dynasties often chose different capitals as their power base).

Chang'an was founded by the Han Dynasty in 203 BCE at the eastern starting point of the Silk Road, an extensive network of trade routes that connected China with the West. The merchants who travelled the Silk Road carried not only foreign merchandise into Chang'an but new cultures, trades, and faiths from across Asia; some also settled there.

A cosmopolitan metropolis

As the capital of the Tang Dynasty (618–907 CE) Chang'an grew into the world's largest and most populous city. By the 8th century CE a million people from China and regions along the Silk Road lived within its walls. It was a place of intellectual and cultural exchange, a mecca for scholars, students, teachers, and philosophers. Musicians and dancers from Central Asian kingdoms performed at court, while Turkish folk songs influenced Chinese poets.

Religious tolerance was a hallmark of Tang rule. Thousands of Buddhist monks lived in the city and it was a centre of Buddhist learning. Persian traders, and refugees who had fled the Arab invasion of Persia, worshipped at Zoroastrian temples, and in 742 CE, Muslim merchants founded the Great Mosque.

The city's golden age ended with the fall of the Tang in 907 CE although it continued as a trade centre. It experienced a revival under the Ming Dynasty (1368–1644), when its Muslim population expanded and became more integrated into Chinese society.

▲▲**This modern mural** celebrates the golden age of the Tang Dynasty. It depicts key buildings in Chang'an and ladies of the Tang court.

▲**The terracotta army**, some 8,000 battle-ready clay warriors, was buried with Qin Shi Huang, China's first emperor, whose capital lay just north of modern Xi'an.

◀**Xi'an's Muslim quarter**, located in what was the foreigners' district during the Han and Tang eras, is home to a 65,000-strong Hui community. Visitors flock to the bustling Beiyuanmen Muslim Market here to sample delicacies from food stalls and restaurants.

> "People crammed into the city, spilled into the suburbs, everywhere streaming into the hundreds of shops."
>
> The *Wen Xuan* ("*Selections of Refined Literature*"), c.520–530 CE

Muslim descendants

Islam was introduced to China by envoys from the Middle East in the 7th century. Muslim traders from Persia and Arabia settled in Chang'an and married Han Chinese women. Their children became known as Hui, now one of China's 56 ethnic groups.

Christian missionaries

Nestorianism, a Christian sect that originated in Syria, entered Chang'an in 635 CE with Alopen, a missionary from the Church of the East, who was permitted to build a church. Although followers were persecuted in later eras, Christianity survived in China and today, there are around 12 million Catholics and 30 million Protestants.

Ming fortifications

Chang'an served as the capital of 10 dynasties, and in response to shifting conditions, it was relocated, rebuilt, and expanded several times on sites within the surrounding region. During the Ming Dynasty new walls were built to protect what had become a much smaller city than under the Tang; the Ming fortifications remain intact today.

Eboracum
Londinium
Massilia
New Carthage
Rome
Italica
Carthage
Athens
Gades
Timgad
Syracuse
Ephesus
Apamea
Palmyra
Uthina
Leptis Magna
Mediterranean Sea
Tyre
Alexandria

KEY
Extent of Roman Empire in 117 CE
Main trade routes
Sea routes

▲ **This Roman sculpture** of the Greek goddess, Artemis, was found in Ephesus. Known as Artemis of Ephesus, it illustrates Greco-Roman cultural mixing.

▲ **Funerary portraits** were an Egyptian burial practice which continued into Roman times. The lifelike portraits were used to cover the head of the mummified person.

The Roman Empire

At its height, the Roman Empire was vast, stretching throughout Europe, across the Balkans to the Middle East and into North Africa. This map shows the main roads and trading routes built by the Romans.

▲ **This Roman manicure set**, found in Bath, England, would have been used for cutting, cleaning, and shaping nails. Roman women carried such tools on belt hooks.

▲ **This Punic stone slab** from the 1st–2nd century CE combines elements from the ancient Punic culture of North Africa with Roman Carthage influences.

▲ **This tondo shows the Severan Dynasty**, the family of Roman emperor Septimius Severus, who was from North Africa and married Syrian Julia Domna.

All roads lead to Rome

LIFE IN THE ROMAN EMPIRE

From its legendary foundation in 753 BCE, Rome was a community that depended on immigrants. Its founder and first king, Romulus, was presented by patriotic writers as a descendant of Aeneas, the hero who escaped from the sack of Troy. In its early days, Rome accepted migrants from neighbouring peoples, such as the Etruscans who provided some of the city's early kings. From these small beginnings, Rome grew until it became a mighty empire of 70 million people, uniting Celts in the far north with Greeks and Arabs in the east and Nubians in the far south. These groups continued to speak their own tongues, but were joined by the rule of a single emperor, common laws, and the Latin language.

The empire's mosaic of provinces and peoples was held together by Roman citizenship, which gave the elite few who were born to Roman citizens enhanced rights, and gave the rest a hope that they too might acquire them. A person living in one of the provinces could be made a citizen as a reward for loyalty or service to the empire – for example, 25 years' service in the auxiliary units of the army gave ex-soldiers citizenship. Veterans were awarded diplomas, inscribed on bronze tablets, which they took with them to the farms or land they were granted – another privilege of former soldiers.

Roman soldiers, local gods

Service in the army led to the large-scale movement of people – in Britain alone there were 55,000 soldiers, many from Germany, the Netherlands, and even a unit of sailors from far-off Iraq. There was also a contingent of troops from North Africa, the Aurelian Moors, that settled in Britain. Many soldiers took local wives – though officially they were not allowed to marry. The occupation led to a mixing of cultures, including the merging of Roman gods with local (in Britain and Gaul, Celtic) deities. For example, Sulis, the divine guardian of the healing spring at Bath, became identified with the Roman goddess of wisdom, Minerva.

Migrants in high positions

It was not just soldiers who travelled: in York (Eboracum), England, in 1901, archaeologists discovered the skeleton of a young woman who evidence suggested originated in North Africa. Buried in a grand sarcophagus (stone coffin), with expensive grave goods including a pair of ivory bangles, she was clearly a person of importance who travelled to Britain and died there in the 4th century CE. By then, the highest offices in the empire were open to migrants. All of the early

▶ **This Roman *scutum* (shield)** is the only surviving example of the shields used by Roman soldiers. Its painted features reflect Roman icons of victory, including an eagle and a lion.

▼ **The Roman ruins of Timgad** are in today's Algeria. Founded by Emperor Trajan, in 100 CE, they are an example of Roman grid planning. Roads were built in straight lines for direct routes.

emperors had been from what is now Italy, but in 98 CE, Trajan, from Italica (in today's southern Spain), became the first non-Italian emperor, and from 193–211 CE, Septimius Severus (from what is now Libya) ruled as the first African Roman emperor. Later rulers came from what is now Britain, Turkey, Bulgaria, and Jordan.

Trade offered another opportunity for travel and cultural interchange within the empire. The Romans sent their wine throughout the Mediterranean on great trading galleys, while in Rome itself so much olive oil was imported that the remains of its shattered pottery containers still make up much of Monte Testaccio – an artificial mound that survives in the heart of the city today.

Most merchants returned to their home ports, but some settled. In South Shields, northeast England, the merchant Barates – from far-off Palmyra (in modern Syria) – set up a tombstone to his beloved wife Regina, an enslaved woman from the southeast of England, whom he had freed. Written in his native Palmyrene, the inscription reads: "Regina, freedwoman of Barates, alas!"

For those enslaved, life was very different from that of a soldier, senator, or merchant. Men captured in battle were often set to gruelling work in mines or on large farms. With little opportunity to return home, some married other enslaved people and gradually assimilated into Roman culture – for example, doctors from Greece, many of whom had been able to purchase their freedom. Some communities of foreigners, such as Egyptian priests of the goddess Isis, or Jewish people, remained apart from mainstream Roman society due to their religion, and retained their own traditions and languages.

Infrastructure and entertainment

As the Roman Empire grew, existing towns took on a more Roman cast, with the construction of buildings for Roman-style law courts; basilicas clustered around a forum; amphitheatres for gladiatorial shows; and circuses for horse-drawn chariot races to provide entertainment for the masses. Some gladiators were enslaved people fighting to obtain their freedom, while others were free migrants hoping to win a fortune. The chariot driver Gaius Apuleius Diocles, who came from Lusitania (now Portugal) and who won at least 1,400 races in the arena over two decades, gained the equivalent of more than £100 million today in winnings.

▲ **This 2nd century CE country life mosaic** is from Uthina, a Roman colony in today's Tunisia. This part of northwest Africa produced and exported wheat, olive oil, and wine to parts of the Roman Empire.

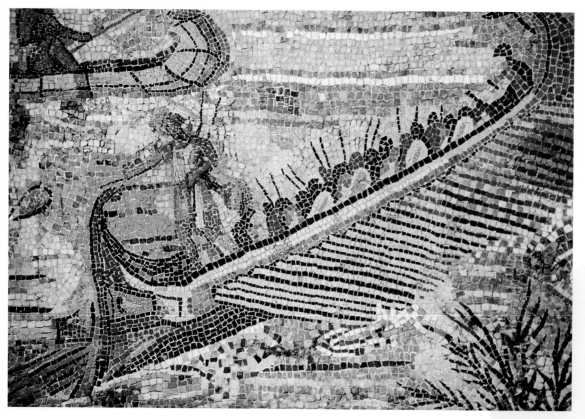

◀ **This detail of a *bireme*** (an ancient warship), is from the Nilotic mosaic of the flooding of the river Nile in Egypt. It shows a multicultural army, with soldiers of different skin tones.

In the east, where the climate was hotter, the Romans built colonnaded streets to provide shade, as at Apamea (in Syria). They also built temples to local gods such as Bel (in Palmyra), and Jupiter, as well as sanctuaries to the Persian god Mithras.

The decline of the empire

In its early days, Rome had seen larger-scale movements of people as Celtic tribes invaded Rome (sacking it in 390 BCE), and as Dacians carried out raids from what is now Romania into the empire. By the 3rd century CE, however, these invasions became more dangerous and the Roman army took in large numbers of Germanic mercenaries to guard against incursions by their countrymen across the Danube and the Rhine. Some Roman citizens became refugees, abandoning their provincial villas to return to the comparative safety of Italy, or moving to the more secure provinces in the east of the empire. In the 5th century, groups trying to flee barbarian attacks founded Venice, finding safety in the maze of islands off the mainland, while in other places, such as Britain, towns were abandoned completely and life reverted to the rural subsistence of the pre-Roman era.

When the Roman Empire in the west collapsed in 476 CE, and its former provinces fell into the hands of Germanic invaders, Roman citizenship ceased. The vast empire within which hundreds of thousands of soldiers, merchants, and pilgrims had been free to travel, mixing their cultures, religions, and languages, was no more, though this model survived to inspire future ages.

▲ **The Great Dish** was found near Mildenhall, Suffolk, England, in 1942. It is part of the 4th-century CE Mildenhall treasure, one of the most valuable collections of Roman silverware.

3

Transcontinental Contact

375–1400 CE

Transcontinental Contact

375–1400 CE

In the millennium from 375 BCE to 1400 CE, migration shaped the world in new ways as powers rose and fell and people moved long distances across continents. The Chinese Han Empire fell in the 3rd century CE and the Western Roman Empire collapsed in the 5th century CE, both in part due to their inability to absorb waves of incoming migrants. In Mesoamerica, the Mayan city-states were abandoned, creating instability which only ended when the Mexica (Aztec) built a new empire based around Tenochtitlan in the 14th century CE. In Europe, from the 8th century CE, Norse warriors from Scandinavia used boats (and horses) to launch long-distance raids into the medieval kingdoms which had emerged in Europe after the fall of Rome.

Religion became a driver of migration in this period, as Jewish people suffered persecution and expulsions that drove them to move across many different states and settle around Eastern Europe. The expansion of Islam from its beginnings in the Arabian peninsula in the 7th century CE created a vast empire stretching from Central Asia to the Iberian peninsula. This expansion spread the Arabic

Byzantine ships are depicted at the Ostrogothic palace of Theodoric (see pp.68–71)

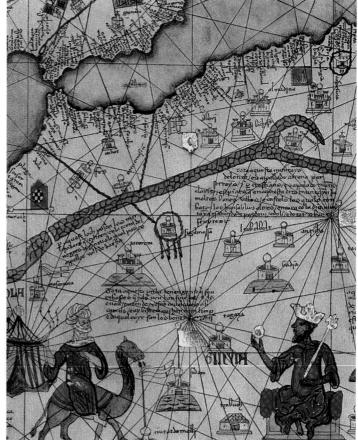

Mansa Musa of Mali is pictured on his journey to Mecca (see pp.72–75)

"[He] went ashore with all his company. Then he said, 'This is beautiful, and here I should like to build me a home.'"

On Thorvald Eriksson's explorations, "The Saga of the Greenlanders", *Flateyjarbók (Flat Island Book)*, c.1387

language and Islamic culture, creating a flow of migrants and pilgrims across the Muslim world as far as West Africa to empires such as Mali (which stretched to the borders of the Sahara Desert).

Many groups migrated huge distances across land and sea. Some movements were peaceful, such as those of the Māori (from Polynesia), who settled New Zealand around the 12th century, and those of the Roma (originally from India), who reached Western Europe by the 15th century. Others were more violent – such as those of the Mongols, who,

through conquest, built a vast multiethnic empire that spanned most of Central Asia, China, Russia, Iran, and parts of Europe, held together by armies of horse-borne archers.

By the time the period ended, merchants, migrants, and simple travellers traversed well-established trade routes, such as the Silk Road, along which cultural influences and people spread. The speed of travel had not varied much for a thousand years, nor the means by which people went. Yet the centuries to come would usher in a new age of migration on an unprecedented scale.

Viking ships cross the seas to the British Isles (see pp.88–89)

Christians massacre Jewish people during the First Crusade (see pp.94–95)

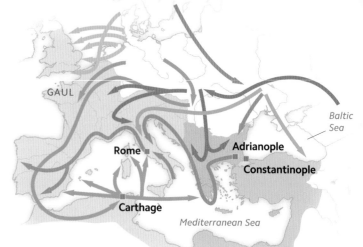

Reshaping the continent

THE GREAT MIGRATIONS

The European continent was reshaped in the centuries between 300 and 700 CE, when waves of migrating tribes moved from Northern Europe and the Russian steppes to settle in the lands of the former Roman Empire. These peoples went on to establish kingdoms that formed the basis of future European countries, including France and Spain.

Entering the empire

From the 3rd century CE, the Romans established treaties with a number of Germanic tribes on the fringes of Roman territory, such as the Vandals and Goths. Soldiers from these tribes had been enlisting in the Roman army since the 1st century CE, and the treaties bound them to fight in exchange for food and money. When the Roman Empire began to struggle economically in the 4th century CE, the warriors were allowed to settle on Roman land in lieu of payment. And as Rome lost political control and became more dependent on its army, Germanic soldiers played an increasingly important role.

The Germanic peoples who had settled at the Roman frontier along the River Danube probably originated from southern Scandinavia or the Baltic coast. They lived in small agricultural villages in forest clearings, and gradually coalesced into larger confederations, such as the Alemanni (meaning "all men") and the Franks. Despite agreements with the Romans, they clashed sporadically. Then, in the 370s CE, a new threat advanced from the east: the Huns, a group of nomadic warriors on horseback who attacked the Germanic groups, driving them south. The Goths at the vanguard of the migrants crossed the Danube and pleaded with the Roman authorities for refuge. They were allowed into the empire, but deteriorating relations with local Roman officials led the migrating Goths to revolt. They advanced towards Constantinople, crushing the Roman army at Adrianople (now in Turkey) in 378 CE and fanning out across the Balkans. Under their leader, Alaric, they sacked Rome in 410 CE. A later group of Goths who invaded Italy came to be known as the Ostrogoths, while those who travelled further west into southern France and Spain were termed the Visigoths.

The collapse of the Roman frontier

By this time, other tribes had breached the Roman frontier. In December 406 CE, the Germanic Suebi and Vandals, and Iranian Alan peoples, crossed the frozen Rhine and swept through Gaul (modern-day France, Belgium, western Germany, and northern Italy) and into Roman Spain. Eventually, 80,000 Vandal warriors and their families crossed the Straits of Gibraltar into North Africa where they formed their own kingdom.

With the frontier now impossible to hold, the Romans began to allow settlement within the empire by those they had formerly regarded as barbarians. The Visigoths obtained land in southwestern Gaul under a system known as *hospitalitas*, but their travels were not over. The Franks conquered what was left of Roman Gaul and pushed the Visigoths over the Pyrenees into Spain.

▲ **Between 300 and 700 CE**, the former Roman Empire was invaded by Germanic tribes and other groups from northern Europe and the Russian steppes.

▼ **The Visigoths** adopted the Roman imperial symbol of the eagle as they migrated. This Visigoth brooch is made of bronze and coloured glass.

"… Now the Vandals… since they were pressed by hunger, moved to the country of the [Franks]."

Procopius, *De Bello Vandalico* (*The Vandal Wars*), III 3–7, c. 550 CE

◄ **This 19th-century woodcut** shows the Franks, a Germanic tribe, crossing the Rhine into Gaul in the 5th century CE, when it was part of the waning Western Roman Empire.

▼ **Vandals, Alans, and Suebi** migrated to Roman Spain in the 5th century CE in search of fertile lands and a better life, as shown in this woodcut from 1873.

A mosaic from the 6th century Basilica of Sant'Apollinare Nuovo, Ravenna, built by Ostrogoth king Theodoric as his palace chapel.

In Italy, the Germanic leader of the Roman army, Odoacer, deposed the last Western Roman emperor, Romulus Augustus, in 476 CE, and declared himself king. But his reign was short; he was defeated by the Ostrogoth chieftain Theodoric, who, as the son of a king, had received a Roman education in the eastern capital of Constantinople after being taken there as a hostage. Theodoric tried to merge Roman traditions and Ostrogoth culture to cement his power in Italy and assimilate his Ostrogoth subjects. He also employed Roman officials, such as the philosopher Boethius, to run his government.

New cultures

Although the Germanic tribespeople had lived in small villages before settling in the former Roman provinces, they took to urban life. Many converted to Catholicism, although the Goths and Vandals initially adopted Arianism – a form of Christianity considered heretical by mainstream Christians.

Within a few generations, the tribes began to assimilate. They converted to orthodox Christian beliefs, and their Germanic languages began to be replaced with a version of the Latin spoken in the provinces, which gradually evolved into Spanish, French, and Italian. In Britain, however, matters were different. By the time boatloads of Angles, Saxons, Jutes, and Frisians crossed the North Sea to Britain in the mid-5th century CE, Roman control there had collapsed. As the newcomers advanced, Roman towns were almost completely abandoned. Latin became a religious and scholarly language only; it was a version of the language spoken by the newcomers, that eventually developed into English.

Further migrations

Western Europe had scarcely begun to create a new hybrid Germanic and Roman culture when it faced challenges from fresh waves of migrants. The Slavs, a non-Germanic group probably originating in southern Russia, began raiding the Eastern Roman Empire across its Danube frontier in the early 6th century CE. With large areas of the empire depopulated by a plague in the 540s CE, they were able to reach the Peloponnese by the early 6th century CE. Even though they were then pushed back, other Slav groups settled large areas of Central and Eastern Europe, including what is now Poland, Russia, Croatia, and Serbia. Their dispersal was accelerated by the arrival of the Avars, invading nomadic warriors on horseback, who formed an empire in Central Europe (centred on modern Hungary), which lasted for around 250 years from 560 CE.

Italy, its prosperity blighted by a Roman reconquest that inflicted two decades of warfare, experienced a new Germanic settlement in 568 CE, when the Lombards, fleeing the Avar advance, surged into Italy. There, they established their own counties and duchies, whose rulers did not, this time, seek to employ old Roman methods of rule. What continuity there was came from the Christian Church, which gave a sense of unity to the very diverse groups whose states developed with the end of the age of migrations in the 9th century.

▲ **The Lombards**, a Germanic tribe, fled southwards to Italy to escape the Avars in the 6th century CE. King Agilulf (r.590–616 CE) is shown seated on his throne in this fragment from his helmet.

Eastern invaders

Persians, Avars, and Slavs laid siege to Constantinople in the Byzantine Empire (the eastern half of the Roman Empire) in 626 CE, but the city held, as shown in the 16th-century fresco below. Other nomadic tribes, including the Bulgars and Magyars, followed from the eastern steppes into Central Europe. The latter raided across Europe until a major defeat at Lechfeld in 955 CE. They then settled down in what is now Hungary.

> "... the Visigoths forced their way into the Roman Empire and seized all Spain..."
>
> Procopius, *De Bello Gothico* (*The Gothic War*), III, 3–7, c.550 CE

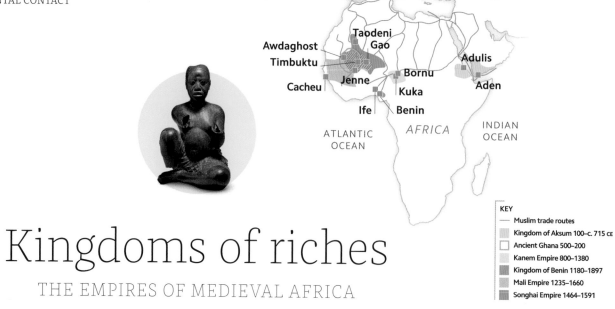

Kingdoms of riches

THE EMPIRES OF MEDIEVAL AFRICA

The varied landscape of sub-Saharan Africa has seen numerous empires rise and fall. Many of these kingdoms were founded by outsiders who migrated across the continent, subjugating and frequently incorporating existing groups into their territories. Almost all these powerful states were supported by trade in the continent's rich resources, including gold, salt, and ivory. Diverse groups of traders also brought new ideas to the continent, including Islam, which spread across much of Africa.

Power, trade, and ideas

The kingdom of Aksum, named for its capital in the Ethiopian highlands, was a major power by the 1st century CE. A cultural crossroads and trading centre on the route between the Mediterranean and India, its exports of ivory, hippopotamus hides, gold dust, and frankincense enriched its rulers who erected enormous stone stelae. In the 4th century CE Aksum adopted Christianity. Brought along trade routes from the Eastern Roman Empire, the religion provided a means of uniting Aksum's diverse peoples, and endured in the form of the Ethiopian Orthodox Church even after the kingdom's decline in the late 6th century CE.

Further to the west, centred on Lake Chad, the kingdom of Kanem was thriving by the 9th century CE. Formed by a confederation of nomadic peoples (some

of whom migrated to the area in the 8th century CE, when the Sahara region became drier), the empire's wealth was based on its control of strategic trade routes and the export of enslaved peoples (see pp.84–85), kola nuts, and ivory. In the 11th century, the kingdom's ruling Saifawa Dynasty converted to Islam, which was brought to the region by Muslim traders and missionaries from North Africa and the Middle East. Most of Kanem's population followed

▲ **Map of medieval Africa** showing the extent and key cities of its main empires, including the early kingdom of Aksum, and later Mali Empire.

▼ **This figure** from the late 13th–14th century was likely made in the royal city of Ife, Nigeria. It uses raw copper brought to Africa from France.

KEY

- — Muslim trade routes
- Kingdom of Aksum 100–c. 715 CE
- Ancient Ghana 500–200
- Kanem Empire 800–1380
- Kingdom of Benin 1180–1897
- Mali Empire 1235–1660
- Songhai Empire 1464–1591

"Many persons... set out on long journeys [from the Roman Empire to Africa]; some for the desire of making discoveries, others from a spirit of commercial enterprise."

Account of travellers to Ethiopia by Rufinus of Aquileia, 402 CE

suit, and had adopted Islam by the 13th century. The state's period of expansion ended in the late 14th century, when civil wars and invasions forced Kanem's court and peoples to relocate to the western edge of Lake Chad. In their new location they founded the state of Bornu, which survived until the 19th century.

West African empires

Trade across the desert (see pp.84–85) also helped establish the West African Wagadu Empire (within modern-day Mauritania, Mali, and Senegal), known as the kingdom of "Ghana" after the title of its kings. It was founded by the Soninke people, who were pushed to the southwestern edge of the Sahara by Berber nomads around 500 CE. Referred to by the Muslim astronomer al-Fazari around 770 CE as "the land of gold", it developed into a strong empire, with its capital at Kumbi Saleh gradually Islamicized by Muslim merchants arriving in trade caravans.

The kingdom of Mali, which had become the predominant power in the region by the early 13th century, also relied on trading gold. Situated

▲**This pendant** of a bird and two eggs (8th–11th century CE), made by the skilled artisans of Igbo Ukwu, Nigeria, uses metals and beads that were circulating on trade routes across Africa, Europe, and the Middle East.

◄**The king of Aksum** took in Muhammad and his followers as refugees in his Christian kingdom. He is depicted here, in an illustrated manuscript by Rashid ad-Din, declining a request from their persecutors to hand them over.

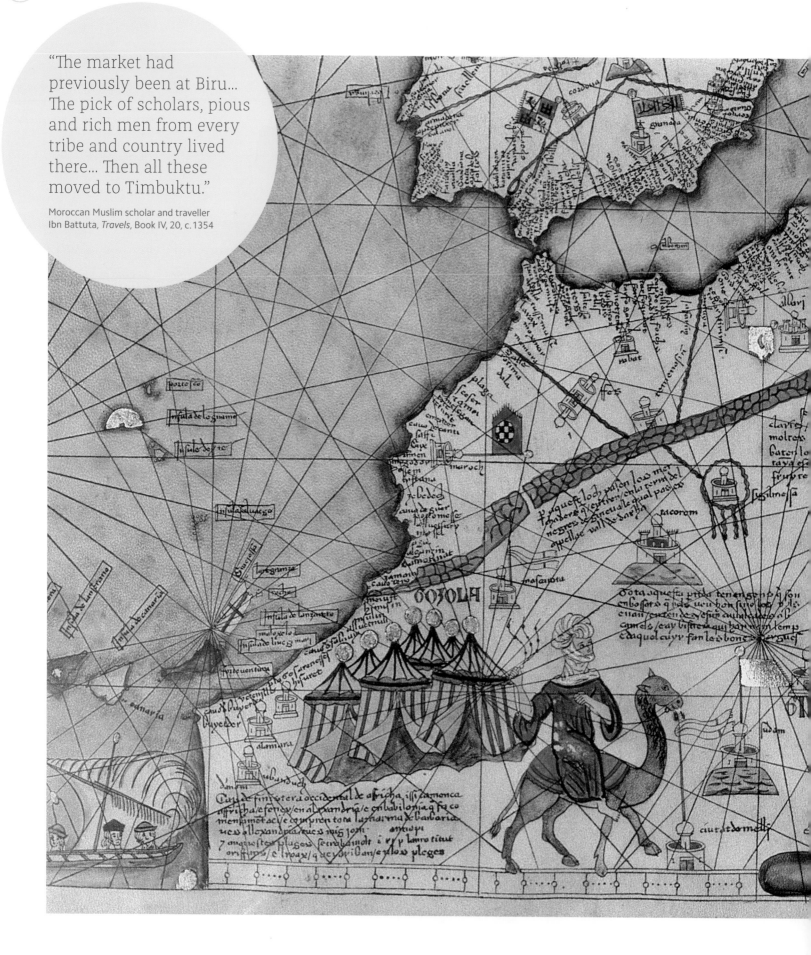

"The market had previously been at Biru… The pick of scholars, pious and rich men from every tribe and country lived there… Then all these moved to Timbuktu."

Moroccan Muslim scholar and traveller Ibn Battuta, *Travels*, Book IV, 20, c. 1354

◀ **Mansa Musa** (ruler of Mali from 1312 to 1337) made such a great impression with his lavish displays of wealth, while en route to Mecca, that his journey was recorded in the *Atlas of Maritime Charts* by Abraham Cresques in 1375.

▶ **Larabanga Mosque**, built in the kingdom of Gonja (in modern-day Ghana), is one of West Africa's oldest mosques. Legends relate it was founded in 1421 by an Arab trader.

between the rainforests of the south and the Muslim states of North Africa, the *mansas* – the rulers of Mali – taxed goods passing through their domains and profited from the rich gold-mining regions, such as Galam and Bambuk, in their territory. Salt and luxury goods were brought to their lands from the north, as well as cultural influences and Islam.

Descriptions of the kingdom of Mali by North African Muslim scholars and travellers such as Ibn Battuta (1304–69), who visited the empire in 1352, reveal the flow of trade, people, and ideas to the region, and the development of Timbuktu as a centre of Islamic learning, as well as a trade hub. Mali's greatest ruler Mansa Musa (c. 1280–1337), a devout Muslim, made the *hajj* to Mecca in 1324, bringing Muslim scholars, a number of *shurafa* (descendants of the Prophet Muhammad), poets, architects, and thousands of books, on his return.

The leaders of the Songhai state, who overthrew the kingdom of Mali in the 15th century, inherited Mansa Musa's legacy of trading and diplomatic relations, religion, and scholarship. By the 16th century, Timbuktu was home to as many as 25,000 scholars and students, who travelled from the Middle East, and North and West Africa to follow both religious and secular studies. The Songhai Empire also took advantage of a new and growing trade in manuscripts and books, which carried knowledge throughout the Islamic world.

Following the Niger River

The trade routes that crossed the Sahara region to the kingdoms of West Africa stretched further south, following the Niger River, to empires in forest regions. Here, powerful states such as the empire of Benin, and cities of Ife and Igbo Ukwu, fed products such as ivory, glass beads, and sophisticated metalwork into the trans-Saharan trade network, while salt, copper, and other valuables were transported to their realms.

Following the arrival of Portuguese merchants in 1489, the kingdom of Benin also began to exploit maritime trade routes, and establish diplomatic relations with European countries. Benin's traders controlled the flow of goods from inland areas to the coast, and exchanged ivory, pepper, artworks – and later enslaved peoples, captured from rival tribes – for resources such as guns and precious metals, particularly brass and copper. These metals, traded in the form of "manillas" – a type of bracelet – became a valued form of international currency. Much in-demand by the metalworkers in Benin, manillas were melted down and cast into elaborate plaques and sculptures.

Changing balance of power

As contact with Europe via the West African coast increased, the old pattern of empires supported by trade across the Sahara began to change. A major factor was the growth of the Atlantic slave trade (see pp.124–27), started by Portuguese traders in the 15th century, which disrupted the long-standing balance of power. Enriching Europeans and some African empires, and destroying others, it generated new trade routes that carried vast amounts of enslaved African labour and wealth abroad.

Benin bronzes

The palace of Benin was adorned with brass and bronze plaques telling the history of the growth of the kingdom's empire. Many depict the Oba (or king) and his attendants. These plaques were later stolen from Benin by the British.

The ruins of the Great Mosque still stand today at Kilwa, a former Swahili city-state on Africa's east coast. Arab settlers founded these coastal trading centres from around the 9th century CE, building magnificent stone houses and mosques.

EUROPE ASIA

Black Sea

Damascus
Cairo Baghdad
Fustat Kufa Basra Syrian Desert

Arabian Peninsula

AFRICA Arabian Sea

Spreading the faith

THE ISLAMIC EMPIRE

KEY
- Muslim lands by 632 CE
- Muslim lands by 656 CE
- Muslim lands by 756 CE

At the start of the 7th century CE, a patchwork of nomadic and settled tribes lived across the Arabian Peninsula and Syrian Desert, sandwiched between the declining empires of the Byzantines to the west and the Sasanians to the east. The tribes had no central organization, but were united by the Arabic language and the idea that they shared common ancestors. As the Prophet Muhammad's influence and the new religion of Islam spread across Arabia, the Islamic Empire began to take shape, and by 750 CE, it stretched across three continents.

The rise of Islam

Muhammad received his first revelations in around 610 CE, and began to spread the word of Allah around his home town of Mecca, in modern-day Saudi Arabia. In idol-worshipping Mecca, however, Muhammad's preaching proved unpopular, and in 622 CE, he and his followers moved to the oasis town of Medina. There, the Muslims set about establishing unquestioned authority, struggling against the Meccans, and forging tribal alliances.

Through a combination of military skill and diplomacy, Muhammad's network of followers rapidly grew, and with it spread Islam. Conversion was not always necessary to join the *umma* (Islamic nation), but people were drawn in by the exciting opportunities it offered. They tended to become Muslim as individuals, rather than as tribes. Some tribal markers, such as names, lingered, but others, especially those that did not fit with Muhammad's teachings, gradually disappeared.

Following the death of Muhammad in 632 CE, successive leaders, known as caliphs, extended Islamic dominion into Iraq, Iran, Syria, and Egypt.

At the end of a campaign, the conquerors settled, joined later by their families and dependents, who migrated from Arabia to live in the new territory.

Cultural mingling

In Syria, Muslims mingled with the native population, with whom they shared the Arabic language. Damascus became the empire's capital in around 661 CE, and Syria's existing heritage flourished alongside Islamic culture. The Umayyad Mosque (Great Mosque) of Damascus (see p.80) is an example of this cultural mixing, with its distinctly Christian architectural features.

By contrast, in Iraq, Muslim soldiers and their families lived in the garrison towns of Basra and Kufa, segregated from the native population. The soldiers were paid a salary, which deterred them from seizing land owned by the local inhabitants. This was also the case in Egypt – to avoid conflict with the local elite, the conquering armies built garrison towns. The most notable of these was Fustat, the remains of which now form part of Old

▲ **The Islamic world** expanded rapidly from the Arabian Peninsula after Muhammad's death. Most of the empire's growth occurred under the Rashidun Caliphate (632–61 CE).

▼ **The astrolabe** was a popular tool with Islamic astronomers, used mainly for navigation. The Caird Astrolabe (c.1300) is thought to have been made in France to an Islamic design.

▼ **The Muslim forces** were victorious in the Battle of Yarmouk in 636 CE, taking Syria from the Byzantine Empire and bringing Islam to the previously Christian region.

> "Whosoever accepts Islam... shall have the same rights and duties as [other Muslims], and they are obliged to... treat him as one of themselves."
>
> Umayyad caliph Umar II, r.717–20

◀ **Persian scientist** Nasir al-Din al-Tusi is depicted at work in the observatory of Maragheh (now in Azerbaijan), which he designed and built with the support of the Mongols.

Cairo. Unlike in Iraq, Arabs remained a minority in Egypt, and Islam and Arabic spread slowly. The province played a limited role in the early empire.

As Muslims pressed further east into the Iranian plateau, taking over land that had been part of the Sasanian Empire, some of the Persian ruling class escaped, and the Persian language, culture, and traditional religions survived. In their former territories, however, Islam came to dominate.

Thriving empire

The Islamic Empire reached its maximum extent under the Umayyad Dynasty (661–750 CE), whose armies conquered North Africa and pushed into the Iberian Peninsula (see pp.86–87). Islamic institutions were exported to every corner of the empire. One of the most important were hospitals, largely secular institutions, many of which were open to all. Major hospitals were built in Baghdad (Iraq), Damascus (Syria), and Cairo (Egypt), enabling Islamic medical knowledge to spread.

Other Islamic institutions spilled beyond the empire's boundaries, spreading alongside Islam. These included the *halqah* (teaching circle) and *madrasa* (formal school). Some cities outside the empire, like Timbuktu in West Africa, achieved such renown as centres of Islamic education that they attracted scholars from across the empire. While scholars moved beyond the empire's borders, plenty of people were travelling in the other direction. These were prisoners of war, captured on the fringes of the expanding empire and sold into slavery. Many were sent to the central provinces of the Arabian Peninsula, where they were resold in slave markets. A steady flow of enslaved people also came from non-Muslim parts of Africa, many of whom were trafficked across the Sahara (see pp.84–85).

Enslaved people had a major impact on the course of Islamic history, having formed part of the army since Muhammad's time. In the 9th century CE, the ruling Abbasid Dynasty began to rely heavily on enslaved soldiers, with the caliph al-Mu'tasim even using them for his personal guard. These soldiers were mostly Turkic nomads, known as *mamluks*, who had been raised on the steppe of Central Asia. They were generally captured by other Turkic nomads, then enslaved and sold to Muslim leaders.

Turkic takeover

Using enslaved Turkic soldiers proved costly for the Abbasid Dynasty. As alien peoples, the *mamluks* had no allegiance but to each other and often founded their own dynasties in charge of increasingly autonomous provinces. The Ghaznavid and Mamluk dynasties both began in this way. With successive Turkic invasions, the Abbasids' authority waned, and they eventually lost political control in 1258 when the Mongols sacked their capital of Baghdad (see pp.96–99).

The invading Turkic nomads wrought destruction on a massive scale, but they also protected and patronized the cultures and religions of the peoples they conquered, building mosques, palaces, and tombs. The Mongols, for example, rebuilt cities, repaired irrigation works, and encouraged farming. They also built observatories and libraries. Even so, they did not abandon their nomadic culture. Under Mongol rule, pastoralism was encouraged, Turkic became the language of the empire's military, and the *yassa* (the Mongols' traditional legal code) maintained a prominent role.

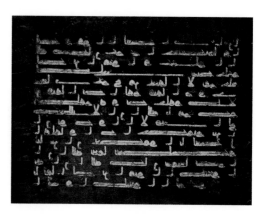

▲ **Early manuscripts of the Qur'an** have been found across the Islamic Empire. This one is from late-9th-century CE Egypt. It is written in Kufic script, an early form of calligraphy.

◀ **This mosaic** is from the treasury dome of the Umayyad Mosque in Damascus, which was built on the site of a Christian cathedral and decorated with mosaics made by Byzantine workers.

An Arab physician treats a patient in this 13th-century miniature from Islamic scholar al-Hariri's *Maqamat*, a collection of stories based in cities across the Islamic Empire.

Baghdad
THE JEWEL OF ISLAM'S GOLDEN AGE

▲▲**The Al-Kadhimiya Mosque** was built by Shah Ismail of the Safavid Dynasty in the early 16th century. The Ottoman sultan Suleiman the Magnificent added ornamentation after 1534.

▲**Mobile coffee stalls** are a common sight in Baghdad, where the first coffee shop opened in 1586, under Ottoman rule. The metal *dallah* used to serve the coffee originates in Baghdad.

▶**This map of Baghdad** was painted by the 16th-century, Bosnian-born polymath, Matrakçi Nasuh, known for his intricate miniatures depicting contemporary Ottoman cities and landscapes. This art form was influenced by small Persian paintings with religious or mythological themes.

The seat of Islamic power had shifted several times by the time the Abbasid Dynasty took control from the Umayyads in 750 CE. While their predecessors had expanded the empire westwards across North Africa and into Europe, the Abbasids, with their army of mostly Persians, looked to the east. In 762 CE, the second Abbasid caliph, al-Mansur, founded a new capital in Mesopotamia (Iraq) called Madinat al-Salaam ("City of Peace"), later known as Baghdad.

Al-Mansur brought in 100,000 architects, engineers, surveyors, and labourers from across the Islamic Empire to build his walled capital. Well placed on the Silk Road linking Asia and Europe, Baghdad soon became a global trade hub. Merchants arrived with goods from across Asia, and some traders, including Indian traders of spices, wood, and cloth, chose to stay.

Centre of learning

Under Abbasid rule Baghdad became the centre of Islamic learning. Muslims, Jews, and Christians worked side by side at the Bayt al-Hikmah ("House of Wisdom"), writing and studying books on mathematics, astronomy, medicine, geography, and the arts, and translating Greek and Roman works into Arabic. This scholarship was made possible by papermaking, a technology invented by the Chinese, passed on by Persians, and streamlined in Baghdad by the Arabs.

Baghdad's Golden Age ended in 1258 when the Mongols, Turkic nomads from Central Asia, ransacked the city, massacring many citizens (see pp.96–99). The Ottomans invaded in 1534 and tore down what remained of the city's round walls and modernized its architecture.

During World War I, the British took control from the Ottomans, and made Baghdad the capital of the newly created state of Iraq in 1920. Baghdad's population boomed as people flocked from rural areas in search of a better life. In the 20th century, the number of Jews in Baghdad decreased drastically, and many foreign Arabs left before the beginning of the Persian Gulf War. Much of the city was destroyed as a result of the Iraq War (2003–11), but efforts are now underway to rebuild its infrastructure and restore order.

CULTURAL INFLUENCES

Persian settlers

Baghdad was once known as "the Round City", after its circular defensive walls. The design is of Sassanian origin and indicates the influence that Persians had on the Abbasids. Many Persian Muslims stayed in the city while on pilgrimage, with some becoming residents. Persians also established the canal system linking the Tigris and Euphrates rivers.

Jewish communities

The Great Synagogue of Baghdad is one of the oldest synagogues in the world. Caliph al-Mansur built his new city on a site that included several Jewish villages, and allowed Jewish settlers to remain. By the 11th century, Baghdad's Jewish quarter (Dar al-Yahud) was home to some 45,000 Jews. Since the 1950s, the city's Jewish population has dwindled.

Eastern Christians

Hunayn ibn Ishaq was a 9th-century CE Nestorian Christian polymath and arguably the forefather of Arabic medicine. He translated many important Greek works (including those of Plato) into Syriac and Arabic. The Abbasid caliphs also employed Nestorian Christians as their private physicians. Eastern Christians form a significant minority in modern Baghdad.

"Baghdad, in the heart of Islam, is the city of well-being... In it are to be found the best of everything..."

Arab geographer al-Muqaddasi, *The Best Divisions for Knowledge of the Regions*, 10th century

Indian scholars

Among the scholars at the House of Wisdom in Baghdad were Indians invited by the Abbasid caliphs to translate Sanskrit texts – especially those on medicine, maths, and astronomy – into Arabic and Persian. The Abbasids also recruited Indian physicians to practise Ayurvedic medicine (a traditional healing system) in their hospitals.

Ottoman district

Al Rasheed Street, in central Baghdad, contains the city's financial district, many government buildings, and copper, textile, and gold bazaars. When it was built by the Ottomans in 1916, it became the first modern avenue in Baghdad's old city. Four years later, it became the scene of protests against British occupation.

Armenian faiths

This church stands in Baghdad's Karrada district, home to a mixed community of Armenian Christians and Muslims. Armenians have been settling in the city since it was built, but today's residents are mostly descended from those who migrated after the 1915 Armenian genocide.

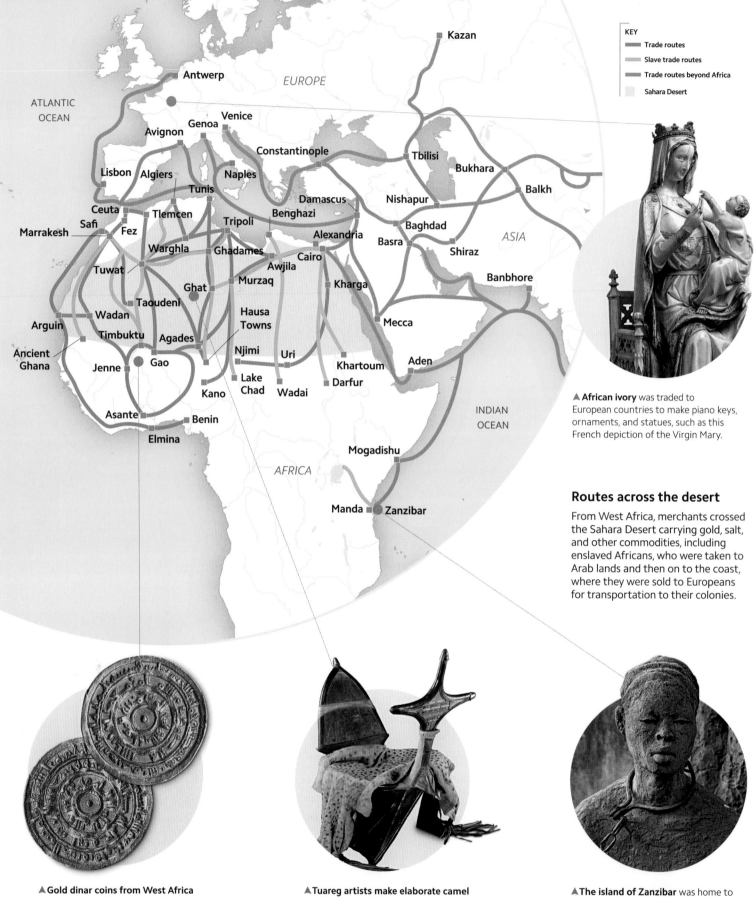

ATLANTIC OCEAN

EUROPE

ASIA

AFRICA

INDIAN OCEAN

Kazan

Antwerp

Genoa

Venice

Avignon

Constantinople

Tbilisi

Bukhara

Lisbon

Algiers

Naples

Damascus

Nishapur

Balkh

Tunis

Benghazi

Baghdad

Ceuta

Tlemcen

Tripoli

Alexandria

Basra

Shiraz

Marrakesh

Safi

Fez

Warghla

Ghadames

Awjila

Cairo

Banbhore

Tuwat

Ghat

Murzaq

Kharga

Taoudeni

Wadan

Hausa Towns

Mecca

Arguin

Timbuktu

Agades

Njimi

Uri

Aden

Ancient Ghana

Jenne

Gao

Lake Chad

Wadai

Khartoum

Darfur

Kano

Asante

Benin

Elmina

Mogadishu

Manda

Zanzibar

▲ **African ivory** was traded to European countries to make piano keys, ornaments, and statues, such as this French depiction of the Virgin Mary.

Routes across the desert

From West Africa, merchants crossed the Sahara Desert carrying gold, salt, and other commodities, including enslaved Africans, who were taken to Arab lands and then on to the coast, where they were sold to Europeans for transportation to their colonies.

▲ **Gold dinar coins from West Africa** were transported across the Sahara and exchanged for salt and other goods that were in high demand.

▲ **Tuareg artists make elaborate camel saddles**, such as this one. Widespread use of camels facilitated trade across and within the Sahara from 200 CE.

▲ **The island of Zanzibar** was home to the largest slave market in East Africa. This monument to the victims stands on the site of the former slave market.

Across the great desert

TRANS-SAHARAN TRADE

Since prehistoric times, goods, people, and cultures have crossed the harsh territory of the Sahara. Peoples from North Africa, including the Berber and Tuareg, and from West Africa, such as the Fulani, Bambara, and Soninke, pioneered trade in the region. Trading activity increased in the 7th century when the Arabs invaded North Africa to spread their Islamic faith. They also sought gold, large quantities of which lay on the West African coast.

Migration across the Sahara

Looking to monopolize trade, Arab and Berber merchants established themselves in the Sahel. For example, many moved to Koumbi Saleh, the capital of the Ghana Empire (see pp.72–75). There, they lived apart from the native population, in the business district. Nevertheless, they led many locals to embrace Islam and were key to Ghana's eventual conversion. Between the 7th and the 11th centuries, trans-Saharan trade carried gold to European merchants on the Mediterranean and brought back Saharan salt (a vital preservative).

Merchants were not the only group to migrate across the Sahara as trade routes developed. Jews travelled to the Sahel from Morocco as they invested in trade. And scholars from the Muslim world, such as Andalusian architect Abu Ishaq Ibrahim al-Sahili, settled in Timbuktu, the fabled centre of learning.

The trade in people

By far the biggest flow of migrants across the desert was linked to the trans-Saharan slave trade, which developed to satisfy a demand for labour in Islamic North Africa, the Middle East, and Europe. As African tribes were conquered by more powerful sub-Saharan empires, their members were taken and sold on to Arab and African traders in exchange for gold, salt, ivory, or other goods. The journey across the Sahara for those enslaved was deadly. It took around 70 days and water was scarce. Three out of four enslaved people died en route from thirst, hunger, illness, or exhaustion. The survivors were taken to markets in the central provinces of Islamic territory, where they were then resold.

Enslaved boys faced further dangers. As eunuchs were widely used in administration and to oversee harems (or women's private living areas), and the price for eunuchs was high, boys faced castration. Nine out of 10 of them died due to unsuccessful operations. Demand was greatest for women, who often became domestic servants, or were chosen to work as courtesans or concubines in harems. This sometimes allowed enslaved women, and their children, a degree of assimilation and social mobility in Muslim society. For instance, Harun al-Rashid, the caliph who ushered in the Islamic Golden Age, was born to a formerly enslaved woman who gained significant influence in state affairs.

Between 650 CE and 1600, about 5 million people were trafficked via six main routes, at a rate of about 5,000 per year. Over the next three centuries, 2.5 million people were taken across the Sahara to Arabia until the trade finally ended in the 20th century.

▼ **Camels transported goods** such as salt across the Sahara. Salt was a prized commodity in North Africa and therefore valuable. Camels were the ideal transport for the desert because they could last for several days without water.

▼ **Enslaved people** were transported across the Sahara Desert in convoys, as depicted in this 19th-century painting. The journey was a long and treacherous one.

The Book of Chess, Dice and Board Games, produced in 13th-century Spain, depicts the peaceful coexistence of Christians, Arabs, and Jews.

IBERIAN PENINSULA

Corsica

Toledo
Lisbon
Córdoba
Valencia
Sardinia
Seville
Granada
Algeciras
Kairouan
Mediterranean Sea
Damascus

Dawn of a golden age
THE MOORS IN AL-ANDALUS

In 711 CE, the Umayyads, a Muslim dynasty from Syria, crossed the Strait of Gibraltar and invaded the Visigothic kingdom of Hispania on the Iberian Peninsula. They soon killed its king and, by 720 CE, had conquered most of the peninsula. They called the area they came to govern Al-Andalus.

Arabs led this Islamic army, which was comprised mainly of Berbers – a North African ethnic group. Following their conquest of Hispania, the invaders (who were known as Moors) settled there. At first, Muslims made up just 1 per cent of the population of Al-Andalus, but they did not remain a minority for long. In 740 CE, up to 10,000 Syrians arrived and from the 8th to the 12th century, a steady flow of Berbers streamed in from North Africa.

Life under Moorish rule
Society in Al-Andalus was stratified according to religion. Muslims formed the top tier, although not all Muslims were treated equally. Arabs came first, then Berbers, then *muwalladun* (Christians who had converted to Islam). At the bottom were *dhimmis* (Jews and Christians), who were treated as second-class citizens. Nevertheless, there was a high degree of tolerance to religious minorities under Islamic governance. Provided they accepted Muslim rule, *dhimmis* could keep their faith, be educated, and could pursue any profession. There is also evidence to suggest they were allowed to marry Muslims. The multiculturalism ushered in by Muslim rule also reached parts of the Iberian Peninsula that remained under Christian control.

Science and the arts flourished in Al-Andalus. The conquerors brought with them Arabic numerals, geometry, Greek philosophy, and the oud (a musical instrument resembling a lute). They prioritized literacy and built public libraries, with the library in Córdoba boasting 600,000 manuscripts. The Moors also drew on elements of Hispania's culture, as evidenced in the fine weaving techniques of the silks produced in Madinat al-Zahra, a palace city near Córdoba.

Christianity restored
From the beginning of the 11th century, civil wars between rival Muslim factions tore Al-Andalus apart. By 1031, it had fractured into several semi-independent states. The resulting instability led to constant border shifts. Muslims suddenly found themselves living in Christian cities, while those from the Christian territories in the north began to settle in areas just beyond their borders. In these uncertain times, Muslim governors withdrew many of the rights *dhimmis* once had, and some Muslims persecuted Jews. In 1066, a Muslim mob massacred most of Granada's Jewish population, some 4,000 people.

By the 15th century, the Christians had regained control of Iberia. The Moors were driven out, but their influence remains. Today, architectural riches such as the Alhambra are among Spain's most important heritage sites. Crops introduced by the Muslims, such as sugar cane, figs, and almonds, have become staples, and Spanish has absorbed more than 4,000 words and phrases from Arabic.

▲ **The Moors** swept across the Maghreb, in North Africa, crossed the Strait of Gibraltar, and spread out across the Iberian Peninsula (modern-day Spain and Portugal).

▼ **The Mosque-Cathedral of Córdoba** was built as a mosque in 785 CE, and combines striking elements of Moorish architecture, such as these horseshoe arches, with the remains of earlier Roman and Visigothic structures.

▼ **An illustration** from the *Cantigas de Santa Maria*, a 13th-century book of songs attributed to Alfonso X, King of Castile and Leon, shows the Muslim conquerors (on horses) and Christian prisoners of war on foot and in chains.

Raiders, traders, and settlers
VIKINGS IN EUROPE AND THE NORTH ATLANTIC

The Norse were a people who lived in Scandinavia. A portion of them who were farmers by trade but acted as warriors became known as the Vikings. They didn't call themselves by this name; it was only used later by others whose lands they attacked from the late 8th century CE. Originally farming and fishing folk, the indented coastline and islands of Scandinavia made them expert seamen who developed longships – vessels with a shallow draught allowing them to sail in shallow waters and up rivers.

Political instability in Scandinavia, as chiefdoms coalesced into kingdoms; a shortage of land as the population grew; and the attraction of the wealth of northwestern Europe, which provided targets for enterprising traders and opportunistic raiders, led the Vikings to venture out of Scandinavia.

From raids to settlement
The first small attack was on the rich monastery of Lindisfarne in northeastern England in 793 CE, but after that the Vikings arrived in larger numbers, staying the winter and extending their raids to cover Scotland, Ireland, and France. From the 840s in Ireland, and 860s in England, they began to settle, dividing up land and establishing farms. It is unclear how many came, but the level of Scandinavian DNA in the north of England and parts of Scotland is quite high (up to 30 per cent in Orkney), indicating that over time perhaps 25,000 to 30,000 Norse settled in Britain. DNA analysis also suggests that once settlements were established, Viking arrivals may have included women and children.

From the Scottish and Faroe islands, the Vikings explored deeper into the North Atlantic. In around 874 CE, a voyage led by Norwegian chieftain Ingolf Arnarson arrived in Iceland. With no Indigenous population there, they were free to settle along the fertile coast.

Into the North Atlantic
Within 30 years, all the good land in Iceland had been parcelled out. Frequent feuds between families erupted over boundary disputes. After one such incident around 980 CE, Erik the Red took ships further west. He travelled across to Greenland and established a small Viking colony. From there, Erik's son, Leif, reached North America, but while legends recount that he established a small settlement there, he later returned home to Greenland.

The Viking colony in Greenland, too, vanished – whether through disease or attacks by Indigenous people, is not known. Elsewhere, the Viking migrants stayed, their descendants gradually merging into the populations of northern England, Scotland, Ireland, and Normandy in France. Their presence can be seen in English place names that end in "-by" and words such as "sky" from Old Norse, the language of the Norse people, as well as in the DNA of the modern inhabitants. In Iceland, they founded a new Norse society, and until recently most people there could trace their descent from people in the *Landnámabók*, an early account of the original Viking settlers.

▼ **This Viking helmet** dates to the 10th century. The Vikings wore strong armour made of iron to protect their bodies when they went into battle.

▼ **A medieval depiction of Viking ships** from c. 1130 depicts an attack on Britain. The Vikings travelled in sturdy longships that could withstand rough waters.

The Viking world

Ocean-going ships allowed the Vikings to sail in search of new lands and trading opportunities. At first they dominated their Baltic neighbours, taking tribute in the form of amber, wax, fish, ivory, and furs. Danes and Norwegians exploited weaknesses in France, England, and Ireland, using their fast and manoeuvrable longships.

KEY

→ Viking routes
▨ Viking homelands
▨ Viking settlement

GREENLAND

Reykjavik

Hvalsey

L'Anse aux Meadows

to North America

to North America

Lindisfarne
Lewis
York
Dublin
London
Paris
Orleans
Bordeaux
Lisbon
Seville
Rome

Birka
Jelling
Novgorod
Bulgar
Kiev
Itil
Constantinople
Baghdad

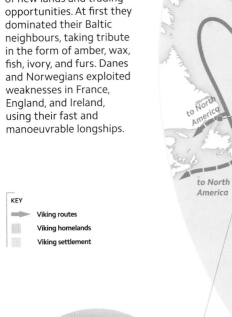

▲**The remains** of a 12th-century Viking settlement Catholic church in Greenland. The majority of the Norse were Christianized between the 10th and 11th centuries.

Viking York

The Vikings ruled York, England, which they called *Jorvik*, for around 80 years until the mid-10th century. Archaeologists have discovered traces of a thriving Viking community in the city centre, where craftspeople produced glass beads, leather goods, and silver and gold jewellery from narrow post-and-wattle workshops. Many York streets still end in the Old Norse word "-gate" (meaning "street"), such as Coppergate, which was the street of the cup-makers.

▲**The Lewis Chessmen**, discovered on the Isle of Lewis, Scotland, are remarkable surviving pieces of evidence that indicate the hobbies of the 12th-century Norse.

▲**This 10th-century silver cup** from Jelling, Denmark, features the type of animal designs that influenced art in Britain following Viking settlement.

The *Sachsenspiegel* is a book of law, written in German in the early 13th century. This illustration depicts the process of choosing a king.

German core territories to c. 1100
German settlement areas to c. 1200
German settlement areas to c. 1250
German settlement areas to c. 1300
German settlement areas to c. 1400
Slavic settlement areas

The Ostsiedlung
MEDIEVAL GERMAN SETTLEMENTS

Between the 10th and 14th centuries, streams of Germanic peasants moved eastwards across Europe in search of agricultural land, accompanying nobles and knights who carved out new territories, often by force. This movement, known as the *Ostsiedlung* ("east settlement") transformed the ethnic make-up of much of Central Europe.

The settlers established farms, villages, and towns as they spread into less populated regions. Brandenburg and Saxony (in modern-day Germany), where Slavs had been the dominant ethnic group, became overwhelmingly German-speaking. Further east, German enclaves sprang up in the Slavic-dominated regions of Poland, Serbia, and Slovakia when miners arrived to quarry newly discovered lodes of silver, coal, and iron.

In some cases, the *Ostsiedlung* was encouraged by colonizing agents known as "locators", who recruited peasants to join the exodus. In others, whole villages of serfs (farm labourers bound to a particular estate) simply uprooted themselves in search of a freer life. The migrants cleared new areas, particularly in the heavily forested lands of southern Germany, laying out fields and regular plots that would eventually grow into great towns such as Nuremberg (founded around 1050).

Religion and resistance

In some established towns, such as Székesfehérvár in Hungary, the Germans were allocated their own suburb (in 1249), where they lived peacefully alongside the existing inhabitants. Yet elsewhere there was resistance. Religion was an important factor in the migrations – the Roman Catholic Church promoted the conversion of pagan groups in Eastern Europe to Christianity, by force if necessary, and saw the movement of Christian German speakers as a means to achieve this.

Many of the Indigenous peoples in the east – Slavic groups collectively known as the Wends – refused to convert to Christianity. When Pope Eugenius III launched a crusade against them in 1147, Prince Nyklot, leader of the Obodrites (a Wendish group), reacted by attacking the region's Christian German settlers. The crusade ended in the 1180s with the flight of the surviving Wends eastwards. Further Baltic Crusades in the 13th century drove out Prussia's native inhabitants, but despite years of Christian campaigns, the Indigenous peoples of Lithuania, Latvia, and Estonia survived.

The legacy of the migration

As German merchants spread across Europe, they built trading bonds, such as the Hanseatic League, which had a monopoly on trade in the Baltic states. Their timbered houses still stand in many Baltic and northern German towns as evidence of these trading communities. By the 13th century, the *Ostsiedlung* had slowed, though settlers continued to spread out as far as Russia's Volga region. Centuries later, the Nazi Party sought to absorb these migrants into a greater Reich, and *Volksdeutche* (people of German origins) were forced to move back to Germany.

▲ **Germans settled** lands further and further east between c. 1100–1400, into areas previously inhabited by Slavic peoples.

▼ **The Hanseatic League** was a confederation of northern European towns and merchant guilds. It monopolized the area's trade for around 300 years from the late 12th century.

▼ **The city of Nuremberg** grew into an important medieval trading centre. This woodcut is from the *Nuremberg Chronicle*, a 15th-century illustrated history of the Christian world.

Changing fortunes

THE ROMA IN MEDIEVAL EUROPE

KEY
▦ Balkan Peninsula
— Modern international borders

▲**The Roma people** originated in India and migrated through the Middle East. After a period in the Byzantine Empire, groups moved through the Balkans to Western European countries.

▼**Luri musicians** (thought to be Roma) who migrated from India, perform at the Persian court in the 7th century CE.

▼**An illustration** from *Travels through Turkey* by Rev. Henry J. Van Lennep (1862) shows a Roma fortune-teller reading the palm – a traditional Roma practice – of a Turkish woman.

As a result of a series of migrations, beginning in India 1,500 years ago, today's 10 million Roma people live in dispersed communities around the world. The word "Roma", which the people use to describe themselves collectively, comes from the Romani for "man", but there are many different named groups within the broad Roma population.

Moving westwards

Persian and Arabic sources from the 10th and 11th centuries appear to contain the earliest references to Roma peoples. They relate how 10,000 musicians (referred to as "Luri") were sent from India to perform at the court of the Persian shah Bahram in 420 CE, and how they later migrated throughout the Persian Empire. By the 8th century, Roma were living in modern-day Iraq. They followed itinerant professions or provided services – such as entertainment, fortune-telling, metal processing, and livestock trading – that allowed them to retain a nomadic lifestyle, one which some Roma communities still practise today. Groups travelled and lived in *itsara*, or caravans, answering first to the *vitsa*, or family, and the larger tribe.

The move west continued, perhaps accelerated by the expansion of the Islamic Empire. Some settled in the Balkan region, but by the early 15th century groups of up to 30,000 Roma were arriving in Western Europe. Accounts from this time imply that the arrivals – such as those led by Andreas, "Duke of Little Egypt", who were given supplies in Brussels in 1420 – were initially greeted warmly. The accounts also explain the origin of the term "gypsy" – now considered to be a slur by some. Groups claimed to be Christian refugees fleeing advancing Muslim Ottoman Turks, and gave "Egypt" or "Little Egypt" as a location of origin.

In the late 18th century, proof of India as the homeland of the Roma was provided by the German scholar Johann Rüdiger, who noticed resemblances between the Romani language and the northern Indian dialects of Punjabi. Subsequently, linguists have found traces of Farsi (Persian) and Armenian in Romani that tell of a migration westward through the Middle East. More recently, DNA sampling has identified genetic links between the Roma and people from South Asia.

Expulsion and persecution

During the 16th century, a changing social and religious landscape fuelled growing intolerance towards the Roma. Accused of being vagrants and spies, Roma peoples were increasingly subject to entry bans and forced deportations across Europe. Their ostracization has persisted over the centuries. During World War II, the Nazis condemned thousands to concentration camps, considering them racially inferior.

Despite continuing challenges, the strong social and cultural traditions of the Roma have endured. Their music, in particular, continues to influence genres including Flamenco and jazz, while their itinerant lifestyle is being re-imagined by a new generation of Romani people (see pp.274–75).

Roma arrive outside Bern in the 15th century. Their Arabic-style clothes and weapons set them apart from the Christian Swiss inhabitants.

A persecuted people
MEDIEVAL JEWISH MIGRATIONS

KEY

Jewish settlement after 1150

Migration routes following expulsions

Jewish people in the Middle Ages experienced enormous hardships, from the threat of forced conversions to violent massacres. While some revolted against their persecutors, many were forced to flee their homes as a result of organized attacks and expulsions by local rulers.

In the 5th century CE, Jewish communities were scattered around the Mediterranean, concentrated in what had been the Byzantine Empire. From the 7th century CE, Muslims took over these lands. Known for their religious tolerance, they allowed Jewish communities to flourish. Some Jewish migrants also moved into Christian kingdoms. In 1023, King Baldwin IV, Count of Flanders, invited a rabbi and 30 of his followers to settle in his lands because, unlike Christians, Jewish people were able to engage in money lending.

An oppressive era

By the 11th century, Jewish communities had settled in England, and in French and German lands. In 1096, Christian soldiers on their way to fight in the First Crusade – an attempt to wrest Jerusalem from Muslim control – violently attacked communities along the Rhine; they forced Jewish people into synagogues and set them on fire. Around 1,000 Jews who had previously fled to the city of Worms – and who had been given sanctuary in the bishop's palace there – were killed in the 1096 massacre as a result of blood libel (false rumours about Jews murdering Christians for rituals). Some Jewish people resisted, joining Arab attempts to defend Jerusalem, or dying by suicide rather than convert to Christianity. Others headed eastwards to escape the massacres.

Despite attempts by the Church to protect Jews, including a Papal bull in 1120 forbidding their persecution, attacks continued, many of them sparked by blood libel accusations. Further crusades eroded religious tolerance, leading to a wave of expulsions in the 13th century. In 1290, King Edward I banished Jews from England. Many fled to France, but were expelled in 1306 by Philip IV.

In Muslim lands, the situation was sometimes no better. The Andalusian Jewish philosopher, Moses Maimonides, fled the Islamic revivalist Almohad movement in the 1140s, avoiding a forced conversion. He eventually settled in Caliphate-controlled Egypt, where he became court physician to the sultan and wrote commentaries on Jewish law and ethics. Another Andalusian scholar, Samuel ibn Naghrillah (993–1055), fled Córdoba when the city was sacked by Berber raiders. He eked out a living selling spices near the vizier's palace in Malaga until his academic skills were discovered and he became the vizier's secretary (and later assistant vizier).

Eastern Europe

The centre of Jewish life in Europe shifted to Ukraine and Poland, where Bolesław the Pious welcomed them in 1264. These Jews became merchants, and founded their own villages in a way that had not occurred in Western Europe. They spoke medieval German, which in turn evolved into Yiddish, and their culture was able to thrive.

▲ **This map shows** the main routes taken by Jewish people after their expulsions from various kingdoms in Western Europe, and the places they settled after 1150.

▼ **A 13th-century illustration** from a French Bible depicts the massacre of Jewish people by Christian participants of the First Crusade in 1096.

▼ **The distribution of matzoh** during Passover celebrations is depicted in this 14th-century Spanish manuscript.

"There was scarcely a house in all the Kingdom of Poland where its members did not... study [the] Torah."

Nathan Hanover, *Yeven Mezullah*, 1653

◀ **The Statute of Kalisz**, issued by Prince Bolesław the Pious in 1264, granted Jewish people privileges in Poland. Confirmed by subsequent rulers, it became a symbol of safety for Jewish families living in Poland.

1. Residents of Baghdad take shelter within the city walls. Before 1258, Baghdad had prospered under the Abbasid dynasty as a centre of culture, commerce, and learning.

2. Baghdad soldiers are hastily assembled to defend the Abbasid capital.

3. Siege engines, technology the Mongols acquired from China, are used to destroy the city's defences, and raze its hospitals, libraries, and places of worship.

4. Mongol archers, known for their prowess, fire missiles over the city walls.

▶**This 14th-century Persian painting** depicts the Siege of Baghdad (1258), when the Mongol army, led by Hulagu Khan, invaded the city. Hulagu constructed a palisade and ditch around the perimeter and took the wealthy capital after 13 days of fierce fighting.

Connecting East and West

MONGOL EXPANSION

In the 13th century, the Mongol army tore across Eurasia, conquering a multitude of city-states and civilizations and establishing a vast empire that united Chinese, Islamic, Iranian, Central Asian, and nomadic cultures under Mongol domination. The Mongols had gained a reputation for annihilating their opponents, and terror and panic spread as news of their sudden, violent conquests preceded them. However, once control was established, the dynasty encouraged economic, cultural, and religious exchange between its diverse territories, creating an unprecedented merging of peoples, faiths, traditions, and ideas.

Aggressive expansion

The great empire began in the steppe of Central Asia, in what is now Mongolia, which in the 12th century was controlled by nomadic Mongol and Turkic tribes. By 1206, a Mongol warrior called Temujin had succeeded in uniting these tribes and created a powerful military force. He took the title Genghis Khan, meaning "universal ruler", and under his leadership a Mongol army invaded China and began to create the largest land-based empire in world history.

The populations in territories that submitted to the Mongols were generally spared, but Genghis's forces wrought destruction on those who resisted. They razed dozens of cities in and around China between 1211 and 1223, killing around 18 million people and causing mass displacement as the inhabitants fled. Following the conquests,

the Mongols captured skilled personnel, whom they took with them on their campaigns. When Genghis toppled Zhongdu (modern-day Beijing), capital of China's Jurchen Jin Dynasty, in 1215, he conscripted their infantry and siege engineers to make his army more versatile. The Mongols also absorbed elements of their new subjects' culture. For example, when Genghis conquered the Uighurs in 1209, he enlisted their scribes to organize the administration of his new empire. He also took their script, adapting it for Mongolian – previously an unwritten language.

Life under Mongol rule

Once the lands had been subjugated, many Mongol warriors settled and began to trade with and marry locals. These ties eventually led the Mongols to adopt local religions. In the western part of the empire, many converted to Islam. In China, a large number embraced a Tibetan form of Buddhism. The *khans* (rulers) were respectful of the practices and traditions of their new subjects, while retaining aspects of their own Mongolian culture. They supported merchants, peasant farmers, and artisans, believing that boosting the economies of their domains would in turn enrich the empire.

▲ **The campaigns** of Genghis Khan and his descendants created an empire that by 1279 extended from the Pacific Ocean in the east to the Danube River and the Persian Gulf in the west.

▼ **This Mongol helmet** was taken as a trophy in Japan, where Mongol fleets – comprised of Korean and Chinese ships – were defeated in 1274 and 1281.

▼ **Hulagu Khan** (centre left) was a 13th-century Mongolian ruler who conquered much of western Asia. His mother was Christian, but he converted to Buddhism, against the wishes of his Christian wife, Dokuz Khatun (centre right).

Once the bulk of Eurasia was under Mongol control, and after achieving relative order and stability in their territories, the Mongols facilitated and encouraged contacts and economic ties between Eastern and Western civilizations. Technology, products, knowledge, and ideas were shared and traded by peoples from Europe to East Asia. This period, which lasted from 1279 (when the Mongols captured southern China) until the empire's collapse in 1368, is known as the "Mongol Peace".

Trade, arts, and culture

Following the fall of the Roman Empire and the Chinese Han Empire, the Silk Road – an ancient trade route connecting Europe and Asia – had fallen out of use. Now, recognizing the importance of trade to the economic survival of their empire, the Mongols revived it. They made roads safe and built extensive infrastructure, including travellers' inns placed a day's camel ride apart along barren stretches. European merchants, craftsmen, and emissaries were able to travel as far as China for the first time in history. Horses, porcelain, precious stones, paper, leather goods, and gunpowder were all traded along the route.

But the most important commodity was silk: the Mongols invested heavily in its production, taking over existing factories and establishing new ones. Their development of the industry led to the migration of artisans. The Mongols sent Chinese silk weavers to the trade hub of Samarkand (in modern-day Uzbekistan) to work with local Muslim weavers. Likewise, Muslim weavers who specialized in silk cloth interwoven with gold were moved to factories in China.

Weavers were not the only group to be resettled. Chinese painters were sent to Persia (now Iran), where they greatly influenced the development of miniature painting. Persian artists began to include Chinese motifs in their works, such as dragons and phoenixes. Their depictions of rocks, trees, and clouds also took on a Chinese style. Similarly, the Mongols relocated officials to culturally distinct parts of the empire. In this way, the Mongols governed China with Muslims and Europeans, and Persia with Chinese and Tibetans. Impressed by Persian advances in medicine, the Mongols also moved Persian doctors to China to establish an Office for Muslim Medicine.

> "I had to seek caves ... to have shelter, while the Tatars [Mongols] rushed through the... heart of the wasteland."
>
> Master Roger, Italian Archdeacon living in the Kingdom of Hungary, c. 1243

All of this served to forge close relations between East Asia and West Asia. Europe, too, was influenced by this cultural exchange. Mongol fashion became popular as far west as Britain. The hennin – the distinctive conical headdress worn by European noblewomen in the 15th century – was likely to have been inspired by the hats worn at the Mongol court. Also, the Knights of the Garter – England's oldest order of chivalry – used dark-blue "Tatar" cloth (so called as it was made by Tatars, Turkic-speaking peoples that were incorporated into the Mongolian empire) for their insignia.

Mongol culture also made its mark on the Chinese, who adopted nomadic cooking styles. A 14th-century court nutritionist, Hu Sihui, wrote a dietary manual called *Yinshan Zhengyao*, in which he encouraged the nomadic traditions of boiling as the favoured means of cooking, and eating all parts of the animal, which became mainstream in China.

The fall of the empire

The Mongol Empire flourished for 162 years, and at its peak controlled about 23 million sq km (9 million sq miles) of land. But eventually, disputes among Genghis's successors resulted in the empire being split into four khanates which,

▶ **In this silk tapestry**, an enthroned Mongol prince is flanked by Persian men. It was created by Chinese weavers sent to Mongol-ruled Iran or Iraq during the 14th century.

by 1368, had all dissolved. In the Ilkhanate, which ruled Persia, the Mongols were absorbed into Persia's Turkish tribal population which, except for a brief hiatus in the 18th century, provided the state with its rulers until 1925. The Mongol Yuan dynasty ruled China until 1368. For centuries, Genghis Khan's descendants ruled various dynasties in Central Asia, the last being the Emir of Bukhara (Uzbekistan), who was deposed in 1920. The Mongol language is still spoken today in Central Asia and parts of northern China.

▼ **Horses** were fundamental to Genghis Khan's military successes, and horse culture spread from Mongolia to other territories throughout the empire, including China.

"These were the canoes of my ancestors, in which they paddled across the Great Ocean of Kiwa..."

From the Ngāti Raukawa chant

Chieftain Tāmati Wāka Nene of the Ngāti Haō people is shown in this 1890 painting by Bohemian artist Gottfried Lindauer. His *moko* (facial tattoo) indicates his status.

from Polynesian islands

AOTEAROA
(NEW ZEALAND)

PACIFIC
OCEAN

Chatham Islands

To the long white cloud
THE MĀORI REACH NEW ZEALAND

New Zealand was the last great landmass on Earth to be settled by humans. The Māori pioneers who arrived around 1250 CE had travelled over 2,500 km (1,550 miles) across the open sea from Eastern Polynesia, most likely beginning their voyage in the Society, Cook, or Austral Islands. It was the final extension of the Polynesian migration which had populated the archipelagos of the South Pacific, and it was likely carried out in double-hulled canoes with outriggers, which could carry up to 50 people.

Foundation legends

Māori tradition suggests that the new land was discovered by a fisherman called Kupe who went in pursuit of an octopus and found himself far from the waters of the Māori homeland of Hawaiki. As he drew close to the North Island, his wife Kuramārōtini gave it the name Aotearoa ("long white cloud"), which has been the Māori name for New Zealand ever since. Kupe returned to Hawaiki and told of his find, and soon other *waka* (canoes) made the journey. Subsequent Māori remembered the names of the occupants of the seven *waka* said to have settled New Zealand, and each member of an *iwi* (Māori kinship group) traces their descent from one of these founders through a process of *whakapapa* (genealogy) that is central to Māori identity.

The newcomers spread rapidly through the North Island and then into the South Island. They had brought with them dogs and rats, together with *kumara* (sweet potato), taro, yam, and paper mulberry, but they were able to supplement their diet by hunting the abundant giant moa (large flightless birds, some over 200 kg (440 lbs) in weight) and seal, as well as catching fish with nets and hooks. They built villages of rectangular gable houses and cultivated crops in some places, while elsewhere they established seasonal camps in their hunt for game.

Later Māori culture

The earliest settlements were sited at harbours or river-mouths where access to fresh water was good and game was plenty. Within a century, however, they had hunted the moa to extinction and, with population levels rising, the society of the first migrants came under stress. Around 1500 CE, some made a further journey, to the Chatham Islands, 800 km (497 miles) east of the South Island, where they established a new culture, the Morori, which continued to be based on hunting.

Back in Aotearoa, society became more hierarchical. Chieftains rose with authority over larger areas, and defensive hill-forts were built as frequent inter-tribal wars erupted. A rich tradition of wood-carving and greenstone sculpture developed as Māori society entered its Classic period.

▲ **The Māori travelled** from the Polynesian islands (see p.39) to New Zealand's North Island by boat, before spreading onto the South Island. Some later travelled east to settle the Chatham Islands.

▼ **This greenstone (jade) carving** uses a spiral *koru* design – a traditional motif in Māori art – which represents a fern frond opening, symbolizing new beginnings, hope, and strength.

▼ **An engraving of a war canoe** (or *waka taua*), by Sydney Parkinson in 1770, shows the typical perforated carvings, front and back, and painted designs used on these powerfully symbolic vessels.

1. The Mexica people are directed by their god Huitzilopochtli to build a city where they see an eagle standing atop a cactus, eating a snake, in the mythical story of the founding of Tenochtitlan.

2. This war shield indicates that the Mexica needed to fight for their territory.

3. The figures in white robes depict the 10 men who led the Mexica to this location.

4. The large warriors indicate the might of the Mexica people against their weaker foes. Their shields carry the same pattern as the war shield above.

▶**The Codex Mendoza** was commissioned in 1541 by Spanish viceroy Antonio de Mendoza as a way to record details of the Mexica Empire. This is the frontispiece showing the founding of the city of Tenochtitlan. Drawn by Indigenous artists, the pages are annotated in Spanish.

Metztitlan
Mazatlan
Teotihuacan
Texcoco
Tlaxcala
Tenochtitlan
Itzapan

from North America
from Spain

Gulf of Mexico

PACIFIC OCEAN

KEY
Extent of Mexica Empire in 1521
Arrival of the Mexica from the mythical Aztlán in the 1300s
Arrival of Hernán Cortés in 1519

Mesoamerican migration

INDIGENOUS EMPIRES IN CENTRAL AMERICA

Between around 500 CE and the early 1500s, a series of powerful societies exerted their influence throughout Mesoamerica (modern-day Mexico and Central America). Successors of earlier civilizations, such as the Olmec, they established large city-states, expanding their authority through conquest, alliances, religion, and trade. As one culture rose to prominence, others declined or were forced to relocate – the victims of warfare, overpopulation, drought, and environmental degradation. Their centuries of domination in the region were finally ended in 1519 by the attacks of Hernán Cortés and the Spanish conquistadors (see pp.114–15).

Zapotec and Maya expansion

Profit from trade networks helped the Zapotec peoples establish a large empire from their base in the Valley of Oaxaca, and to build the first large city in Mesoamerica, Monte Albán. By 500 CE, this religious and cultural centre had a population of over 17,000, and its combination of palaces, temples, housing, and ball courts (where teams played a ritualistic ball game) influenced later cities built by other societies across the region.

Southeast of the Zapotec, the Maya peoples were establishing a large empire, at its height between 250 and 900 CE. Encompassing most of modern-day southern Mexico, Guatemala, and northern Belize, it included as many as 10 million people. The Maya made great advances in mathematics, astronomy, architecture, agriculture, and irrigation that later influenced societies throughout Mesoamerica, but by the end of the 9th century CE, most Maya city-states appear to have declined or collapsed. Survivors migrated to other parts of the region, while their former cities were covered by forest vegetation (though some Maya city-states in the Yucatán peninsula survived into the 1500s).

Inheritors of Toltec culture

In the mid-10th century, the Toltec peoples, who had migrated from the deserts of the north-west to the centre of the Yucatán peninsula, began waging a religious war, spreading the cult of their god, Quetzalcóatl, throughout their growing empire. Trade links extended their influence, with pottery, textiles, and obsidian carried south by Toltec merchants. While their power had collapsed by the mid-11th century, the Toltec's cultural heritage continued through the Mexica peoples (later called the Aztecs by Europeans) who venerated Toltec society and adopted many of their practices.

Oral histories recount that the Mexica travelled south from Aztlán, finally settling on an island in Lake Texcoco. Directed by their god Huitzilopochtli they founded the city of Tenochtitlan in 1325, which grew into one of the great Mesoamerican capitals (see pp.106–07). The Mexica went on to dominate the region until their defeat by the Spanish in 1521. While this ended their power, the traditions of the Zapotec, Toltec, Maya, and Mexica still live on in the political, artistic, culinary, and religious, life of the region today.

▲ **Although the Mexica**, who built their famous city at Tenochtitlan, are among the most famous cultures of Central America, many others made their mark on the region and have left behind spectacular sites.

▼ **A ball court and players** are shown in this manuscript, which probably dates from before the arrival of the Spanish. Ball courts were built across Mesoamerica.

▼ **Teotihuacan**, a vast city-state that flourished during the 5th century CE, attracted many cultures including the Zapotec and Maya peoples. The city's art, religions, and architecture would influence the later Toltec and Mexica peoples.

The 500-year-old Q'eswachaka bridge was constructed by the Inca to cross the Apurímac River in what is now Peru's Cusco region. The bridge is woven from twisted straw ropes, which are renewed every year by Quechua-speaking peoples – Indigenous descendants of the Inca.

CULTURAL INFLUENCES

Indigenous religions

By the early 1500s, the Mexica ruled up to 500 small states in Central Mexico. Their belief system shared aspects with other Indigenous Mesoamerican religions, including that of the Toltecs, the culture that had dominated the region. This relief is from the Toltec Temple of Quetzalcóatl (or Feathered Serpent), a god also worshipped by the Mexica.

Spanish colonizers

From the rubble of Tenochtitlan, the Spanish built their centre of power in the New World. European planners laid out Mexico City on a grid pattern of neighbourhoods and plazas, and later, Mexica ruins were included in the central district. Today, Spanish colonial architecture sits beside 19th-century and modern Mexican buildings.

French architecture

Mexicans of French origin are largely descended from the migrants and soldiers who settled when France invaded Mexico in 1863 and created the short-lived Second Mexican Empire. In the late 1800s, Mexico City was modernized, incorporating French Art Nouveau elements in its buildings, such as the Palace of Fine Arts.

Mexico City
THE CITY OF PALACES

In 1325, the Mexica (or Aztecs), a Nahuatl-speaking group who had migrated from northern Mexico or the southwestern US many years earlier, built a settlement called Tenochtitlan on an island in Lake Texcoco in the Valley of Mexico (see pp.102–03). After bringing other Indigenous peoples in the region under their control, the Mexica became a dominant force in Mesoamerica. Tenochtitlan grew into a city-state with canals, plazas, intricately carved palaces and temples, and 100,000–200,000 inhabitants.

In 1519, Spanish conquistadors arrived in Tenochtitlan and, with the help of local groups resistant to Mexica rule, overthrew the great empire. The Spanish destroyed Tenochtitlan and built Mexico City on the same site.

A multicultural megacity

The Spanish colonial period (1535–1821, see pp.114–15) saw voluntary and involuntary migration to the city. Spaniards were drawn largely by economic opportunities, while enslaved people from Africa and Asia were trafficked there to provide labour. Waves of Spanish immigrants – priests, soldiers, administrators, traders, and artisans – settled in the city. Non-Spanish immigration was prohibited during the colonial era, but after Mexican independence in 1821 other Europeans began to arrive, including many from France. The city expanded massively in the late 19th and early 20th centuries, as the last sections of Lake Texcoco were built over.

The population also boomed when industrialization drew Mexicans from rural areas and migrants from countries and regions such as China and the Middle East, as well as Central America and the US. These movements shaped the culture, architecture, and economy of a megacity that is now home to more than 9.2 million people.

▲▲ **This 1825 painting of Mexico City** by Pedro Calvo was created shortly after Mexico gained independence and reveals the city's Spanish colonial architecture.

▲ **People in skull-faced costumes** parade to mark the Day of the Dead, a festival that honours the departed, and which blends Indigenous and Christian beliefs.

◀ **This colourful piece of 21st-century street art** on a wall in Mexico City, features traditional Mexica masks. Their use extends back thousands of years to Mesoamerican ceremonies and rituals that predate the arrival of Spanish colonists.

> "There is no Mexico City without those ... who constantly build rich cultures and histories every day."
>
> Ignacio M. Sánchez Prado, Professor of Spanish and Latin American Studies, 2020

Chinese immigration

During the colonial era, a few Chinese sailors settled in Mexico City. Enslaved Asians, including Chinese people, were also brought to the city by Europeans. Greater numbers of Chinese migrants came in the late 19th and early 20th centuries to work on industrial projects such as the railways. A flourishing Chinese community exists in the city today.

US entrepreneurs

In the late 19th and early 20th centuries, US businessmen, engineers, and entrepreneurs were encouraged to migrate to the city to help Mexico industrialize. New businesses were established, such as the Sanborns chain – American-style diners that were first established in Mexico City.

Cuban migrants

Café La Habana in Mexico City was once a meeting place for Cuban revolutionaries. Fidel Castro and his supporters used Mexico as a launch point for the revolution. Many Cubans fled to Mexico after the Cuban Revolution (1953–59), and more followed to escape the Communist regime that ensued.

4

Colonization and Conquest

1400–1800

Colonization and Conquest

1400–1800

Long-standing patterns of migration were radically disrupted from the 15th century as Europeans – armed with gunpowder weapons and equipped with ocean-going ships – explored and then occupied many lands by force. In Mexico and Peru, the Spanish conquered Mexica (Aztec) and Inca territories, bringing with them diseases and an exploitative plantation system that caused the death of up to 90 per cent of the Indigenous population. A similar disaster unfolded in North America, where British and French settlers, often themselves fleeing religious persecution in Europe, built colonies in the 17th century. The invaders encroached steadily and aggressively on Indigenous territory, fought wars that would push Indigenous peoples from their lands, and in places used them for forced labour.

From the 1520s, European powers established the Atlantic slave trade as a source of forced labour in the Americas. They transported 12.5 million enslaved people across the Atlantic from West Africa to the Americas – the largest number going to Brazil – before the slave trade ended in the 1830s, having devastated and depopulated the West African coast.

Peruvians convert to Christianity under Spanish colonial rule (see pp.114–15)

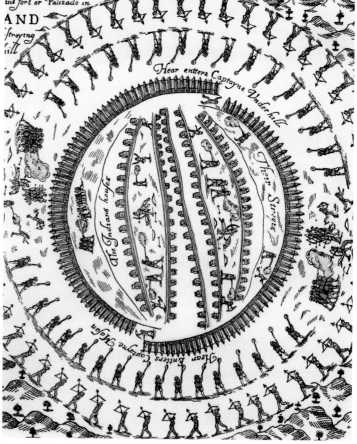

English settlers wage war on the Pequot people in New England (see pp.118–21)

> "Why should you take by force that from us which
> you can have by love? Why should you destroy us...?"
>
> Powhatan, chief of the Powhatan Confederacy, writing to English colonizer John Smith, 1609

In India, the Muslim Mughals (who originated in Central Asia), built an empire that would cover almost the whole Indian subcontinent, creating a culture that fused Indian and Persian, Hindu, and Muslim influences. Within this and the Ottoman Turkish Empire, different peoples co-existed, but the advent of Europeans – first as traders in search of spices such as nutmeg, and then as occupiers – destabilized the political systems and led to the establishment of European colonies. Further European settlement took place in southern Africa as Dutch-speaking migrants took land from the Khoi, San, and Xhosa peoples. Further north, the English colonial regime in Kenya fought with the cattle-herding Maasai people over their migration routes.

Europe itself was in a state of flux in the 18th century, as the Industrial Revolution led to an explosive urbanization that pulled millions of people from the countryside into the towns. Improved communication technology made links with home easier, so leaving for work became more attractive. This pattern of urbanization would be replicated as industrialization spread around the world.

Russian Cossacks invade Siberia in 1580 (see pp.132–33)

Enslaved Africans labour on a coffee plantation in Brazil (see pp.124–27)

A search for grazing lands

THE MIGRATION OF THE MAASAI

◄ This beaded neckpiece, made in the early 20th century, is an example of those worn in layers by married Maasai women. Gender, hierarchy, and marital status are all identified by beaded jewellery – a custom that has lasted for centuries.

▼ In Maasai communities women are responsible for milking the cows and looking after the home, while the men are in charge of protecting and herding the cattle.

Between the 15th and 18th centuries, the Maasai people – a semi-nomadic Nilotic group – migrated south from the area now known as South Sudan. They set off on foot with other ethnic groups – including the Tutsi – in search of pasture lands for their cattle to graze, more cattle to build up their herds, and water. By the 17th or 18th century, they inhabited a long stretch of land reaching from northern Kenya to northern Tanzania.

Maasai lifestyle and culture

As the Maasai moved southwards, they forcibly displaced earlier inhabitants, such as the Datoga and Chagga, although other groups assimilated into Maasai culture. By the 19th century, Maasai territory had expanded to cover most of Kenya and northern Tanzania, the largest its extent has ever been.

The Maasai have always believed that land is owned by everyone and should be shared equally, and their way of life is very dependent on their cattle. Traditionally, the Maasai people rely on their herds for all their basic needs, including food, clothing, and shelter. Cow hides are used to make clothes as well as walls or roofs of temporary homes, and more permanent houses are made from cow dung and urine. Cattle are also the main form of currency in Maasai society.

Facing challenges

Between 1883 and 1902, the Maasai endured much hardship, and it is estimated that over 60 per cent died as a result of smallpox and famine caused by drought and rinderpest, the highly contagious viral disease that wiped out their herds.

The Maasai faced further threats in 1895, when British colonists arrived in Kenya. The British persuaded the Maasai to sign a treaty (in 1904), giving the British the best Maasai lands for settlement in exchange for exclusive rights to two reserves. Several years later (in 1911) the British and a small group of Maasai signed another treaty, in which yet more land was given to the British. The British forcibly drove the Maasai from their land and confined them to reserves in drier areas. The Maasai's loss of autonomy continued with the independent Kenyan and Tanzanian governments, and much Maasai land has since been turned into national parks and wildlife reserves for tourism.

Today the Maasai, who number around 1 million, continue to celebrate their culture. They have maintained their oral traditions in terms of history, law, and politics, continue with cultural traditions such as singing and performing dances, wear traditional clothing, and carry out body modifications. Many continue to live a semi-nomadic, pastoral lifestyle and have resisted settling in permanent homes in towns, although some Maasai have assimilated into urban living and mainstream education.

SUDAN

Lake
Turkana

KENYA

TANZANIA

KEY
Modern Maasai territory

◀ **The Maasai** made the
long journey, over centuries, from modern-day
South Sudan, through the Kenyan highlands,
past Lake Turkana in northern Kenya, to their
most recent location in southern Kenya and
northern Tanzania.

▼ **Women and children** gathered in the
traditional village of Mto Wa Mbu in
northern Tanzania, painted in typically
colourful and expressive Maasai style.

"You know where
you are coming
from, but not where
you are going."

Maasinta, the first Maasai,
according to their oral literature

Our Lady of Cocharcas, painted in Peru, 1765, reflects the emergence of a new school of Indigenous art that melded Catholic and local narratives.

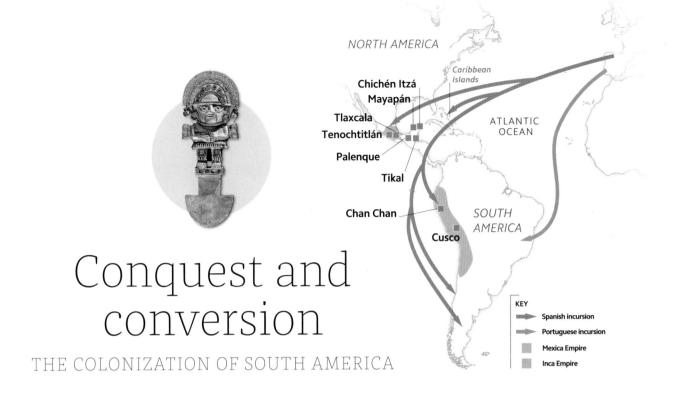

Conquest and conversion

THE COLONIZATION OF SOUTH AMERICA

Fifteenth-century Central and South America was home to some of the most advanced, powerful, and wealthy civilizations in the world. The Mexica (Aztecs) had founded a sophisticated state in what is now Mexico, with a magnificent capital city at Tenochtitlan; further south in Ecuador, Peru, Bolivia, and Chile, the Incas ruled a vast empire of 12 million people from their administrative centre of Cusco. These were highly organized societies with complex religions, efficient methods of farming, and effective military might. When European colonizers seized control of these lands in just a few decades, they effected a complex interchange of wealth, influences, and ideas that refashioned life in the Americas.

Conquistadors and colonizers

The arrival of Italian navigator Christopher Columbus in the Caribbean on 12 October 1492 marked the first contact between Europe and South America. His expedition to find a westward route to Asia, funded by the Spanish monarchy, had not achieved its intended aim, but his favourable reports of the lands, wealth, and peoples of the Americas sparked centuries of European colonization.

Spanish settlers, including farmers and artisans, priests, and conquistadors – military leaders seeking their fortunes in the conquest of new lands – were quick to arrive in the Caribbean, establishing colonies that became bases for the conquest of the mainland. By 1533, both the Mexica and the Inca empires had fallen, defeated by a combination of brute force, local rivals, political manipulation, and the importation of European diseases such as smallpox and measles. It is estimated that by the early 1600s European contact had caused the death of around 90 per cent of the Indigenous population.

Exchange and integration

Disease was just one element of a new series of exchanges (later termed the "Columbian exchange") created by colonial contact. Spanish settlers brought crops and animals, including wheat, horses, and cattle to the Americas. Mineral and agricultural riches, including silver, gold, potatoes, and tobacco flowed in the opposite direction.

The culture and social fabric of Indigenous societies were also transformed by these exchanges of people and goods. European colonizers imported millions of enslaved African peoples to join forced Indigenous labourers on plantations and mines. They also brought Christianity.

Religion was the colonizers' main justification for conquest and, though colonizers enforced conversion, Indigenous cultures adapted and survived. Missionaries learned local dialects in order to spread Christian teachings but traditional beliefs continued alongside newly adopted religions. Colonialism had a devastating impact, but a synthesis of European, Indigenous, and African cultures has since evolved.

▲ **European colonizing powers** seized control of Caribbean and Latin American territories from 1492, with Spain taking most of Central and South America, and Portugal invading from the east coast into what is now Brazil.

▼ **Gold ceremonial treasures**, like this knife from Peru, were looted by conquistadors and melted down into bars to finance further expeditions.

▼ **Spanish conquistador** Hernán Cortés and Mexica emperor Cuauhtémoc face each other in battle in 1521.

CULTURAL INFLUENCES

Phoenician ruins

Much of Lisbon's ancient and medieval history was destroyed during the earthquake of 1755. But the survival of this site, in the cloisters of Lisbon's Cathedral, has confirmed a Phoenician presence in the city, then known as Alis Ubbo, from about 1200 BCE. Phoenician pottery has also been found at the nearby São Jorge Castle.

Roman architecture

This magnificent aqueduct, built between 1731 and 1799, mostly follows the course of the Roman original. Under the Romans, Lisbon (called Olisipo), became Lusitania's primary port, providing fish, olive oil, and wine to the rest of the empire. The Romans inspired some of Lisbon's iconic features, such as its limestone cobbled pavements.

Moorish influence

From the hilltop above the town of Sintra, the Palace of Pena is a striking blend of Muslim and Catholic architecture. One of the Moors' most visible legacies is the wall of arches in front of the chapel. Many districts in Lisbon have Moorish names, such as the Alfama neighbourhood.

Lisbon

THE CITY OF LIGHTS

In 1200 BCE, the Phoenicians, maritime merchants from the Levant (see pp.44–45), are said to have founded a trading outpost in the Tagus estuary, on the west of the Iberian Peninsula. The Romans occupied the outpost from 138 BCE until 409 CE, and it was awarded the status of a city by Octavian (the future emperor Augustus) around 30 BCE. Over the next few centuries, Lisbon was conquered by the Alani, the Suebi, and the Visigoths. In the 8th century, it was ruled by the Moors (see pp.86–87) who held the city for 433 years. Moorish architecture and district names survive in Lisbon today.

The Moors were finally overthrown by the Portuguese in 1147, who made Lisbon their capital in 1256, but it wasn't until the Age of Exploration that the city really flourished. A diverse community of merchants settled in the city, which soon grew very wealthy. Much of Lisbon's money came from the slave trade, with around 2,000 enslaved people arriving from Africa annually from 1490. Following a devastating earthquake in 1755, Lisbon never returned to its former glory, and from the 19th century many people left in search of better economic opportunities.

A resurgence of immigration

In the 1960s, African workers started to arrive from Portugal's colonies, in particular Cape Verde, to fill labour shortages. When these colonies gained independence between 1974–76, Portugal received half a million people, many returning Portuguese citizens.

Since the 1980s, thousands more have arrived in Lisbon from Portuguese-speaking Brazil, Angola, and Guinea Bissau, seeking better lives. And in the 1990s, there was an influx from Eastern Europe, with migrants drawn by job opportunities, which helped further transform Lisbon into the multicultural metropolis it is today.

▲▲ **These glazed tiles** depict Lisbon's Praça do Comércio as it was before it was destroyed by the earthquake of 1755.

▲ **Fado, a mournful genre** of music, developed in Lisbon in the 19th century. Some suggest it has Moorish roots; others say it grew out of an Afro-Brazilian dance style.

◀ **One of Lisbon's iconic features**, *azulejos* (tiles), arrived in Portugal in the 15th century, when parts of the country were under Moorish rule. The word comes from the Arabic *al-zulayj* (a small polished stone). This modern tile mural depicts Lisbon's busy port.

> "For the traveller arriving by sea, even from afar Lisbon is a beautiful and dreamy sight, shining against the vibrant blue of the sky, which the sun excites."
>
> Fernando Pessoa, literary figure and a native of Lisbon

Jewish synagogue

In 1497, King Manuel I forced Portugal's Jews to convert to Christianity. Decades later, the Inquisition persecuted families thought to be practising Judaism in secret. The procession below is passing the Shaare Tikvah, the first synagogue built in Portugal since the Middle Ages, and the culmination of Portuguese Jews' long fight for recognition.

African population

Many people of African descent live in Lisbon, due to centuries of slave trading and Portugal's colonial links with the continent. Despite their diverse backgrounds, immigrants of African descent explore similar experiences through *kuduro*, a style of music and dance that originated in Angola but flourished in Lisbon's suburbs.

Brazilian community

Today, Brazilians are Portugal's biggest migrant community. They have brought their rich culture with them. One import, the soap opera, is so popular that Brazilian slang has flooded the Portuguese language. This mural of a Indigenous Brazilian activist, Raoni Metuktire, was painted by Brazilian artist Eduardo Kobra in 2019.

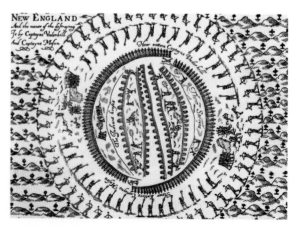

NORTH AMERICA

Quebec

Roanoke
Delaware ●
Jamestown
Powhatan ●
Choctaw ●

ATLANTIC OCEAN

Timucua ● **St Augustine**

KEY

▪▶ English incursion
▪▶ Dutch incursion
▪▶ French incursion
▪▶ Spanish incursion
● Indigenous groups

Indigenous language groups

Algonkin
Siouan
Iroquoian
Muskogean

European invasion
THE COLONIZATION OF NORTH AMERICA

Before the 16th century, North America was home to hundreds of Indigenous nations, with a complex array of languages, cultures, and ways of life. The Indigenous cultures of America that survived the next four centuries did so in spite of, rather than because of, the European invasion of the continent.

This invasion began in 1565, when Spanish *conquistador* ("conqueror") Pedro Menéndez de Avilés established St Augustine in Florida. Avilés wanted to create a base from which to compete with the French colonizers, who were also looking to exploit resources in the region. And so North America, where Indigenous peoples had lived peacefully for more than 10,000 years, became a battleground between European powers.

A foothold in the New World
Over the next 100 years, the French, Swedish, Danish, Norwegian, Dutch, and English would compete with the Spanish to establish a foothold in what they called the New World. Each European power had its own goals, so their interactions with Indigenous peoples differed. Sweden bought land in what is now Delaware from the Lenape and Susquehannock nations, only to be ousted by their Dutch competitors, who seized the land by force. The Spanish were looking mostly for gold, so were primarily focused on land in the southwest. When the French founded Quebec in 1608, they were looking to develop the fur trade, so often sought to work with Indigenous people to sustain a supply. The English wanted furs, too, but they also wanted land – initially just to use its natural resources, but later to settle on and build new communities far from home.

Jamestown colony
In 1585, Englishman Ralph Lane established a short-lived colony in Virginia named Roanoke after the Indigenous people there (see box, p.120), which he soon abandoned after stirring up conflict with the nearby Secotan people. A second colony, set up here in 1587, also failed. The first lasting colony was Jamestown, on Chesapeake Bay, which began with 104 colonists in 1607. Over the next 15 years, 10,000 people arrived, but not all would survive. More than 80 per cent of the population died in 1609–10 in what was known as the "starving time", due to food shortages. They were unable to grow the crops they were familiar with; they had no knowledge of local natural resources; and they brought with them diseases that they could not always treat.

Jamestown, with its famine and struggles, was not an attractive prospect for female settlers. In order to create a sustainable and thriving society, the Virginia Company – the key English company in the colonization of the east coast of North America – went to special measures to bring women to the colony. Ninety "tobacco wives" arrived in Virginia in 1619, their passage paid for by the company. Once they married a colonist, their husband would reimburse the company for their travel fare in tobacco. Some women were sent to

▲ **When colonists** from England, France, Spain, and the Netherlands arrived in North America they took land from established Indigenous communities.

▼ **Deerskins were an important** trading item for Indigenous peoples. This deerskin mantle with shell patterns belonged to Powhatan, an Indigenous chief.

▼ **This woodcut depicts the destruction** of a Pequot village by colonial militia in 1637, during the Pequot War in New England. Around 400 Pequot were killed in less than an hour.

See-non-ty-a, an Iowa Medicine Man is a work by American painter George Catlin (1796–1872). Catlin specialized in portraits of Indigenous peoples, striving to capture what he feared was a "vanishing race".

Virginia against their will, and of the almost 150 sent to Jamestown between 1619 and 1622, only 35 survived their first six years there. Still, the arrival of women in Jamestown marked its move from a temporary home – where men could make fortunes before returning to England – to a permanent one.

Indigenous relations

Relations deteriorated between the Jamestown colonists and Powhatan, the *mamanatowick* (head chief) of a confederacy of at least 30 Indigenous nations in the area, who provided him with military support and paid taxes. The Powhatan confederacy had initially welcomed the English, giving them food and the use of land, but ceased friendly contact in 1609, when the English began to steal from them.

Indigenous peoples often helped the early colonists to survive, supplying food until their crops were established. Crucially, the Europeans learned from the locals how to grow tobacco. A lucrative tobacco industry would develop in Virginia, bringing more settlers, and later, enslaved people, to work on plantations, and clearing large areas of land once occupied by Indigenous nations.

For the most part the Europeans took what was profitable from Indigenous peoples and made no attempts to integrate with them. They retained their cultures, rather than learning Indigenous languages or adapting to their beliefs. The Indigenous peoples, on the other hand, were encouraged by the colonists to assimilate to European ways. Powhatan's daughter Matoaka (also known as Pocahontas), was captured by the English in 1613. She was baptized as a Christian and married to an English tobacco planter. It is probable that she had no choice in either conversion or marriage, but she was later used by white Americans as an example of how Indigenous people could become "civilized".

English dominance

As more Europeans arrived in North America, deadly confrontations became the pattern as Indigenous nations fought for their homelands and the European empires competed for domination. In 1675, the Pequot people launched a war – the last major effort by the Indigenous people of New England to stop the European invasion.

Over the next century, Dutch and Scandinavian nations lost influence, and it was the English who won out between the remaining English, Spanish,

▲ **A painting showing English Quaker William Penn** making his treaty with Tamanend, a chief of the Lenni-Lenape nation, and founding the colony of Pennsylvania in 1681.

and French. In 1763, England took control of the former French colonies, including Quebec, in what is now Canada. English farms and settlements grew into cities, and the English area of occupation moved further into the North American interior, with greater waves of settlers making the journey across the Atlantic. By the mid-18th century, virtually the entire east coast was under the direct control of the English, forming the 13 colonies which were to combine to battle for independence and eventually found the United States of America.

The Lost Colony

In 1587, around 115 colonists, led by English explorer John White, made a second attempt to settle on Roanoke Island in today's North Carolina Sound. With the colonists near starvation, White returned to England to seek help. When he was able to reach Roanoke again, three years later, the only sign of the colonists was a mark on a tree saying "Croatoan". Their fate is a mystery, but it is thought that they went to live with the nearby Weapemeoc (Croatoan) nation.

"You see us unarmed and willing to supply your wants, if you will come in a friendly manner, and not with swords and guns, as to invade an enemy."

Chief Powhatan, letter to English colonizer John Smith, 1609

The city of Quebec during the construction of *l'habitation* (a series of buildings) in 1608. The work was overseen by the city's founder, French explorer Samuel de Champlain.

CULTURAL INFLUENCES

Indigenous cultures

French explorer Jacques Cartier's first encounter with the Iroquois peoples at Hochelaga, now Montréal, took place in 1535. Cartier, who claimed Canada for France, is credited with naming the country using the Huron-Iroquois word *kanata*, meaning a settlement. In 1535, Hochelaga was home to around 1,500 Iroquois people, who lived in traditional longhouses.

British takeover

Marché Bonsecours, designed by British architect William Footner, is a two-story domed public market in Montréal. The development of new industries was sparked by the arrival of large numbers of British settlers from the late 18th century, when France ceded Canada to Britain in 1763, following the Seven Years' War (1756–63).

Black culture

Many Black Americans arrived in Montréal in the late 19th and early 20th centuries to work on the city's expanding railways. Communities such as Little Burgundy – nicknamed "the Harlem of the North" – with a thriving jazz scene, flourished. Below, a jazz quintet plays at Club St Michel, an important cabaret located on Rue de la Montagne.

Montréal

THE CITY OF SAINTS

The second-largest city in Canada, Montréal sits on a large island at the confluence of the Saint Lawrence and Ottawa rivers. This area has been occupied by First Nations peoples for thousands of years. From around 1000 CE, nomadic Iroquois communities began to adopt a more sedentary lifestyle, cultivating maize and later building villages, including one that became known as Hochelaga, on the land that is now Montréal.

By the time French missionaries established the colony of Ville-Marie – later renamed Montréal – in 1642, Hochelaga had disappeared and the Indigenous population had been depleted by European diseases, violence, and warfare with neighbouring peoples. Despite attempts by the Iroquois to defend their territory, Ville-Marie grew into an important fur trading station, and the French settler population slowly expanded.

The city grows

In 1760 British colonial forces took control of Montréal, and British immigration grew. After the American War of Independence (1775–83), Loyalists, who had supported the British, also settled in the city. They were followed by migrants from Ireland fleeing starvation, disease, and poverty wrought by the Great Famine of 1845–49, while later, large numbers of Italians – particularly from the impoverished south – began to arrive. They and other migrants helped to build and staff the city's crucial transport infrastructure, as well as work in its burgeoning industries.

Montréal's first Black communities emerged in the 19th century, made up of former soldiers, people who had escaped from slavery, and later Black Americans recruited to work on the rail networks. Since the 1960s, people fleeing unrest, conflict, and dictatorial regimes have sought refuge in the city, including from the Middle East, North Africa, and Haiti. Today, immigrants account for 28 per cent of Montréal's inhabitants.

▲▲ **Rue Saint-Paul and Rue Saint-Vincent**, still major thoroughfares, were built by the French in the 1670s. The French influence remains strong in Montréal.

▲ **The first recorded public ice hockey game** was played at Montreal's Victoria Skating Rink in 1875. Ice hockey merged British and Indigenous sports.

◄ **Street art by Cedar Eve Peters** – an Anishinaabe (Ojibway) artist from the Saugeen First Nation – in Montréal's Saint-Henri district honours Peters' ancestors. The spirit beings depicted here are inspired by Indigenous beliefs.

> "Montréal... like Canada itself, is designed to preserve the past, a past that happened somewhere else."
>
> Leonard Cohen, *The Favourite Game*, 1963

Italian migrants

Between the 1880s and 1920s and after World War II, millions of Italians – mainly from the south – emigrated to the Americas to escape poverty. Many came to Montréal, resulting in the growth of neighbourhoods such as La Petite-Italie (Little Italy), where this grocery store owned by an Italian family was located in 1910.

Asian communities

A Chinese-Canadian marching band, dressed in the colours of the Québec flag, parades down Sainte-Catherine Street, Montréal, on Canada Day. The city has one of the oldest Asian communities in North America. Its Chinatown emerged in the late 19th century, when Chinese railway workers and miners migrated from western Canada to escape discrimination.

Middle Eastern refugees

Montréal's Arab World Festival celebrates the arts of the Arab world. The most significant population movements from the Middle East and North Africa began in the late 1970s, prompted by events such as the Lebanese Civil War (1975–90). Since 2011, more than 40,000 refugees from Syria have arrived in Canada.

EUROPE

US
ST DOMINGUE
CUBA
MEXICO
JAMAICA
COLOMBIA
BARBADOS
BRAZIL

Senegambia
Sierra Leone
Windward Coast
Gold Coast
Bight of Benin
Bight of Biafra
West Central Africa

The Middle Passage

THE ATLANTIC SLAVE TRADE

KEY
Number of enslaved people

0–1,000,000

1,000,000–4,000,000

4,000,000–8,000,000

The Atlantic slave trade was the biggest forced movement of people in history. When Europeans arrived in the Americas they decimated Indigenous populations, which meant there were always labour shortages on the colonial plantations and mines. In response, the British, Portuguese, Spanish, French, and other European colonial powers turned to enslaved Africans.

From the 16th century, European traders sailed to the West African coast and bought enslaved people from African and African-European dealers. Most enslaved Africans were originally captured in battle, kidnapped, or sold as punishment or to pay off a debt; Europeans also conducted their own slaving raids. This practice escalated into a vast commercial operation, and between the 16th and mid-19th centuries the Europeans sent at least 12.5 million Africans from West and Central Africa to the "New World" – North America, South America (especially Brazil), and the Caribbean.

Triangular trade

As the demand for cheap plantation labour grew in the 17th and 18th centuries, European traders set up bases along the west coast of Africa. Here, manufactured goods such as guns, textiles, and alcohol were exchanged for enslaved Africans. Most of these captives had been forcibly marched, chained together at the neck, over hundreds of kilometres from inland areas to the port – a trek known as the "First Passage". Imprisoned, inspected, and finally sold to traders, they were then loaded onto boats for transport across the Atlantic (the "Middle Passage"), before enduring a "Final Passage" from

port to their place of enslavement in the colonies. Delivered of their human cargo, ships returned to Europe with sugar, tobacco, coffee, and cotton produced by enslaved labour. This "triangular trade" transformed economies, political systems, and culture in the Americas and generated vast wealth in Europe, but devastated African states.

The economic incentive for rulers of West African kingdoms or merchants to start wars or launch kidnapping raids destabilized African society. Around two-thirds of captives were young men, many of them farmers, which decimated local economies and led to food shortages. Severe depopulation destroyed many communities; others were forced to flee inland to remote areas in an attempt to escape raiding parties and enslavement.

An intolerable journey

For Africans who survived the forced march to the coast and incarceration before transportation (and many did not), the Middle Passage inflicted further suffering. Stripped, branded, and shackled with leg irons, captives spent the six- to 11-week Transatlantic journey packed below deck, often in conditions so cramped they could not sit upright.

The overcrowding, stifling heat, and lack of sanitation led to epidemics of diseases including dysentery, smallpox, and measles,

▲ **Enslaved people** were taken from West Africa and shipped to Portuguese-controlled Brazil, the Spanish-dominated Caribbean, and southern parts of the US.

▼ **The "Door of No Return"**, in the prison on Gorée Island, Senegal, was the final door that enslaved Africans would step through on their home continent before they boarded the ships that would carry them to the Caribbean and the Americas.

▼ **A Ghanaian mural** depicts enslaved Africans at Assin Manso, one of the country's largest slave markets.

"I feared I should be put to death... for I had never seen among any people such instances of brutal cruelty..."

Olaudah Equiano, describing the crew on a slave ship, 1789

One of the 4 million enslaved Africans sent to Brazil is pictured here in a photograph taken at the port of Recife c. 1869.

while poor food caused scurvy and malnutrition. Men and women were separated on board, with women sometimes left unchained and allowed a bit of freedom, such as access to fresh air on deck. However, crew members often treated these women with extreme violence, raping and sexually assaulting them. Before slavery was abolished in the 19th century, more than 1.8 million enslaved Africans died on the Middle Passage from illness, abuse, lack of food, or while resisting their captors.

Resistance and identity

Onboard rebellion was common, with mutinies occurring on one in every 10 voyages. Occasionally, enslaved mutineers successfully overpowered the crew, as in the uprising on the Spanish slave ship the *Amistad* in 1839, but more often resistance was viciously crushed. Individual acts of defiance, which ranged from refusal to eat to attempts to jump overboard, were also dealt with harshly. Captives could be brutally force-fed or beaten until they ate, and captains often placed netting around the sides of the ship to prevent death by suicide.

Attempts at resistance on the Middle Passage reflected a new sense of community forged between Africans from different ethnic groups, brought together by dehumanizing treatment. Many did not speak the same language, and the development of methods of communication using song, call and response cries, and percussion enabled information and stories to circulate. These systems continued as a means of transmitting instructions, warnings, and oral culture among enslaved communities in their final destinations.

Religion was another source of shared identity and subversion. Many enslaved Africans invoked the supernatural power of ancestral spirits, and used curses to try to harm their enslavers. The links between spirituality, music, and dance were inadvertently sustained by brutality on the journey. On many boats, the crew forced enslaved Africans to dance on deck to maintain their health (or rather their commercial value) during the long voyage. The result was the transferral of ritual, rhythms, and culture across the Atlantic.

Final Passage

On arrival in the Caribbean and the Americas, enslaved Africans were auctioned or sold directly to traders or business owners who transported them to their final places of work, including sugar,

coffee, rice, and tobacco plantations, gold and silver mines, and private farms and households. A period of "seasoning", involving deprivation, violence, and hard labour was used to acclimatize arrivals to their surroundings and new jobs.

Although the enslavers attempted to strip Africans of their identities, they did not succeed. Instead, new cultural identities emerged, which created the foundations for later Black American and Caribbean cultures. New religions emerged in the Americas and Caribbean, such as Candomblé in Brazil and Vodou in Haiti, which reconfigured African beliefs, healing, music, and dance in a new context – in stories, folklore, spiritual songs, and music such as samba and jazz.

▲ **Continuing traditions** of dance and music were a way of maintaining cultural links with Africa, and provided enslaved Africans with a small degree of agency and even a subtle means of rebellion, sometimes using coded messages in songs.

▶ **This photograph** shows enslaved people working on a coffee plantation in the Vale do Paraíba region in Brazil in 1882. Brazil was the last country in the Americas to abolish slavery (in 1888).

Olaudah Equiano

Born in Essaka (now Nigeria), Equiano was kidnapped at age 11 and sold into slavery. Later released from slavery and living in London, UK, he became active in the British abolitionist movement and wrote his life story (1789), which helped the abolitionist cause.

"Before I entered the house, two slave women, hired from another owner, who were at work in the yard, spoke to me, and asked who I belonged to? I replied, 'I am come to live here.' 'Poor child, poor child!' they both said; 'you must keep a good heart, if you are to live here.' When I went in, I stood up crying in a corner. Mrs. I----came and took off my hat, a little black silk hat Miss Pruden made for me, and said in a rough voice, 'You are not come here to stand up in corners and cry, you are come here to work.' She then put a child into my arms, and, tired as I was, I was forced instantly to take up my old occupation of a nurse. I could not bear to look at my mistress, her countenance was so stern."

Mary Prince, an enslaved Bermudan woman, in *The History of Mary Prince, A West Indian Slave, Related by Herself*, 1831. In 1828, Prince's enslaver, Thomas Wood, took her to London. She was legally free there (slavery was abolished in Britain) but stayed with Wood until the local anti-slavery society helped her to leave and find work. As far as we know, Prince was never able to return to her family in the West Indies.

Two women are photographed on Saint Croix, in the Danish West Indies. After the Danish abolition of slavery in 1848, formerly enslaved people there earned wages – but many did the same gruelling work and lived in the same poor lodgings as before.

CULTURAL INFLUENCES

Portuguese colonizers

This view of Guanabara Bay and the entrance to the city of Rio, painted in 1816, is as seen from the terrace of the Convent of Santo Antônio, which was built by the Portuguese in 1608 to house Franciscan monks. Portuguese naval captain Gaspar de Lemos arrived in the bay in January 1502, making the first European contact with the region.

Enslaved West Africans

Slavery was central to colonial Brazil. Between the 16th and 19th centuries, the Portuguese trafficked some 2 million enslaved West Africans to Rio – more than any other city in the world. The food, language, music, dance, art, and culture of the city have been shaped by African influences, notably *capoeira*, a form of martial arts, shown below.

German infrastructure

Migration from Germany was encouraged by the Brazilian government from the early 19th century. Germans initially moved to the rural south, and later to urban areas, including Rio. German engineering firms played a key role in the development of the city: for example, Siemens built long-range telegraph lines and Rio's first telephone exchange.

Rio de Janeiro

THE MARVELLOUS CITY

▲▲ **Costumed dancers** take part in the main Rio de Janeiro Carnival – the city's major cultural event and a fusion of African and European celebrations.

▲ **A samba band from the Mangueira** *favela* holds a jam session. Samba music and dance originated in Black communities in Rio and draws on African influences.

◀ *Ethnicities* **by Eduardo Kobra** is the world's largest piece of street art, spanning 3,000 sq m (32,292 sq ft) in Rio's port area. Unveiled in 2016 to mark the city's hosting of the Olympic Games, it features five faces, each one representing a different continent.

Rio de Janeiro sits on the shores of Guanabara Bay, in an area originally occupied by Tupinambá communities, who lived in large villages and fished the rich waters offshore. Many place names in the city have Tupinambá origins – Ipanema, for example, means "bad water". Europeans arrived there at the start of the 16th century, devastating the Indigenous population. In the 1550s, French colonists founded a settlement on an island in the bay, before being evicted by the Portuguese, who established Rio de Janeiro in 1565.

The Portuguese relied heavily on enslaved labour, initially of Indigenous peoples, who built much of Rio. From the 16th to the 19th centuries, Rio became synonymous with the Atlantic slave trade (see pp.124–27): more enslaved Africans arrived here than at any other port in the Americas, while sugar, gold, diamonds, coffee, and other goods produced by enslaved people in Brazil were shipped to Europe.

Modern migrants

In 1808, following Napoleon's invasion of Portugal, the Portuguese royal court moved to Rio, which became the only European capital outside Europe. As the 19th century progressed, the city began to modernize and industrialize. Migrants from Europe, the Middle East, and Japan (see pp.188–89) arrived in large numbers, particularly in the late 19th and early 20th centuries. At the same time, working-class settlements known as *favelas* sprung up on the hillsides around the city centre. Initially inhabited by soldiers who had fought in the Canudos War (1895–97), they became home to millions of Black Brazilians. Many domestic migrants from rural areas have since joined them. Today, Rio, with a population of 6 million people, is one of the world's most diverse cities, with a blend of Indigenous, African, and European influences evident in everything from Carnival and samba to football and the martial art of *capoeira*.

> "We are Blacks, Indians, whites – everything at the same time – our culture has nothing to do with the European."
>
> Hélio Oiticica, Brazilian visual artist

Italian labourers

Political and economic crises led Italians to migrate to Brazil en masse in the late 19th and early 20th centuries. Hundreds of thousands arrived in Brazil and, although most headed to the south of the country or to the São Paulo region, a significant community grew up in Rio. Many worked in the coffee industry, which boomed during these years.

Middle Eastern traders

Migrants from the Middle East – in particular from Lebanon and Syria – started to settle in Rio from the end of the 19th century. Many worked as traders and peddlers in local markets, such as this one at Carioca Viaduct. Events including the collapse of the Ottoman Empire, World War I, and World War II later increased the flow of arrivals from the region.

Japanese workers

Escaping rural poverty, Japanese migrants flocked to Brazil in the early 20th century. Most travelled to the São Paulo region to fill labour shortages on coffee plantations, but a sizeable number settled in Rio. People of Japanese descent are shown here dancing during the Carnival parade in 2008.

ARCTIC OCEAN

Baltic Sea · Archangel · Siberia · Kamchatka · St Petersburg · Moscow · Tomsk · Yakutsk · Sakha · Okhotsk · Irkutsk · Kiev · Azov · MONGOLIA · Sea of Okhotsk · Black Sea · Caspian Sea · PACIFIC OCEAN

KEY
- Muscovy
- Acquisitions to 1505
- Acquisitions to 1584
- Acquisitions to 1682
- Acquisitions to 1725
- Acquisitions to 1796

Relocation and Russification

RUSSIA EXPANDS UNDER THE TSARS

Today, Russia is the largest country in the world, covering an eighth of the Earth's inhabited area. Six hundred years ago, however, it was just the small dukedom of Muscovy, centred on Moscow under Tatar domination. But in the late 1400s, Muscovy began to expand – first westwards to take over other ethnic Russian territories, then eastwards claiming Tatar lands and beyond, eventually taking over all of Siberia to build a Russian Empire with hundreds of ethnicities under its control.

Although Russian control grew ever wider, its expansion rarely involved the voluntary movement of ordinary people. In the late 1500s, Russian peasants were made serfs, effectively the property of their overlords and forbidden to move freely. Accounting for over a third of all Russians, most serfs worked their whole lives on the land in one place, often in grinding poverty. Landowners, though, could move their serfs – transfer them to a neighbour, or to the newly conquered lands in Siberia. Only a tiny minority moved east voluntarily.

Famine and conquest

The biggest migration happened suddenly, and catastrophically, between 1601 and 1603. Freezing Russian summers made the harvests fail, bringing a famine that killed 2 million people, a third of all Russians at the time. Refugees flooded into the cities, and the countryside emptied. Many peasants escaped serfdom through this disaster by moving off the land forever to build new lives in the cities.

Over the next two centuries, Russian expansion into Siberia caused further population movements. Russia's elite became rich through the conquest of Siberia, as they exploited the region's rich resources;

but they also brutally suppressed the Indigenous peoples in the region. To enforce their control, the Russians set up *ostrogs* (forts) across Siberia to exact *yasak*, a tax paid in furs. The Sakha people of the northeast and the Ainu of Kamchatka suffered badly. Their treatment is now considered a genocide, as 70 per cent of Indigenous people were killed in a short time – either directly by the Russians, or by the smallpox they brought with them. The Russian demand for fur also took its toll on local wildlife.

Cultural domination

In the 1700s, the Russian state began to offer peasants land at the empire's fringes in return for military service – a bid to "Russify" (make Russian culture pre-eminent in) Siberia and "Little Russia" (modern-day Ukraine). Initially, Russian farmers struggled in these unfamiliar environments, and the Sakha way of farming reindeer, used in Yakutia for thousands of years, was unsustainable on a large scale. Yet over time, Russians made their homes in these territories: they became the dominant population and Russian the main language. This remains the case today over a vast swathe of northern Asia, where other ethnicities are now minority populations.

▲ **The Russian Empire grew** to cover a vast expanse, from Poland and Finland in the west to Alaska and Sitkain the east. The movement of people to the east was not voluntary.

▼ **Russian Cossacks** attack the army of Mongol ruler Kuchum Khan on the River Irtysh in 1580. This offensive marked the beginning of the Russian conquest of Siberia.

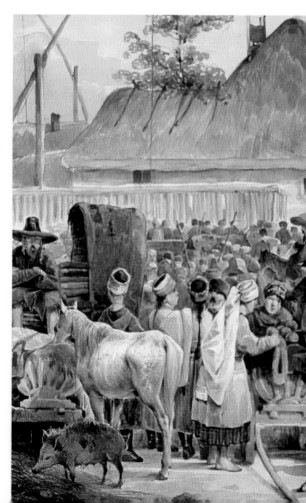

◀ **On the border guard of Muscovy** by Russian painter Sergei Ivanov, shows Crimean Tatars preparing to attack. From the 16th to the 18th century, the Tatars repeatedly invaded Muscovy.

▼ **A country fair in Ukraine**, painted in 1836 by Russian artist Vasily Sternberg, illustrates Russian migrants thriving in "Little Russia".

"...most of the best land passed into the hands of the Russian population... the [Indigenous] tribes of Siberia were moved to the north..."

Siberian activist N.M. Yadrintsev, *Siberia as a Colony*, 1881

Protestants flee persecution

THE HUGUENOT MIGRATIONS

In 16th-century Catholic France, Protestants who followed the teachings of French theologian John Calvin became known as Huguenots. Calvinism was popular among the French elite, including the future king Henry IV, and by 1562 there were more than 800,000 Huguenots in France. However, when persecution of this sizeable minority reached a peak in the 1680s, tens of thousands of Protestants secretly left France to find refuge.

Religious tensions and violence had erupted as early as the 1560s, and soon culminated in the St Bartholomew's Day massacre of 1572 that saw 3,000 Huguenots murdered by Catholics in Paris. Violence continued over the next two months, sparking the first wave of Huguenot departures.

Hostilities continued until the Edict of Nantes was issued by Henry IV in 1598 following his accession to the French throne and subsequent conversion to Catholicism. The Edict was unusual, and unpopular, since it promoted religious tolerance, and Huguenots were granted civil rights as well as freedom of worship in many parts of France. But growing resentment among the majority Catholics made life difficult for them, and when King Louis XIV revoked the Edict in 1685, they were deprived of all religious and civil liberties.

A dangerous escape and its impact

Despite the hostile environment, Huguenots were banned from leaving France, so those who chose to do so faced a perilous journey to other European countries, not knowing if they would be accepted or not. Many left in the middle of the night on small rowing boats to meet Dutch and English boats offshore. Children were smuggled out hidden in wine barrels. Often a man would go ahead to prepare things, and his family would follow. Those who were caught were executed or sentenced to hard labour at the oars of the French fleet's galleys (low ships powered by sails and oars). Nonetheless, 200,000 Huguenots escaped.

The French economy was badly damaged by the departure of the Huguenots, many of whom were rich and were skilled craftspeople – wool and silk weavers, clockmakers, bookmakers, artists, carvers, and clothes designers. Some towns lost a high proportion of their most industrious and skilled artisans and struggled to recover.

Building a new life

Around 50,000 Huguenots settled in England, where they met a mixed reaction. Some English people resented this sudden influx of immigrants, perceiving them as a threat to their livelihoods. Others were sympathetic, recognizing that many Huguenots had lost everything as they fled. In 1708, the refugees were accorded the right to full citizenship

▼ **A stone relief** above the door of the French Protestant Church in Soho, London, UK, depicts a Huguenot family fleeing France by boat.

▼ **French Protestants fled** not only to England, but to other non-Catholic areas, such as the Dutch Republic, Germany, and Russia.

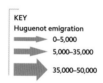

KEY
Huguenot emigration

→ 0–5,000

→ 5,000–35,000

→ 35,000–50,000

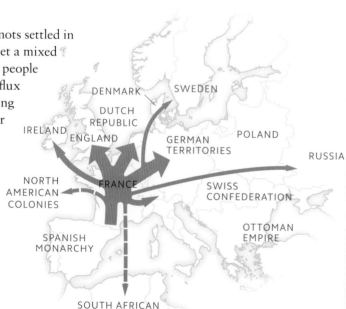

under the Foreign Protestants Naturalisation Act. Meanwhile, those who settled in the Dutch capital, Amsterdam, were given full citizen status in 1705. Huguenots were also welcomed in some German states, and in Geneva – though only those in the clock trade chose to remain. Anti-Catholic sentiment in these nations did much to further the immigrants' cause.

The Huguenots brought craftsmanship and money to their new home countries. London's Spitalfields area, where many Huguenot weavers settled, became a hive of industry, and the effect of their innovations rippled throughout the British economy. Huguenots were also influential in art and fashion, and in Britain's move to a capitalist economy based on banks, credit, and stocks and shares. By about 1760, the Huguenots scattered across Europe were no longer regarded as foreign.

◄ **Around 3,000 Huguenots** were massacred by Catholics in Paris on St Bartholomew's Day in 1572, as shown on this Dutch engraving from 1696.

Dutch artist Jan Antoon Neuhuys's 1566 artwork shows the sorrow experienced by Huguenots leaving family members behind.

Colonizing the Cape

THE DUTCH IN SOUTH AFRICA

▲ The Dutch created the first European settlement in South Africa at Table Bay, in the Cape of Good Hope region. It was populated by Dutch colonists and enslaved people from other Dutch colonies.

Between 1588 and 1672, Dutch trade, science, art, and ships were the envy of the world and the Dutch Republic experienced a "Golden Age". It became very rich from its trade links around the world, with Dutch ships sailing to Asia and the Americas, bringing back spices and silks.

The Dutch East India Company (VOC in Dutch) ran operations in Indonesia, and the West Indian Company (WIC) in the Americas. They set up ports and trading centres such as Batavia (now Jakarta) in Indonesia and Surat in western India, and the Cape of Good Hope in South Africa, used by trading ships as a stopping-off point to collect provisions as they sailed between Asia and Europe.

The VOC established its first settlement in the Cape in 1652. At first, it was more a trading hub than a colony, but the company soon realized that, in order to provide their ships with sufficient fresh produce, it needed farmers to settle there as well. Accordingly, it encouraged employees and their families in the Netherlands to try out a new life in the colony, giving them free passage and work as independent farmers. By the mid-18th century around 13,000 Dutch people had established themselves in South Africa.

Indigenous communities

The Khoikhoi and the San (known collectively as the Khoisan) were the Indigenous people of the Cape. They lived as hunter-gatherers and herdsmen but the Dutch forced them to work, without pay, on their farms, subjecting them to brutal treatment and preventing them from leaving. As well as taking Khoisan land and denying them access to water, which displaced

many from the area altogether, the settlers also exposed them to diseases, such as smallpox, to which they had no immunity. The settlers perpetrated at least two massacres of Khoisan people, to which they responded by attacking the settlers and burning their farms.

Need for labour

The hot, dry climate proved very challenging for the Dutch farmers (called Boers and, later, Afrikaners in Dutch), who were unable to cope with the growing need for crops and livestock by the VOC ships and the settlers. To meet demand, the Dutch increased their workforce

▼ This brick from the Castle of Good Hope, the Dutch East India Company's base in the Cape, bears the initials VOC, which stand for Vereenigde Oost-Indische Compagnie, the company's name in Dutch.

▼ The settlement of Cape Town expanded in the 17th century, as increasing numbers of Dutch ships called in for supplies during their voyages between Europe and Asia.

by transporting enslaved people from their other colonies: Angola and the Ivory Coast and Indonesia and Malaysia. In 1692, there were about 300 enslaved people in the settlement, but by 1793 the number had grown to 14,000. They mostly worked on the rural estates but also in the newly formed port city of Cape Town.

The influence of these diverse groups of people is evident in the Afrikaans language, which grew out of the Dutch spoken by the settlers. It was adapted by the enslaved people and their enslavers as well as being added to by other South African peoples.

Change of rule

By the end of the 1700s, the VOC had become financially unviable. The British seized the Cape settlement in 1795, but permitted the Dutch to continue governing it; in 1814, the Dutch ceded the colony to Britain. Although the British abolished slavery in their territories in 1808, they allowed the Dutch to keep their enslaved people until 1838.

Dutch opium trading

The powerful Dutch East India Company dominated trade with the East Indies (now Indonesia), with opium a key commodity. Used as a painkiller, the drug was also given to the company's sailors to treat typhoid, among other diseases. This painting, c.1650, shows Dutch captains and officers of the Dutch East India Company indulging in alcohol and opium in Indonesia between voyages to Europe via Cape Town.

▲ **The Dutch governor** of the Cape settlement, Jan Willem Janssens, is pictured meeting the leaders of the Khoisan in 1803, when the British briefly returned the Cape to the Dutch.

▶**This allegorical painting** by Mughal artist Basawan (c. 1590) depicts a scene of chaos, yet Akbar the Great, who is riding barefoot on a wild elephant, is shown in full control. Akbar's success as a ruler lay in his cooperation with all his subjects – Muslims, Hindus, Persians, Central Asians, and Indigenous peoples.

An age of wealth and welcome

THE MUGHAL EMPIRE EXPANDS

KEY

- Extent of Mughal Empire in 1530
- Expansion of Mughal Empire to 1605
- Expansion of Mughal Empire to 1707
- Mughal expansion into Babur's Afghan Kingdom
- Routes of Mughal expansion campaigns

At its height, the Mughal Empire spanned most of modern-day India, Pakistan, Bangladesh, and Afghanistan and was home to about 100 million people. It lasted for more than two centuries, and became one of the wealthiest empires in history.

The Mughal dynasty was founded in 1526, when Babur, a Muslim ruler of Turkic-Mongolian origin from modern-day Uzbekistan, in Central Asia, invaded northern India via Afghanistan. Islam had arrived in the Indian subcontinent in the 7th century, but Mughal rule played a key role in spreading, cementing, and integrating the religion in a region with a large Hindu majority.

Central Asian and Persian migrations

The original soldiers from Central Asia included members of the Turkic Chagathai tribe and Uzbeks. Many settled in India, and thousands more Central Asians migrated throughout the 16th and 17th centuries to take up service in the Mughal Empire, particularly in administration.

There was also significant Persian immigration. Babur's son and successor Humayan, who had a high regard for Persian culture, invited nobles and administrators from Persia (now Iran) to India, and Persian became the language of the Mughal court and administration. Many immigrants were Sunni Muslims, who felt discriminated against in Persia where Shia Muslims increasingly dominated. Over the following centuries, Persians with varied skills migrated to India to seek work, including physicians, painters, architects, and craftspeople.

The Mughals felt strongly connected to their roots, and both Central Asian and Persian influences are evident in Mughal art and architecture, which flourished under Akbar the Great (r. 1556–1605). Elements of these cultures, combined with both Islamic and Hindu styles, can be seen in Mughal constructions such as the Taj Mahal, commissioned by Emperor Shah Jahan (r. 1628–58).

Akbar's reign was also a high point for religious tolerance. The emperor had a keen interest in other faiths, and invited Hindus, Buddhists, Christians, Zoroastrians, Jews, and Muslims to his court. He abolished the tax (*jizya*) on non-Muslims, allowed Hindu pilgrimages, and appointed Hindu nobles to senior positions. One legacy of the Mughal Empire was the establishment of large Muslim communities, particularly in northern India, which lasted until Partition (see pp.218–21), and, in some areas, beyond.

Decline of the empire

A lack of religious tolerance among Akbar's successors may have been a factor in the Mughals' decline, which began around 1700. Under the conservative rule of Aurangzeb (r.1658–1707), the *jizya* was reintroduced and Hindu leaders revolted. Invasions by Persians (1738) and Afghans (1761) dealt the Mughals further critical blows. The weakened empire continued for another century, but in 1858 it was finally dissolved by the British.

▲ **The Mughal Empire** expanded as far as the Himalayas in the north and the Deccan plateau in the south, and from Kabul in the west to Bengal in the east.

▼ **A jewelled ornament**, called a *sarpech*, was worn on the front of turbans at the Mughal court and in Persia.

▼ **Nur Jahan**, whose family emigrated from Persia to India, married Jahangir, the fourth Mughal emperor. She is believed to have been the true power behind the throne, had great political skills, and was highly cultured and creative.

Mohican
Pennacook
Massachuset
Pocumtuc
Boston
Massachusetts Bay
Nipmuc
from Englar
Plymouth
Cape Cod Bay
Wampanoag
Nauset

ATLANTIC
OCEAN

KEY
- Route of the Pilgrims in 1620
- Modern state boundaries
- Massachusetts Bay Colony
- Plymouth Colony

Pilgrims and Puritans

ENGLISH PROTESTANTS COLONIZE NEW ENGLAND

On 16 September 1620, the *Mayflower* set sail for North America from the English port of Plymouth. Of the 102 passengers on board, almost half were Protestant Separatists (later called the Pilgrims). They were radical Puritans whose extremist views had led them to break from the Church of England.

The *Mayflower* was bound for the Hudson River, in northern Virginia. However, bad weather drove the ship away from the English colony there and towards Cape Cod, where it landed in what is now Provincetown Harbor. Before going ashore, the passengers drew up the Mayflower Compact, an initial set of rules for self-governance. Pilgrims and non-Pilgrims alike agreed to remain loyal subjects to the English king, James I, and to establish a lawful and Christian society.

On shore, the Pilgrims came across Indigenous graves, which they plundered for supplies and offerings of corn. They went on to found the Plymouth Colony on land that had been inhabited for more than 10,000 years by the Wampanoag people. The Wampanoag had already suffered greatly from contact with European traders, who had brought with them a deadly disease (its identity unknown) that killed around 90 per cent of the region's Indigenous residents between 1616–19.

Relationship with the Wampanoag

The first winter in the Plymouth colony was brutal. More than half of the colonists died and the rest only escaped starvation thanks to the Wampanoag, who taught them how to cultivate corn and hunt. In turn, the Wampanoag sought an alliance with the colonists to provide protection from rival Indigenous nations. After a good harvest in 1621,

the colonists celebrated with a feast, attended by Wampanoag leader Massasoit and 90 of his people. This feast is known as the first Thanksgiving, which is now celebrated in the US as a national holiday. Many Indigenous people, however, see Thanksgiving as a reminder of the theft of their lands and the deaths of millions of their ancestors.

Further migration and tensions

In 1630, another group of Puritans arrived in New England, building the Massachusetts Bay Colony – a strict, theocratic society – north of Plymouth. Unlike the Pilgrims, these Puritans wanted to "purify" the Church of England of any remaining Catholic practices from within. Further Puritan groups soon migrated from England to New England, so that by the 1670s, the colony's capital, Boston, had a population of 4,000.

As more colonists arrived – both Puritan and otherwise – they subjected the Indigenous peoples to increasing violence, displacement, and diseases. Tensions rose, leading to King Philip's War in 1675 (see pp.118–21), named after the Wampanoag leader Metacom (called Philip by the English). The war crushed the Wampanoag and other Indigenous groups. Thousands were killed or sold into slavery by the English – the very people they had once helped to survive.

The Puritans of the *Mayflower*, who later became known as the Pilgrim Fathers, were glorified in white American folklore and artworks, such as this 19th-century engraving of their landing.

> "We, the Wampanoag, welcomed you, the white man, with open arms, little knowing that it was the beginning of the end."
>
> Frank James, Wampanoag leader, 1970

◄ **The Pilgrims** established a colony based around Plymouth, while later Puritans built the Massachusetts Bay Colony around Boston. However, New England was already the traditional homelands of many Indigenous nations.

◄ *Mayflower* **passengers** John Alden and Priscilla Mullin were some of the first Pilgrims to marry in the Plymouth Colony, where they were given 4 acres to build a house in 1623.

◄ **Tisquantum** teaches the Pilgrims how to plant corn and fertilize it with dead herring. Squanto, as he was known, was a Patuxet man enslaved by the English in 1618. He had been taught English by his captors.

From country to town

THE INDUSTRIAL REVOLUTION

▶ **Bradford's Salt's Mill** and Saltaire village were built with workers' welfare in mind. Mill owner Titus Salt's industrial town included a hospital, school, and public washhouses.

The Industrial Revolution that began in Britain in the 1700s brought about a profound change in human society around the world. Factories appeared in the rural landscape, and millions of people left the land to work in the new industrial cities.

Various factors contributed to the migration from country to city. Innovations in agriculture reduced the demand for farm labourers, while advancements in technology led to the creation of factories in the towns and cities, which required lots of workers (or "hands" as they were called). The new technology also produced food surpluses to sustain population growth in the cities, and as Britain's empire expanded, vast new markets for the manufactured goods opened up.

British entrepreneur Richard Arkwright seized the opportunity, opening the world's first factory, Cromford Mill in Derbyshire, in 1771. There, water-powered machines spun cotton on a huge scale, operated day and night by a workforce of men, women, and children. By the late 18th century, industrial cities such as Manchester and Bradford sprawled across the coal fields of northern England, and steam-powered rail and canal networks were built to transport goods and people between them.

City life

Pushed by increasing rural poverty and pulled by the chances of work in the factories, whole families left the land and moved to the cities. Manchester's population swelled sixfold between 1771 and 1831, and reached 2.3 million by 1911.

While wealthier families moved to the suburbs, away from the growing pollution, urban life for the working classes was hard. City centres were noisy and dirty. Workers' housing was overcrowded, with poor ventilation and no sanitation. Diseases such as tuberculosis and cholera were rife. Working conditions in most factories were also dreadful and dangerous. Until the Factory Act was passed in 1833, children as young as six worked 16-hour days. The alternative was to starve in the countryside. When the Great Famine struck in the 1840s, thousands emigrated from Ireland to Britain (and to the US, see pp.174–77).

Although millions left the countryside, the cities mostly grew from an accelerated birth rate. Young people could meet and marry like never before, and economic growth encouraged them to have families. Their children could be educated, enabling them to get better jobs and higher wages. Slowly conditions improved. In 1750, 15 per cent of Britain's population lived in towns; by 1900 it was 85 per cent.

Unstoppable trend

The rest of Europe soon began to industrialize, with Belgium and France, then Germany undergoing their own revolutions. The US industrial revolution began in the late 1700s with a second wave in the mid-1800s – by the 19th century it was an industrial powerhouse. Echoed around the world, this movement from country to city has gathered pace ever since.

"I have done twice the quantity of work that I used to do, for less wages. Machines have been speeded [up]..."

Charles Aberdeen, worker in a cotton mill, Salford, north of England, 1832

▶ **Britain's cities grew rapidly** throughout the 19th century, especially in the Midlands and northwest England; this map shows the major industrial cities.

KEY

▧ Coalfields

◀ **Filthy, overcrowded slums** in the city of Glasgow in Scotland became home for poor immigrants from the Scottish countryside as well as from Ireland.

London's industrial growth centred on the River Thames. This image from 1863 shows iron workers and machinery beside the river in Blackfriars.

"We don't cross the Nomugi Pass for nothing / We do it for ourselves and our parents.
 When the season of painful reeling is over / The world will be bright again / And maybe I'll be able to get married. Because I am poor, at age twelve / I was sold to this factory / When my parents told me, 'Now it is time to go' / My very heart wept tears of blood... Mother! I hate the season in the silk plant; / It is from 4 p.m. to 4 a.m. ...
 I wish I could give my parents rice wine to drink, / And see their happy tears fall into the cup. ... Their letter says they are waiting for the year's end. / Are they waiting more for the money than for me?"

"My Two Parents", a song by a Japanese silk worker c. 1900

Japanese women work in a silk factory in this colourized version of a photograph from c. 1900. Girls were recruited from peasant families by agents who claimed the work would allow the girls to earn a good wage. In reality, these girls slept as little as four hours a day, working long hours for little compensation.

London
THE BIG SMOKE

▲▲**These colourful mosaics** at Tottenham Court Road tube station were created by pop artist Eduardo Paolozzi. The son of Italian migrants to Scotland, he moved to London in the 1940s.

▲**The Shri Swaminarayan Temple** in Neasden, London, was carved piece by piece in India and assembled in London. When completed in 1993, it was the largest Hindu temple outside India.

▶**The Notting Hill Carnival** has taken place in late August since 1966, when it was organized by community activists Rhaune Laslett and Andre Shervington. Inspired by carnival culture in the Caribbean, its floats, costumed dancers, and music stages bring hundreds of thousands onto the streets.

Although there were earlier settlements in the area around the River Thames, the first true city there was built by the Romans (see pp.60–63). "Londinium" was established in the 40s CE, with stone buildings and the first known bridge over the river. The city was abandoned after the fall of Rome, but by the 7th century CE, the port town of "Lundenwic", was growing in what is now Covent Garden. By the Middle Ages, London had become a major trading hub, and the nation's capital. It drew in migrants from across Britain and overseas, from 14th-century Flemish weavers to the 17th-century Huguenots (see pp.134–35).

By the 1780s, London was home to as many as 20,000 enslaved and free Black African people. Industrialization (see pp.142–43) also swelled the population of London, and it became home to Irish people fleeing the Great Famine of the 1840s and Jewish families escaping persecution in Eastern Europe (see pp.160–61). Migration from South Asia began on a small scale in the 19th century, with lascars (seamen) living around the docks, joined by the first Chinese community in Limehouse in East London as sailors settled and started businesses such as laundries and restaurants.

20th century migrations

The decline of the British Empire led to further changes. In the 1940s, London's labour shortage led the government to actively recruit migrants from the Caribbean (see pp.232–33) and South Asia to work in the new National Heath Service or London's public transport system. Large numbers of Italians migrated to work in factories and in catering. Some suburbs experienced successive waves of immigration – such as Brick Lane, in the East End, which has been home to French Huguenots, Jewish migrants, and Bangladeshis. In recent decades, London has welcomed refugees from civil wars in Syria (see pp.270–71) and Afghanistan (see pp.256–57), and drawn migrants from across the European Union (see pp.254–55). Today, London is a vibrant cosmopolitan city, and is home to people speaking over 300 languages, making it one of the most linguistically diverse cities in the world.

CULTURAL INFLUENCES

Irish construction workers

The construction of St Pancras Station (seen here in 1867), and other similar projects, were often carried out by Irish migrant labourers, many of whom came after the Great Famine of 1845–49 made life intolerable at home. By 1851, London had become home to over 100,000 Irish people, who still have a strong presence in the city today.

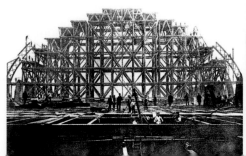

Jewish community

London's East End was home to a large Jewish community in the late 19th century, as Jews fled from pogroms in Russia and Eastern Europe. They joined smaller numbers who had settled when Jews were readmitted to England in 1656, and set up synagogues and businesses – such as these steam baths – but often faced antisemitic discrimination.

South Asian religions

Southall High Street, where these South Asian immigrants are shopping, became the centre of a new migrant community after World War II as many fled India, Pakistan, (and later Bangladesh) to escape war or poverty, or sought opportunities for work in Britain. They founded Hindu temples, mosques, and Sikh Gurdwara, increasing London's religious diversity.

> "I came to London. It had become the center of my world and I had worked hard to come to it."
>
> V.S. Naipaul, Trinidadian writer, *An Area of Darkness*, 1964

Windrush generation

Migrants from the Caribbean first arrived in large numbers on the HMT *Empire Windrush* in 1948. They swapped homes on islands such as Jamaica, Trinidad, and Barbados for areas such as Brixton in south London, bringing Caribbean and African music and produce to its venues and markets, along with a host of Caribbean eateries.

Arab immigration

Many Arabs from Gulf countries made rich by oil wealth in the 1970s invested or settled in London, making Arab dress, as seen here in South Kensington, a familiar sight. Others fled instability in the Middle East – Palestinians came after the wars in 1948 and 1967, followed by Libyans, Syrians, and Iraqis – to create a highly diverse Arab community.

Nigerian South London

A wave of Nigerian migrants to the UK settled in Peckham, southeast London, in the 1970s and 80s. They left Nigeria when the economy plummeted following the end of the oil-boom, and established a vibrant community in London. In 2011, there were 115,000 Nigerian-born Londoners – around 13,600 in the borough of Southwark.

5

Mass Movement
and Freedoms

1700–1900

Mass Movement and Freedoms

1700–1900

The mass migrations sparked by the growth of European empires reached new levels in the 19th century. Britain sent convicts to Australia from the 1780s – later supplemented by free settlers and prospectors in search of gold – who drove First Australians from their traditional lands. In South and West Africa, Indigenous Africans fought wars against the Europeans, who had firearms and well-trained armies. But by the end of the century, European powers controlled almost all of Africa, with significant numbers of white settlers in South Africa, Kenya, and French North Africa.

In Europe itself, political refugees became a significant phenomenon for the first time, with émigrés from the French Revolution, exiles from Latin American independence movements, and people fleeing the Russian Tsarist rule. The most significant migration, however, was out of Europe; a huge number of Europeans moved to the United States, whose growing economy pulled in millions of migrants. Some fled political persecution, others extreme economic hardship – such as the million people who left Ireland during the Great Famine of 1845–49.

"Voortrekkers" prepare for conflict in South Africa (see pp.162–63)

New York City bustles with migrants in the 19th century (see pp.174–77)

"Give me your tired, your poor, / Your huddled masses yearning to breathe free."

Emma Lazarus, Jewish American poet, in "The New Colossus", 1883

Many of these new settlers in the US moved west, driving Indigenous peoples off their traditional lands, and forcing many to migrate to arid territory in Oklahoma. Meanwhile, large numbers of enslaved people in the American South sought refuge in free states in the North using escape routes known as the "Underground Railroad".

Much migration in this period was driven by labour. Chinese workers moved to the US to build railroads in the western states, but they also migrated extensively within Southeast Asia, either as merchants or as urban labourers.

From the 1830s, the British lured Indian labourers to the Caribbean, giving them exploitative contracts as indentured workers on plantations, while from the 1860s, many Japanese workers migrated to nearby regions, such as Korea, or took labour contracts in Brazil, the US, and Hawai'i.

Migration was made easier by a transport revolution. Steamships, canal-boats, the first railways, and improved roads meant that travel became faster and cheaper, while improvements in healthcare also meant people were more likely to survive even the most arduous journeys.

A convict train is overseen by a British soldier in Australia (see pp.154–57)

Chinese labourers arrive in Singapore (see pp.164–65)

Fleeing the Terror

ÉMIGRÉS OF THE FRENCH REVOLUTION

▲ Those fleeing the French Revolution migrated to many parts of Europe, including England, Ireland, Denmark, Sweden, and Prussia – and also to North America.

The French Revolution began with the storming of the Bastille, a royal prison in Paris, on 14 July 1789. This defining act symbolized the anger and desperation felt by ordinary people who, unlike the ruling classes, were facing starvation while burdened with taxes they could not afford to pay. The uprising prompted members of the aristocracy to flee France, fearing for their lives; some left immediately, more followed as violence escalated.

Fleeing the Revolution

This first wave of emigration was typically made up of aristocrats directly opposed to the Revolution, including members of the royal family. They, and all others fleeing, came to be known as "émigrés". The Reign of Terror (1793–94), during which the revolutionary government publicly guillotined Louis XVI and his queen, Marie Antoinette, as well as ordering the guillotining of thousands for treason initiated a larger, second wave of refugees. Creating a total of more than 100,000 exiles, most were professionals and wealthy, educated business owners whose increasing influence aroused conflict with the revolutionary government. Meanwhile, the new regime confiscated the émigrés' property and condemned them to death if they returned.

Life abroad

All of France's close neighbours took in refugees, particularly Austria, the German states, and North America, but it was England that accepted the most: over 40,000. The country had a reputation for tolerance, and the distance provided by the English Channel gave an added sense of security. The refugees tended to gravitate to certain areas of London, including Soho, where there was already a French presence (see pp.134–35).

At first, the English establishment was suspicious of these incomers from its enemy France, with a number believing they had come simply to spread dangerous revolutionary ideas. Some young radicals welcomed that possibility, but reports of mass killings conducted without trial during of Reign of Terror changed attitudes, and even those initially sympathetic to the revolutionaries turned against them. Meanwhile support for the refugees grew, and by 1792 an Emigrant Relief Committee to collect funds for their care had been established. Even so, life for the émigrés was tough – most had arrived almost destitute – and many aristocrats were compelled to earn a living as dance, art, and fencing masters, and French teachers.

Returning to France

Napoleon Bonaparte came to power in 1799 after a coup d'état, marking the end of the French Revolution. He granted émigrés a degree of clemency, and many took the chance to return to France at once. When the French monarchy was finally restored to power in 1815, the émigrés became a powerful political faction. Some, though, chose to stay abroad, especially in North America and England, where they created a cultural legacy that influenced art, literature, fashion, and food.

▼ A cartoon from 1789 lampoons the social order and burden of taxation before the Revolution, showing an ordinary man supporting members of the nobility and clergy.

Artistic reaction

Elisabeth Vigée Le Brun, an artist who fled France, produced this self-portrait. While in exile in Europe and caring for her daughter, Julie, she continued to paint European royalty. In order to support themselves abroad, some émigrés became tailors, seamstresses, hatmakers, and artists.

"The émigré only left his country to seek war against it, the Refugee only quitted it when it had made war on him."

Pierre-Louis Roederer, Member of the Constituent Assembly, 1795

▲ **The guillotine** was used during The Reign of Terror, when the French government took harsh measures against suspected enemies of the Revolution. The threat of the guillotine led many to flee.

▶ **The Duchess of Polignac** was a close friend of Marie Antoinette, Louis XVI's queen, and an unpopular member of the nobility. Fearing for her life, she fled France in 1789.

Colonizers and convicts
THE BRITISH IN OCEANIA

Before 1776, transportation to the American colonies had been a standard punishment for British convicts. However, after the colonies gained their independence the newly formed US would no longer take them. As prisons in Britain became overcrowded, the British government turned to Australia as a potential penal colony.

Captain James Cook had claimed Australia for Britain, but it was already home to a thriving population of First Australians (the modern term for Indigenous peoples, see pp.18–19). Disregarding these inhabitants, Britain sent 11 ships of the so-called First Fleet to Australia in May 1787 with more than 750 convicts on board (about a quarter were women), and 250 free men, mainly marines. The fleet landed at Port Jackson (now Sydney Harbour) in January 1788. More fleets followed in 1790 and 1791.

For the Eora, First Australians living in the area around Sydney, this invasion was devastating. Their way of life was steeped in their deep respect for nature, which the colonists discounted, clearing land for farming, and overfishing and overhunting, nearly starving the Eora as a result. European settlers massacred the Eora to steal their land, and infected them with diseases, most notably smallpox and fatal venereal diseases, which they transmitted to the women they raped. Within 10 years, 90 per cent of the Eora were dead, their culture and histories largely lost.

Life for the new arrivals
The settlers struggled in the early New South Wales colony: the weather was unpredictable and the soil infertile. Male convicts laboured on government projects, usually on farms or in construction. Women were usually employed as domestic servants to the officers, made clothes, or did the washing. Convicts who worked hard could earn a "ticket of leave", which afforded some liberty and a chance to earn money. Those granted an absolute pardon gained complete freedom. By the 1820s these "emancipists", including those who had completed their sentences, outnumbered convicts.

The end of transportation
The transportation of convicts to eastern Australia ended in 1853, and the social structure of the New South Wales colony began to change as former

▶ **The First Fleet sailed** around 24,000 km (15,000 miles) on its journey to Australia, making three stops for provisions; subsequent fleets went onto New Zealand.

▼ **Convict love tokens**, like this penny carved in 1825 by 19-year-old Cornelius Donovan, were given to friends and loved ones as mementos before transportation to Australia.*

▼ **By 1823, Sydney was a** thriving farming community and expanding rapidly through a public works programme that used convict labour.

KEY
→ Route of first fleet
→ Route of subsequent fleets

convicts started to gain equality with the increasing number of free settlers who emigrated by choice. However, the colonies still needed people to work in the Australian interior, including unmarried women, who would balance out the discrepancy in numbers between the sexes. The solution for the British government was assisted emigration.

Between 1832 and 1850 around 127,000 poor Irish and Scottish farmers and other British emigrants were given assisted passage to Australia, and made up 70 per cent of all arrivals. Some arrived with little money and transformed their fortunes but, for others, life was difficult. Assisted migrants could live on board their ship on arrival while they sought

work. After 10 days they had to fend for themselves. For women there were limited opportunities as governesses, dressmakers, and ladies' maids, so some turned to sex work. Others became farm hands.

Life for the First Australians

While life improved for many colonists, it did not for the First Australians. Settlers continued to commit atrocities against them and were rarely punished. The First Australians tried to fight back to retain their lands and ensure their survival, but by this point their numbers were severely depleted due to colonial settlement, and they gradually withdrew from the settlers' frontier.

▲ **Woollarawarre Bennelong**, a senior man of the Eora who was abducted from his community by First Fleet colonists in 1789, acted as a mediator between the Eora and the British government.

Passengers on the *Sobraon*, the fastest ship plying the England–Australia migration route from 1866 to 1891. The vessel catered to first- and second-class passengers only.

> "We can't put you on a boat and send you back home, so we've all got to share and care for this country."
>
> Allen Madden, Elder of the Gadigal people of the Eora nation, 2009

▲ **The Māori community** on Lake Rotorua, New Zealand, agreed to lease land to the British government in 1880, to build a European-style spa resort for visitors and settlers.

South Australia became the first colony not founded with convicts; it aimed to attract settlers with farming and trade opportunities. In Victoria, a gold rush encouraged migration from across Australia and Britain in the 1850s and 1860s, compounding the disruption to First Australians caused by the introduction of sheep and cattle. The miners cut down trees, polluted rivers, and pitted the landscape with holes. Indigenous guides did, however, work with the settlers, showing them new gold fields and finding food and water. They even traded in gold themselves. Meanwhile, the British middle classes started to see Australia as a chance to become part of the colonial upper class. Between 1851 and 1861, the European population of Australia grew from 450,000 to 1,150,000.

Annexation of New Zealand

European colonists, or Pākehā, settled in New Zealand in increasing numbers during the early 19th century, drawn to the islands by their rich natural resources. In 1840, Britain effectively annexed New Zealand through the Treaty of Waitangi, a pact signed with over 500 chiefs of the Māori Tangata Whenua who had been the traditional custodians of New Zealand for 700 years (see pp.100–101). Māori society was based on well-established customs and a sense of respect and guardianship towards the natural world, much at odds with the colonists' behaviour. The Māori recognized that developing a positive working relationship with the British should benefit them economically, but although the treaty was drawn up in Māori and English, there were differences in translation. The treaty ostensibly gave equal rights to both peoples, but many of the rights guaranteed to the Māori were ignored. The British later interpreted the treaty as giving them absolute sovereignty. British settlers who had bought land in New Zealand were now joined by government-assisted arrivals. By 1867, more than 200,000 migrants had arrived, attracted by the discovery of gold and farming opportunities. They were accompanied by missionaries, whose aim was to replace the pantheistic Māori religion with Christianity. The government imposed English literacy, and confiscated large areas of land. It also abolished the Māori's traditional communal claims to land and individualized land titles, so land could be traded easily. As in Australia, with the settlers came disease. By 1870, after decades of conflict, there were too few Māori left to resist colonization.

Colonization of Hawai'i

The first settlers arrived in Hawai'i 1,500 years ago by boat from Polynesia. When the British captain, James Cook arrived in 1778 a new era of colonization began. In the 1800s, Protestant missionaries and settlers arrived from Britain and the US. This scene depicts the baptism of King Kamehameha II's prime minister, Kalanimoku, against the backdrop of the Hawaiian flag. The colonists established sugar plantations and bought up land, and in 1898 the US annexed Hawai'i.

Sydney
THE HARBOUR CITY

Sydney, now a coastal city in New South Wales, Australia, was already occupied by First Australians when ships bringing British convicts and marines arrived in 1788 (see pp.154–57). Drawing on the First Australians' knowledge of the land, and using them for labour, the colonizers slowly turned Sydney – which had poor, infertile soil – into a thriving settlement. They built English-style cottages with gardens, and erected grand public buildings in colonial Georgian style.

Attracting new settlers

Between the 1830s and 1850s, many poor British and Irish farmers migrated to Sydney on government-assisted migration schemes. In 1851, a gold rush in New South Wales attracted a new wave of migrants from Europe, the US, and China. Many Chinese prospectors stayed on and settled in the modern-day Sydney Central Business District (CBD) and Haymarket.

Labour shortages after World War II (1939–45) led to a "Populate or Perish" campaign – an attempt by Australia's government to encourage white European and Middle Eastern immigration. These migrants created close-knit communities in Sydney's suburbs, and established a new culture of food. In the 1970s, the White Australia policy was abandoned (see pp.236–37), and many migrants from Asia arrived – especially from Vietnam (see pp.240–41). In the 21st century, most newcomers are Indian migrants with IT, healthcare, and engineering skills; and migrants from China, many of whom have set up businesses. All have made Sydney a diverse city with one of the largest immigrant populations in the world – today more than 40 per cent of its residents were born overseas.

> "Farewell to old England for ever... Farewell to the well-known Old Bailey... And we're bound for Botany Bay."
>
> Popular folk song, 19th century

▲▲ **Sydney's Greek Orthodox community** parade to celebrate the 200th anniversary of Greek independence in 2018 – part of an annual festival that is now one of Sydney's largest cultural events.

▲ **Traditional Fijian Meke dancers** perform for their elders at Sydney's annual Fiji Day Festival. More than half of Australia's Fijian population are based in New South Wales.

▶ **Wandjina figures, projected onto Sydney Opera House**, in 2016, showcase the work of First Australian artist Donny Woolagoodja and promote First Australian culture. The figures are mythological cloud and rain spirits associated with the creation of the world.

CULTURAL INFLUENCES

British institutions

The British colonized Sydney in 1788. During the 19th century, they established many of its cultural institutions and constructed many public buildings, such as the General Hospital (today the Mint) and St Mary's Cathedral. Sydney's steam tramway opened in 1879; by 1930 it was one of the largest tram systems in the world.

Chinese heritage

In 1851, thousands of Cantonese men arrived in Sydney in search of wealth in the gold rush. Many stayed and became market gardeners, cabinet makers, bankers, and traders. Sydney has a strong Chinese heritage, with a large Chinatown and a Ming-style garden in the city. Chinese people are one of the largest migrant groups.

Italian neighbourhood

Small numbers of Italians lived in Sydney in the late 19th century, but numbers grew in the 1920s and, especially, after World War II. Many Italians worked in the construction or food industries. They set up shops, patisseries, delicatessens, and restaurants – mainly in Leichhardt (an area known as "Little Italy") and made olive oil and broccoli popular in Australia.

Lebanese refugees

The first Lebanese arrived in Sydney in the late 19th century, fleeing the Ottoman Empire. They settled in the Redfern area, where they set up warehouses and factories. Larger waves arrived after World War II and during the Lebanese Civil War (1975–90). In 1972, Lebanese Muslims built the Imam Ali bin Abi Taleb mosque in Lakemba.

Vietnamese small businesses

After the end of the Vietnam War, asylum seekers fleeing Communist persecution started to arrive in Sydney. Most settled in the Cabramatta district, where they established small businesses – mainly grocery stores, bakeries, and restaurants.

New Indian wave

In the 21st century, Indian migrants arrived in Sydney to work as doctors, nurses, IT specialists, and engineers. Today, they make up one of the largest groups of arrivals. They introduced large-scale Hindu festivals, such as Diwali and Holi, and Bollywood dancers take part in the multicultural Parramasala Festival.

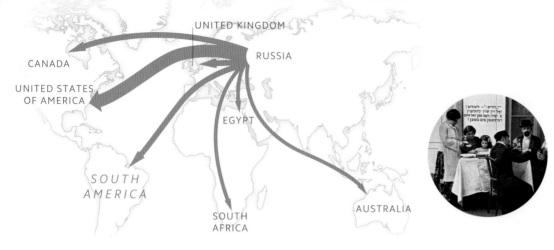

Pogroms and the Pale

JEWS FLEE PERSECUTION IN RUSSIA

KEY
Jewish Migration
- 0–50,000
- 50,000–250,000
- 250,000–2,000,000

▲ **Russian Jews fled** mainly to North and South America, the UK, Africa, and Australia between 1880 and 1924.

◀ **An American postcard** from the early 20th century shows a migrant family settled in the US celebrating the Jewish New Year. The backdrop is a toast to the occasion, written in Yiddish: "Here's a toast; good riddance to a bad year."

▼ **Jews in Kishinev** (now Chişinău, Moldova) ceremonially bury Torah scrolls desecrated during a pogrom over Easter 1903. The Kishinev Pogrom attracted global attention to the persecution of Russian Jews.

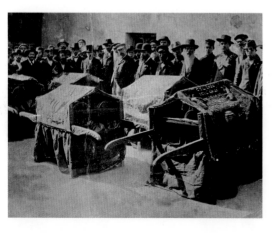

Very few Jewish people lived in Imperial Russia in the early 18th century. However, after the partitions of Poland (1772–95), Russia acquired a large Jewish population. Judeophobic sentiments led Catherine the Great to put economic and residence restrictions (known as "disabilities") in place. These designated an official, limited area in which Jews could live, called *Cherta Osedlosti* – known in English as the Pale of Settlement. This included areas of residence in the western regions, inhabited by Jews for many centuries, as well as land around the Black Sea.

Life in the Pale

Created by decrees in 1783, 1791, and 1794, the Pale of Settlement lay on the western edge of the empire and included land in Poland, Lithuania, Latvia, Byelorussia (now Belarus), Moldavia (now Moldova), and Ukraine. By the 1880s, around 95 per cent of Russia's 5.3 million Jews lived in the Pale – the other 5 per cent lived outside it without legal residence permits – but even within this area, settlement was restricted. Jews were forbidden to reside in large cities, such as Kiev (now in Ukraine), and most of the countryside. This concentrated the Jewish population in just a few towns, which included Minsk (now in Belarus) and Warsaw (now in Poland).

With access to education restricted, and a ban on farming, Jews were limited to a few occupations, including commerce and crafts, such as tailoring. These meagre economic opportunities and a rapidly growing population pushed Russian Jews into extreme poverty. In the 1860s, Tsar Alexander II permitted some Jews to temporarily leave the Pale, namely merchants, academics, war veterans, and craftspeople.

Flight from the Pale

Conditions reached breaking point in the late 1880s, when a series of violent massacres (pogroms) took place. False rumours that the assassination of Alexander II in 1881 was a Jewish plot triggered a wave of attacks. Often with official encouragement, mobs raped and murdered Jews, and looted their property. Jews fled Russia in their thousands, often without passports or any possessions. Expulsions from Moscow and Kiev in 1890 and further pogroms only increased the tide. Between 1880 and 1914, over 2 million Russian Jews escaped from Europe by boat, heading to the US, Canada, Argentina, Australia, Egypt, and South Africa. Hundreds of thousands more fled to the UK and France. Those who stayed in the Russian Empire would later face religious restrictions under the Soviet Union and the Nazi occupation of Poland.

Men often went first to secure work and lodgings before sending for their wives and children. They typically headed for districts in big cities, such as London's East End and New York's Lower East Side, where there were already Jewish communities. For most of them, life was a struggle – they arrived with a limited set of skills and few spoke English, communicating instead in Yiddish. However, in time, the Russian Jewish communities and their culture came to thrive in their new homelands.

"Never in the history of Europe has a political cataclysm torn such huge numbers... from their mother country."

Ariadna Tyrkova-Williams, 1921

Jewish children gather on a narrow street in Warsaw in 1897, when the city was part of the Russian Empire.

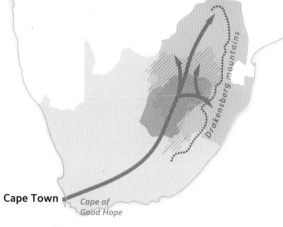

KEY
- → Route of Voortrekkers
- Cape Colony
- Orange Free State
- Natal
- Transvaal
- Highveld Plateau

Cape Town
Cape of Good Hope

Drakensberg mountains

Crossing the Highveld
THE VOORTREKKERS IN SOUTH AFRICA

▲**The Voortrekkers** travelled northeast from Cape Colony, then spread to the modern-day Free State and KwaZulu Natal provinces, and across the Highveld to the Transvaal.

◄ **Whole families fought** in clashes with the Indigenous African peoples, with men firing muskets and women and children loading. The guns gave the Boers a huge advantage over the Africans, who used spears and sticks.

▼ **The Xhosa people** were forced out of Cape Colony by European colonizers, and fought a series of wars over land from 1779 to 1879.

Between 1835 and 1845, around 15,000 Dutch-origin farmers, or "Boers" (the Dutch word for farmer), along with 10,000 enslaved Africans and large herds of cattle, left their homes in the British-controlled Cape Colony (in modern-day South Africa) and migrated northeast in search of new land. This mass migration became known as the Great Trek, and its participants as the *Voortrekkers* ("the first ones to trek"). A century later, its history was co-opted by Afrikaner nationalists, to support their imposition of Apartheid in South Africa.

From Dutch to British control
The Boers were descended from Dutch colonists, who had arrived in the Cape of Good Hope region in 1652. As their number grew, they moved inland and up the coast, in many cases driving Indigenous African peoples, such as the Xhosa, off their land.

In 1806, Britain took control of the area and began a brutal campaign to displace the Xhosa. The Xhosa retaliated, but by 1879 the British had annexed Xhosa territory. In order to boost the English-speaking population and establish further control, in 1820 the British government introduced a settlement scheme, to entice British people to settle in South Africa. The resulting influx caused resentment among Boer farmers, who disliked the Anglicization. Also, once the British abolished slavery in 1834, the Boers could no longer run their farms in the same way, as they relied on enslaved African labour. To retain their way of life, Boer farmers decided to move away in search of new land outside British control.

Disputed territory
The first procession of Voortrekkers set off to settle new lands in 1835, travelling mostly by horse and large ox-drawn wagons. It was a difficult journey into wild landscape. The farmers disagreed over where to settle, and the procession divided.

One group went to the north of the modern-day Free State province, where they clashed with the Ndebele people who were living there. In 1837, they drove the Ndebele north over the border of the modern-day South Africa.

Another group, led by former army commander Piet Retief, crossed the Drakensberg mountains into Natal in 1837. Since the eastern coastal area the Boers had set their sights on was just south of Zulu territory, Retief asked the Zulu king Dingane whether he would grant the Boers land. Dingane signed an agreement, but viewing the Vortrekkers as invaders who would challenge Zulu sovereignty, Dingane launched a surprise attack and massacred the group. In 1838, the Boers took revenge at the Battle of Blood River, killing over 3,000 Zulu.

After the Battle of Blood River, the Zulu king Mpande gave the Boers permission to settle in some areas in exchange for their help in ousting Dingane. They created three independent states: Natalia (Natal), annexed by Britain in 1843, the Orange Free State, and the South African Republic (Transvaal).

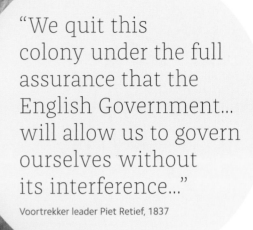

"We quit this colony under the full assurance that the English Government... will allow us to govern ourselves without its interference..."

Voortrekker leader Piet Retief, 1837

◄**The Voortrekkers' route** was often treacherous. Their wagons, called *kakeebeenwaen* ("jawbone wagons") had an ingenious design feature: the large rear wheels could be removed and heavy branches tied beneath to prevent the wagon hurtling down steep mountain slopes and ravines.

Traversing the
South China Sea

FROM CHINA TO SOUTHEAST ASIA

▲**The first Chinese migrants** to Southeast Asia came from southern China. Groups settled in Malaysia, Indonesia, and Singapore, and later in Thailand and Vietnam.

▼**Chinese New Year** is celebrated by the ethnic Chinese communities in Indonesia with traditional fireworks and performances.

▼**Chinese merchants** ran successful businesses in the 19th century in Southeast Asia, such as this general store in King's Bazaar, Mandalay, Burma (now Myanmar).

From at least the 15th century, Chinese merchants from the trading centres of Fujian and Guangdong, in southern China, travelled and settled in other countries in Southeast Asia. By the 17th century, Chinese settlers were well established in different forms across the region. Many were still traders; some in Java, Indonesia, had become successful farmers; a few held local administrative positions. The migrants were mostly men, and many married local women. Over centuries, their descendants formed ethnic groups such as the Peranakans (meaning "local born" in Malay and Indonesian), who live in Malaysia, Indonesia, and Singapore.

Upheaval associated with the fall of the Ming Dynasty, in the mid-17th century, resulted in a new exodus of Chinese refugees to Southeast Asia that lasted until the 18th century. Mostly uneducated farmers, many reached Vietnam and Cambodia, where they eventually earned a good living, particularly by working as rice farmers.

Chinese labour in European colonies

A period of mass migration to Southeast Asia took place in the 19th century, as the Qing government allowed traders to settle in Singapore and Malaya. Meanwhile, European powers established colonies in the region. The colonizers needed labour, while in China, economic depression caused by population growth and disruption to trade as a result of the Opium Wars (1839–60) was pushing people to seek work elsewhere. Defeat in the wars also forced China to open a number of its ports to foreign trade and residents. This facilitated emigration, allowing easier recruitment and transportation of Chinese labourers to Southeast Asian colonial destinations.

The British, in particular, favoured Chinese labourers, who they considered hardworking; and many Chinese migrants moved both voluntarily and involuntarily to British colonies as "coolies" (cheap, unskilled workers). By around 1850, Singapore had become a hub from which Chinese middlemen supplied Chinese labourers to mines and plantations in British Malaya (Malaysia) and the Dutch East Indies (Indonesia).

Typically, labourers were transported via two Chinese brokers, one on the Chinese side and the other in the European colony. The workers received little pay; the costs of transportation, food, and

accommodation were charged to them, plus added interest, and the debt was deducted from the salaries paid by their European employers. The work was hard and they were treated poorly.

Chinese communities and influence

While early Chinese settlers in Southeast Asia adapted to local traditions, the immigrants who arrived from the 19th century onwards maintained their own customs, building temples and schools which taught in Chinese languages. Hokkien,

spoken in Fujian province from where many immigrants originated, is still spoken in parts of Southeast Asia today.

Siam (Thailand) was never colonized, but also encouraged large numbers of Chinese migrants to work on its roads, railways, in mines, and on plantations. As the Chinese community grew, the government began to restrict their influence and encouraged assimilation. By the 20th century, however, some Chinese immigrants had established large businesses and dominated the Thai economy.

▲ **Chinese labourers** arriving in Singapore in the early 20th century by boat from Fujian province in China. These mostly poor men were put to work constructing roads, railways, and civic buildings. This photograph has been colourized.

The Trail of Tears

INDIGENOUS REMOVAL IN THE UNITED STATES

▲ **This map shows the lands** of the five nations before their removal, and the routes they took when they were removed to Indian Territory.

▼ **This quilt, by Chris Wolf Edmonds**, was inspired by the story of the Cherokee people. The phoenix symbolizes hope for the future, while the male figure represents the despair of the journey.

Aside from the sedentary Puebloan Nations in the southwest, most Indigenous nations in the US have experienced forced relocation. The migrations of the "Five Civilized Tribes" are some of the best known Indigenous migration stories. They involve the nations who had converted to Christianity and adopted many European ways: the Choctaw, Chickasaw, Cherokee, Seminole, and Muscogee (also called Creek). White Americans tried to justify Indigenous removal through Manifest Destiny (see pp.168–69). In 1830, the Indian Removal Act set in motion the US government's relocation of Indigenous people from the south-central US to a newly defined "Indian Territory" (now Oklahoma).

Walking west

The Choctaw was the first of the five tribes to be removed, forced out of Mississippi in 1831. A song about the removal, reported by Choctaw historian Muriel Wright, laments: "I saw a trail to the big river and then I cried". The Seminole removal from Florida began in 1832, but the nation fought back – helped by several hundred Black Americans, some of whom had escaped slavery in Florida – in what is called the Second Seminole War. Unlike other removals, the Seminole did not take one long walk west. Their removal took about 20 years, costing the US government thousands of dollars as troops were brought in to hunt the Seminole with hounds and force them onto ships on the Mississippi River. About 4,400 went to Indian Territory, but around 500 Seminole people remained in Florida.

The Muscogee Nation were forcibly moved to Oklahoma in 1834–35, although only 11,500 of the 15,000 who relocated survived the journey.

In 1837, the Chickasaw were removed, and around 16,000 Cherokee people were forced to move to the west of the Mississippi River from 1838–39.

The name "Trail of Tears" comes from Cherokee accounts of their removal to Indian Territory. The Cherokee people were forced into camps while soldiers looted their homes. Conditions in these camps were often fatally unsanitary. From there, the Cherokee were forced to travel, largely on foot and often without shoes, for 1,600 km (1,000 miles) westwards to Indian Territory. Many died on this three-month trek from disease, starvation, or exposure to the elements; others were killed by white people en route. Between 4,000–8,000 Cherokee did not survive the journey.

Life in "Indian Territory"

Once they had arrived in "Indian Territory", the Indigenous nations tried to make the best of their new beginnings. The Cherokee built a strong infrastructure and prospered during a period some called a "golden age" – but this prosperity came as a result of adaptation to white American ways, at the expense of Cherokee culture. The Five Civilized Tribes built new schools in Indian Territory, often in conjunction with Christian missions, where Indigenous children were taught to assimilate.

Today, Oklahoma is home to around 14 per cent of all Indigenous people in the US. Despite their history, the Cherokee are currently the largest nation in the country, with 141,000 Cherokee people still living within the boundaries of their Oklahoma reservation and another 149,000 residing outside it.

▲ **This panel of the Trail of Tears Mural** painted by Muscogee artist Johnnie Diacon for the Museum of Native American History, Arkansas, depicts the long walk of the Muscogee to Indian territory in harsh winter conditions.

◄ **The Armstrong Academy** in Chahte Tamaha was founded by the Choctaw Nation as a school for boys in 1845. The Choctaw placed a high priority on education and saw it as necessary in order to survive in the white world.

The quest for gold drew tens of thousands of immigrants to the "Wild West" in the 1840s. Most gold seekers were men, and life could be lonely and violent. Deadwood, a mining town in the Black Hills of South Dakota, was notorious for its lawlessness and corruption.

Wagons head West

THE AMERICAN FRONTIER

Throughout the 19th century, large numbers of European colonists packed their food and meagre belongings into wagons (or "prairie schooners" as they were known) and headed out West, across America to find new land to farm and open space in which to hunt. Mining also attracted new settlers to the West, and some migrants, such as the Mormons, moved to escape religious persecution in the Midwest. From 1843 to 1869, more than half a million settlers travelled along just three main trails – the Oregon Trail, the California Trail, and the Mormon Trail.

Expansion of territory

The settlers expanded westwards, disregarding the fact that the lands had been occupied for thousands of years by Indigenous peoples, who were now being evicted from their homes and corralled into ever-smaller areas by the military. Many believed in Manifest Destiny, the erroneous idea that it was God's will that the Europeans should colonize America, as they were racially and culturally superior and had a duty to "civilize" and convert the "heathen" native population to Christianity.

The most famous route west was the Oregon Trail, which started in Independence, Missouri, and ran 3,200 km (2,000 miles) across the plains and the Rocky Mountains to Oregon City in the northwest. Attracted by pamphlets telling of fertile land to be claimed, the first dozen or so wagons set out in 1841, along a trail blazed by fur traders. But within a few years, huge trains a hundred wagons strong were regularly heading off at the start of summer, hoping to cross the Rockies before winter set in. The journey took five months and was arduous, with the wagons pulled by oxen and families walking alongside. At the height of the movement, in the mid-1800s, tens of thousands of people died on the trails, mainly from disease, or in accidents in steep mountain passes. Then, in 1869, the Transcontinental Railroad was completed, making it possible to travel coast to coast in eight to 10 days.

Homesteads and cattle towns

For many farming families, their first home out West was a shelter dug into a hillside. On the plains, where there were few trees, early houses were made from sod squares cut from the soil (such houses were known as "soddies"). The first settlers had to be self-sufficient, but as more people arrived, small towns developed: retail businesses and banks emerged to serve the growing population, as did schools, churches, and saloons. Small frontier settlements, known as cattle towns, also sprang up. Catering to the cattle industry, and often located at railway junctions, these were where the cowboys, who drove up their herds from Texas on a seasonal basis, would sell their cattle to ranchers (who lived on the plains and raised livestock for meat) or to meatpackers, who would then transport them by train to the cities.

▲**The most popular trails** set off from Nauvoo (Illinois) or Independence (Missouri) heading northwest to Portland, west to San Francisco, or southwest to Los Angeles, avoiding Texas.

▼**Wagon trains** were formed by hundreds of settlers who banded together for protection and support.

◄**The discovery of gold** drew many adventurers to California to seek their fortune.

The Donner Party

In 1846, 87 settlers, led by George Donner, set out from Missouri. They left late in the season and took a "short cut", which in fact took two weeks longer. En route they lost their cattle, were attacked, and got trapped in snow; some resorted to cannibalism. Only 47 survived.

"I could watch our house go up, our sod house. What a thrill on the occasions when we all rode the lumber wagon across to take a look up close... We felt we had a whole new house again... it was heaven, and we enjoyed it.

We had two big problems, the dirt and the flies. Summertimes we twisted newspapers and lit the tip... Grandpa Meehan added a crowning touch to his soddy, he plastered the entire inside, no one had a home as easy to keep clean as my grandma...

The negro pioneers worked hard, besides raising plenty of corn, beans and what vegetables they had, everyone raised cattle. It was too sandy for grain so the answer was cattle."

Ava Speese Day, an African American homesteader whose family settled in the Sand Hills region of Nebraska in 1907. She was a descendant of Moses Speese, a formerly enslaved man who settled in Custer County, Nebraska, in the 1880s.

The Shores family sit outside their sod house in Custer County, Nebraska, in 1887. Jeremiah Shores (second on the right) was a brother of Moses Speese (see above), and was also formerly enslaved. Shores and Speese were part of a group of Black migrants known as "Exodusters", who started new lives in Nebraska – a safe haven for Black settlers.

The Underground Railroad
BLACK AMERICANS ESCAPE SLAVERY

In 1860, there were nearly 4 million people living in slavery in the American South. Forced to labour mainly on cotton and sugar plantations, they were trapped by a system that took away their human rights and treated them as chattels of their enslavers.

The South was hostile territory for enslaved people – under the Fugitive Slave Act of 1793, local authorities could pick up those seeking freedom and send them back to their enslavers, even if they were found in so-called free states. Authorities gave harsh punishments to any freedom seekers they caught, and there was no way for those escaping slavery to earn a legitimate living. Enslavers also placed bounties on freedom seekers, making hunting them a lucrative business.

Between 1750 and the start of the American Civil War in 1860, between 40,000 and 100,000 enslaved people made it to the North (where slavery was outlawed, though Black Americans did not have the same rights as white people) and Canada (where slavery was abolished), aided by an operation called the Underground Railroad. This was a secret network of routes and safe houses run by formerly enslaved people and abolitionists.

Routes to freedom

The operators of the Underground Railroad used railroad terminology to hide their true purpose. Freedom seekers had to make it to the border states between the North and South alone, but once there they could make contact with a "conductor" who would guide them to hiding places known as "stations" in private homes, churches, or schools, which were run by a "station master". Operators established routes in the west up through Ohio to

Indiana and Iowa and in the east via Pennsylvania. However, the routes were dangerous for freedom seekers and those helping them. Those fleeing carried little with them and faced hunger, cold, and treacherous river crossings on their journey northwards, which could take weeks to complete. Travelling at night in small groups, freedom seekers were not safe en route or even once they reached the North. Bounty hunters tracked them down and had their own routes via which they smuggled kidnapped freedom seekers back to the South.

For many, the destination was Canada, where bounty hunters were banned and communities of former enslaved people established their own farms and churches. Here, those escaping slavery had a lot more freedom than in the North of the US; they could even seek public office and sit on juries. Many worked to help others find freedom or taught new arrivals the skills they could use to find a job.

Helping others escape

Those who helped freedom seekers risked fines, imprisonment, or even being lynched by an angry mob. A few white Quakers played a key role in the Railroad, but most conductors were Black Americans, including former freedom seekers. The most famous was Harriet Tubman (see box, right), who ventured back to the South many times.

Political pressure to abolish slavery grew until, on 1 January 1863, President Abraham Lincoln issued the Emancipation Proclamation, to begin, at last, the process of freeing millions of enslaved people. Slavery was finally legally abolished on 18 December 1865, when the 13th Amendment to the US Constitution was ratified by Congress.

▲ **Routes for freedom seekers** from the Southern slave states led to the free states of the North and on to Canada, where slavery had been abolished.

▼ **Levi Coffin**, Quaker and abolitionist, (centre with hat), and his friend Jonathan Rummel (far right) are surrounded by a group of formerly enslaved people they have rescued.

Harriet Tubman

Born into slavery in Maryland, Harriet (1822–1913) fled to Philadelphia in 1849. She returned to Maryland to help others escape, making 13 journeys in all and assisting 70 people on the Underground Railroad to Canada.

▲ **An Underground Railroad mural** in Dolgeville, New York State, depicts a group of freedom seekers being guided by a "conductor" at night.

◄ **Levi Coffin's home** in Cincinnati, Ohio was a "station" along the Underground Railroad where freedom seekers could rest on their journey north.

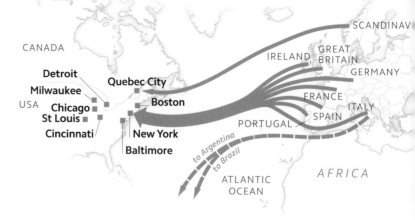

To the land of the free

THE GREAT ATLANTIC MIGRATION

One of the largest movements of people in history took place between 1846 and 1940 when 55 million Europeans crossed the Atlantic, most settling in the US, some heading to Canada and South America. The reasons for this mass migration were complex, but included poverty, hardship, and political and religious oppression in European countries, and the lure of better pay, farmland, more opportunities, and freedom in the US.

The first wave

The majority of North American arrivals during the early 19th century came from Ireland. Life held few prospects for young Irishmen, especially younger sons who could not inherit land, and nearly one million boarded ships for the US and Canada in the 1820s and 30s. Lured by the prospect of work on the Erie Canal, and new roads and railroads, most settled in east coast cities.

The Great Famine that devastated Ireland in the 1840s swelled Irish emigration. A potato blight and the cruel response by landlords and the British government, since referred to as a genocide, left hundreds of thousands destitute and starving, driven from their cottages with no source of income. In desperation, whole families set sail for the US.

By 1847, hundreds of "Coffin Ships" were leaving Liverpool for North America, packed with Irish migrants. Shipowners took advantage of their plight, using vessels of all kinds, whether suitable or not. Conditions on board were dire. Passengers spent most of their two-month journey crammed below deck in the dark, with little access to food or water. Disease on board was rife. A contemporary account describes "the foulness of the air breathed and

rebreathed by the gasping sufferers." On arrival, many migrants were held at quarantine stations, such as Grosse Île in Quebec, in an attempt to halt the spread of infectious diseases. In one notorious incident in the summer of 1847, a typhus epidemic at this station caused the death of over 5,000 Irish immigrants before spreading to Quebec City.

Searching for hope

Mostly unskilled, with no money, few clothes, and little hope, the Irish immigrants of the 1840s and 50s were among the poorest people in Europe even before the Famine, and on arrival in North America they found conditions little better. Often crammed into rundown tenements, they faced hostility from prospective employers, and religious discrimination for their Catholic faith, especially in the US.

But the US and Canada still offered more opportunities than Ireland, and many migrants built lives for themselves working in construction, mining, the army, police force, or as domestic servants. Irish migration continued long after the Famine, and Ireland lost more than two-thirds of its population to North America in the 1800s.

The development of steamships in the 1860s made the transatlantic crossing much quicker, taking less than 10 days, but conditions on board were little improved.

▲**Transatlantic migration** from the 1820s onwards offered destitute Europeans the chance of land and jobs in North and South America.

▼**Inspection cards** issued by shipping companies proved immigrants had undergone a health check on departure, but many fell sick en route.

▼**In the 1880s, Land Wars** between landowners and Irish tenant farmers struggling to pay rent led to evictions. Left with nothing, families followed earlier Irish migrants to the US.

Immigrants entering the US through New York from 1886 were greeted by the sight of the Statue of Liberty, which came to symbolize their hopes for refuge and new opportunities.

Other groups crossing the Atlantic at this time were German, Norwegian, Swedish, and Dutch migrants driven by economic hardship, political upheaval, and a desire for greater religious freedom.

Before 1840, most of these northern European arrivals were experienced farmers who chose to settle in the American Midwest and created some of the country's most productive farms. After 1848, political unrest and unemployment in Germany encouraged urban immigration to cities such as Chicago, Milwaukee, Cincinatti, and St Louis.

A second wave

By the 1890s, migration from Northern and Western Europe was slowing, but even larger numbers were coming from Southern and Eastern Europe. These regions were slow to industrialize and the lure of a better future across the Atlantic was too tempting to ignore. Many Jews from Russia and Eastern Europe were fleeing persecution; Hungarians, Poles, Czechs, Serbs, Slovaks, and Greeks, along with non-Europeans from Syria, Turkey, and Armenia left to escape agricultural crises, political repression, and the effects of overpopulation. Most settled in cities such as New York, Boston, and Detroit, finding jobs in the rapidly growing industrial sector.

The most numerous arrivals during this period were Italians, with around 7 million crossing to the Americas. Migrants from southern Italy and Sicily were mostly farmers, and many made their way to

Fit for entry

Immigration stations were set up at ports of entry such as Ellis Island in the Hudson River in the US, and Grosse Île in the Gulf of St Lawrence in Canada (below), to process new arrivals. Thousands passed through each day waiting in long queues for medical and legal inspections. For most, the ordeal lasted just a few hours, though some were detained for weeks, especially if suspected of illness. Lone women and girls could not leave without a male chaperone.

"An enterprising man, desirous of advancing himself will despise everything for coming to this free country, where a man is allowed to thrive and flourish..."

John Doyle, letter to Ireland, 1818

◄ **Cramped tenement rooms** provided both housing and a place of work, with many immigrant families supporting themselves with piecework, such as stitching garments or crafting small items.

South America, especially Argentina, where they still hoped to find land after immigrants to the US had "filled" land across the country to the Pacific coast. Italians from the more urbanized north were attracted to northeastern US cities, such as New York, Baltimore, Boston, and Philadelphia.

Many Italians were young men not planning to stay abroad, but looking to build up savings until they could return home and work on or inherit the family farm. More than half ended up staying in North America, preferring to support family in Italy by sending back money. Italian immigrants found themselves facing the same prejudices as the Irish a generation earlier; and found employment in manual jobs and public works. "Little Italys" grew up in many cities – close-knit communities often housed in cramped tenements, and with families from one village or region in Italy sometimes clustered around a few streets.

A transatlantic legacy

By 1900, entry to the US and Canada was becoming more difficult, as governments responded to growing anti-immigrant sentiment, even from former immigrants themselves. At first Asian immigrants were targeted, with legislation that allowed entry but denied citizenship in the US, and levied taxes on entry in Canada. After World War I (1914–18), restrictions tightened further, limiting transatlantic arrivals from European nations too.

Immigration slowed to a trickle, but by then the fabric of society on the American continent had changed. A century of migration had transformed cities and rural landscapes, driven industrialization, and created a multiethnic melting pot that formed the basis of a new American culture.

◄ **Mulberry Street, Manhattan**, was by 1900 one of the largest Italian enclaves in the US, with immigrant street vendors, shop owners, and residents creating a "Little Italy". This photograph has been colourised.

Steelworkers pose atop a beam during the construction of New York's RCA building in 1932. Many of those who built the city's iconic skyline were immigrants or from immigrant families. Research into the iconic "Men at Lunch" (colourized here) suggests that two of these men might be Irish immigrants Matty O'Shaughnessy (far left) and Sonny Glynn (far right).

CULTURAL INFLUENCES

Dutch colonizers

In 1626, Dutch colonizers founded the town of New Amsterdam on Manhattan island. They built a Dutch-style city hall and a port, where beaver pelts were loaded onto ships that sailed to Europe and returned with European goods to trade in North America.

Italian enclave

There were several waves of Italian immigration to the US, starting in the 1820s. In the late 19th and early 20th centuries, about one-third of Italian migrants who arrived in the US settled in New York. At first they settled in East Harlem and Lower Manhattan, where the neighbourhood around Mulberry Street (pictured, colourized) became known as "Little Italy".

Jewish businesses

Although there were some Jewish settlers in New Amsterdam, many more arrived from Europe from the 1880s. By 1920, the Jewish population of New York was around 1.5 million, with most living in the Lower East Side, where they established kosher shops and eateries. Today, more Jewish people live in New York than in any other city in the world.

New York City

THE BIG APPLE

▲▲ **New York's skyline** is depicted in this 1943 painting by Black artist William H. Johnson, who moved to the city from Florence, South Carolina, aged 17.

▲ **In 2018, the Lenape peoples** held their first powwow in Manhattan since being forced out of the area by Dutch colonists in the 17th century.

◀ **Street musicians play jazz** in New York's Central Park. Although jazz originated in the Black communities of New Orleans, it became synonymous with New York in the early 20th century, thanks to famous musicians and popular venues, such as Harlem's Cotton Club.

The area that is now New York City was occupied by Indigenous Lenape communities long before the arrival of European colonists in the early 17th century. The first colonizers were the Dutch, who in 1626 made a deal with the local peoples for Manhattan. They founded a fur-trading settlement on the island, which they named New Amsterdam. They steadily pushed out the Indigenous inhabitants, and used enslaved Africans as forced labour – first to build the colony's infrastructure and protect the Dutch from retaliation by Indigenous peoples, then to work on the docks and as domestic servants.

In 1664, English forces seized the settlement, renamed it New York, and encouraged migration from Britain. Slavery remained central to the colony – in 1703, 42 per cent of households in the city contained enslaved Africans. New York continued to expand after the US won its independence; by 1790, it was the biggest city in North America.

Mass migration and growth

During the 19th and early 20th centuries, there was mass immigration from Europe, including Irish immigrants leaving behind the Great Famine (see pp.174–77), and Jews escaping pogroms in Russia (pp.160–61). Between 1910 and 1970, many Black Americans arrived from the southern states (see pp.202–03). New York rapidly expanded. In 1898, its five boroughs – Manhattan, Queens, Brooklyn, the Bronx, and Staten Island – were merged to create a single city. By 1920, New York's population surpassed 5.6 million.

From the 1950s, large numbers of Puerto Ricans settled in the city, while in the late 1960s there was immigration from China and Southeast Asia. Recent decades have brought migrants from Latin America, Asia, Africa, and Europe. Today, more than 800 languages are spoken in this city of 8.8 million.

> "The city seen from the Queensboro Bridge is always the city seen for the first time, in its first wild promise of all the mystery and beauty in the world."
>
> F. Scott Fitzgerald, *The Great Gatsby*, 1925

Harlem's Black culture

In the early 20th century, the Great Migration of Black Americans from southern to northern states, and the arrival of Caribbean migrants, transformed the area of Harlem. During the 1910s, 20s, and 30s, it was the site of the Harlem Renaissance – a flourishing of Black music, literature, theatre, and political activism.

Chinese celebrations

Many Chinese migrants drawn to the US by the California Gold Rush or jobs on the railroads settled in New York in the 19th century. The US government limited Chinese migration from the 1880s to late 1960s, but it has since grown. Today, New York has the largest Chinese population of any city outside Asia, and has multiple Chinese New Year parades.

Puerto Rican heritage

The island of Puerto Rico became a US territory in 1898. Puerto Ricans gained limited US citizenship 19 years later and many settled in New York. More arrived in the 1950s. Around 9 per cent of New Yorkers now have Puerto Rican heritage, which they celebrate at the annual National Puerto Rican Day Parade.

Colonial exploitation

INDENTURED LABOUR IN THE CARIBBEAN

By 1830, the Industrial Revolution was ruining the economy in India. Imports of cheap manufactured goods from Britain were destroying Indian handicraft industries, while the growth of commercial agriculture to supply Britain with raw materials – such as cotton, tea, and indigo – was diverting land from food production and displacing farmers. The result was widespread unemployment and food shortages, escalating to famine during the late 1830s and 1860–70s, when droughts occurred.

For British plantation owners in the Caribbean, high unemployment in India appeared to present a solution to the labour shortages they faced following the abolition of the slave trade. Under a system of indenture, they offered to pay for the transport of Indian labourers, who would be bound to work for them for a minimum of five years. For Indians facing poverty and starvation this promised much-needed economic stability, and more than 400,000 travelled to the Caribbean between 1838 and 1917.

Misled and mistreated

Indian labourers were promised a set wage, decent standards of living, healthcare, and repatriation at the end of service. In reality, most were severely mistreated. Around 17 per cent of migrants died of disease due to poor conditions on the 17,700-km (11,000-mile) voyage to the Caribbean, which took 10–20 weeks by ship. On arrival, they endured long working days, heavy labour, and poor, overcrowded living conditions. Employers frequently withheld wages and food, inflicted harsh punishments, and

▶ **Migration of Indian workers** to the Caribbean and Mauritius was followed in the 1860s by flows of labour to Fiji, Malaya, and East and South Africa.

KEY
Colony

▬▶ British

▬▶ French

▬▶ Dutch

▼ **A ticket of registration**, issued on arrival, certified that migrants had been brought by a licensed carrier and inspected by an immigration agent.

▼ **Migrants harvest bananas** in Jamaica in 1910. Labourers previously indentured on sugar plantations also took up this kind of work.

▼ **Hindu temples in Trinidad** began to be constructed by migrants in the 1890s, as they finished their indenture, moved off estates, and settled freely.

reneged on repatriating migrants at the end of their contract period. With no means of returning to India, some labourers were forced to renew their indenture agreements and remained trapped on plantations in a vicious cycle of servitude.

Pressure for change

Towards the end of the 19th century, many Indian labourers began protesting against the unjust system and their poor treatment. Under pressure from the nationalist movement in India and a series of official enquiries, the British government abolished indentured labour migration in 1917.

Most workers who had completed their contracts elected to stay in the Caribbean running small independent farms, and their continued presence created a lasting legacy. Large Indian communities developed in countries such as Guyana and Trinidad and Tobago, and a new Indo-Caribbean culture emerged that meshed Indian food, music, customs, festivals, and celebrations with Afro-Caribbean and European traditions.

"With a pillow on my shoulder, I began my perilous journey. Sailing a boat... across the seas, leaving behind wife and sisters in search of money..."

Cantonese folk song on the American experience, 19th century

Chinese migrant labour made up the majority of the workforce at the eastern end of the Transcontinental Railroad. As many as 15,000 Chinese men worked in harsh conditions from 1863 until the railway was completed in 1869.

KOREA

CHINA

Omaha

Sacramento

Los Angeles

KEY
---- US Transcontinental Railroad

East to West

ASIAN MIGRATION TO THE US

The first large emigration from Asia to the US occurred in the 1850s, when, lured by the Gold Rush in California, around 25,000 people from China arrived on the West Coast. Mostly young men, the migrants soon discovered that California was not the land of dreams they had hoped for. Gold was hard to find, work was scarce, and they were not welcomed by American gold prospectors. Having left their families in China, and now too poor to return, the men found work as labourers on the Transcontinental Railroad. Between 1863 and 1869, around 15,000 Chinese labourers toiled to build this line. While their American co-workers slept in train cars and earned double their wages, Chinese workers lived a nomadic life in tents. Hundreds were injured or died as a result of working long hours in dangerous conditions.

Hostility and exclusion

Some US citizens resented the presence of the new Chinese settlers, and attacked and even lynched them, especially when an economic depression hit the US in the 1870s. The 1882 Chinese Exclusion Act banned further Chinese immigrants to the US, though a loophole – allowing entry to students and permitting Chinese business owners in the US to bring over employees – led to around 200,000 men and women arriving from China during the ban.

While exclusion from society brought hardship, it also encouraged Chinese immigrants to build their own strong communities, leading to the growth of Chinatowns in urban areas. In the 20th century, as these Chinese populations grew and their children were granted US citizenship, their status and sense of belonging increased. Japan's invasion of China

in World War II (1939–45) prompted many Chinese Americans to join the United States Army. This helped to dispel anti-Chinese sentiment in the US, leading to the repeal of the Exclusion Act in 1943.

Korean War

After World War II, the division of Korea between US-supported South Korea and communist North Korea initiated a flow of immigrants to the US. The outbreak of war in the region led to more arrivals. Korean wives of US troops ("war brides") moved to the US, as did thousands of displaced Korean people and war orphans, including those fathered by US soldiers. Between 1955 and 1977, around 13,000 such orphans were adopted by US families.

In 1965, the new Immigration and Naturalization Act allowed more immigrants from non-European countries, which led to an influx of skilled workers and scholars from China and Korea. Many of these Korean arrivals were high-school educated yet spoke little English, so they set up small but successful businesses such as dry cleaners and convenience stores. Korean communities grew in Los Angeles and New York throughout the 1980s.

While the number of Korean migrants moving to the US fell after 1990, as the South Korean economy stabilized, numbers from China continued to rise, reaching 2.1 million in 2016. Today, the US is home to 5.2 million Chinese Americans and 1.9 million Korean Americans.

▲ **Emigrants from Asia**, especially from China and Korea, have travelled east to the US in search of a new life since the 19th century.

▼ **Korean Americans celebrate** their heritage at the annual Korean Day parade and festival on 6th Avenue in New York City.

▼ **"War bride" Yoong Soon** and her husband, who was stationed in Korea during the Korean War (1950–53), present their first child – the first to be born to a Korean bride and GI father in the US.

After the abolition

MIGRATION TO BRAZIL

The coup d'état that established the First Brazilian Republic in 1889, initiated a new era of economic and social change. The transformation included the arrival of around 4 million immigrants from 1889 to 1930. This migrant population provided labour for Brazilian plantations and for newly industrializing cities, and also changed the ethnic make-up of Brazil and helped create a modern multicultural nation.

European arrivals

A pressing concern for the new republic was filling the labour shortage created by the abolition of slavery in 1888. Demand for Brazilian coffee was increasing and, desperate for cheap labour to grow the economy, the government looked abroad for a new workforce. Embracing the racist ideology that "whitening" Brazil's population was a noble ideal, the regime decided to recruit Europeans.

The Brazilian government began investing money in European immigration projects, even subsidizing steamboat passages across the Atlantic. With much of Europe in economic or political crisis, labourers from Portugal, Spain, Germany, and especially Italy (Italians accounted for nearly 70 per cent of arrivals), were eager to take advantage of the opportunities available.

Most Italians made the journey in family groups. Some took up offers of land in the south of Brazil, where they established Italian communities based on self-sufficient smallholdings. The majority settled in the São Paulo region, where they played a key role in expanding coffee production. For these families, conditions were often poor, and after scathing consular reports described treatment akin to slavery,

the Italian government passed the Prinetti Decree in 1902, which forbade subsidized emigration to Brazil. This temporarily slowed arrivals, but by the 1920s, restrictions on entry to other countries, such as the US, and fresh agreements between the Italian and Brazilian governments, boosted immigrant numbers once more.

Diversifying society

At the same time, a new wave of immigrants was arriving from Lebanon and Syria, driven from the Levant by the collapse of the Ottoman Empire's economy, violence against the Christian community, and the threat of conscription. These immigrants were mostly Christian and, resembling Brazilians, quickly assimilated into society. Attracted to fast-expanding cities rather than the countryside, most Arabs worked as peddlers, or in the textile industry, eventually setting up their own businesses.

With European immigration slowing at the start of the 20th century, Brazil faced another labour shortage. This time the government looked to Japan for labourers. By 1933, almost 150,000 Japanese had arrived, mainly to work on coffee plantations. On completing their contracts, most became small independent farmers, with families banding together to buy and work plots of land. Invested in developing their local communities, and driving the economic growth of the country, these Japanese migrants carried Brazil forward into the 20th century, contributing to a new sense of Brazilian identity based on diversity.

▶**The majority of migrants** to Brazil in the early 1900s came from Portugal and Italy, although significant numbers came from Germany, Spain, the Lebanon, and Japan.

▶**A pamphlet** advertising assisted migration, published in 1908 by the state of São Paulo, which hoped to encourage settlers from Europe.

"We left the masters in Italy and we own our own lives. We have as much as we want to eat and drink as well as fresh air, and this means a lot..."

Paolo Rossato, Italian immigrant, 27 July 1884

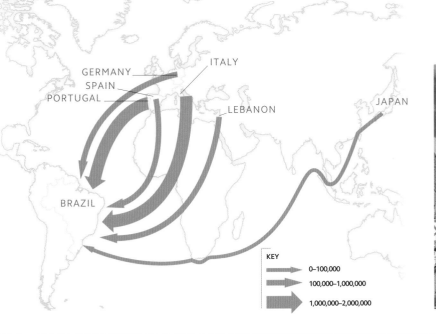

▲ **Culture, food, festivals, and architecture** imported from Europe characterized German towns in southern Brazil, such as Blumenau, which attracted successive waves of settlers.

◀ **Japanese migrants** boosted the economy of the São Paulo region by labouring on coffee plantations and by developing new land for market gardens as smallholders.

Exporting a workforce
JAPANESE LABOUR MIGRATION

Japan saw its first significant wave of emigration in 1868, the year of the Meiji Restoration, which began a process of modernization in the country after over 200 years of seclusion. The previous policy of isolation had meant little migration in or out of Japan, but in 1868, Japan sent 147 men and 6 women to the Hawaiian Kingdom to work on the sugar plantations there. Agricultural workers in Japan were suffering extreme hardship, and Hawai'i had lost many of its labourers to disease, so the two governments agreed that Japanese workers would go to Hawai'i on three-year work contracts.

Despite poor treatment on the plantations, poverty in Japan prompted a further 27,000 people to move to the Hawaiian Kingdom before its demise in 1894. Many did not plan on staying – some moved between Hawai'i and Japan, or returned home after their work was complete – but others stayed in Hawai'i, becoming involved in its growing coffee industry.

To the Americas
Japanese workers next began to move to the US mainland, where they found work on farms, in canneries, on railroads, and in the sawmills of California. As their community grew, many Japanese immigrants started their own farms and other businesses. However, growing anti-Japanese sentiment among Americans who felt threatened by their economic successes put a halt to further immigrants under the Gentlemen's Agreement in 1907 – an informal agreement between the US and Japan. As family members of immigrants were still allowed to join them, Japanese men in the US

began to seek out women in Japan to bring over as their wives, having only seen their pictures. By 1920, more than 10,000 "picture brides" had arrived.

As restrictions and social conflicts increased in the US, the Japanese government began to organize immigration to Latin America instead, starting with Mexico in 1897; Peru and Bolivia in 1899; and Brazil in 1908. Working on plantations, immigrants faced diseases, discrimination, and poor wages. But their numbers continued to grow in the 1920s, and many gradually transitioned to independent farming.

Colonial expansion
In the early 19th century, Japan expanded its empire in Southeast Asia, and the government promoted emigration to its territories as another solution to what it saw as its surplus of farmers. Korea became a protectorate of Japan and foreign ownership of Korean land was legalized in 1906. This prompted Japanese migrants to acquire large plots of arable land. By 1910, when Japan formally annexed Korea, there were 170,000 Japanese people living there. In just over a decade, this increased to 400,000.

Between 1932 and 1945, 270,000 Japanese settlers also moved to Japanese-occupied Manchuria in northeastern China. Many were poor farmers seeking a better life. By 1945, however, this flow of colonizing migrants had ended. War with China and World War II had caused thousands of Japanese deaths across the empire, and many surviving immigrants made the choice to return to Japan.

▶ **A propaganda poster** from 1927 promotes Japanese emigration to Manchuria by advertising the rich harvests available ahead of Japan's invasion of the region in 1931.

▶ **Hundreds of thousands of people** migrated from Japan to parts of Asia, North America, and South America in the late 19th and early 20th centuries.

▲ **Agricultural workers** harvest pineapples on a plantation in Hawai'i in 1920. Farm labour was a common choice for Japanese immigrants, and many launched successful agricultural businesses.

◄ **Japanese immigrants**, in 1920, arriving in San Francisco, California by boat. From the 1880s, labour shortages drew increasing numbers of migrants to California and Hawai'i.

439. - À la Frontière

Le Père et ses Fils, dont l'un sert au 2e Etranger,
l'autre dans l'Afrique Occidentale Allemande

DEUTSCHES·REICH

▲ **Colonial soldiers** from the French army and the German army meet at the German East Africa border. The European colonial powers shared out land between them. This image has been colourized.

◀ **The Herero people** resisted colonial rule in German Southwest Africa (now Namibia). As a result, from 1904–07, German colonists murdered around 75 per cent of the Herero population and sent survivors of this genocide to concentration camps.

The Scramble for Africa

EUROPEANS COLONIZE A CONTINENT

Since the 15th century, Africans had endured European encroachment on their land, first through trading posts established by the British, Dutch, and Portuguese, then by missionaries and by explorers seeking their fortunes. Then in the 19th century, rivalries between the Europeans for ownership of Africa's rich resources led to the Berlin Conference, convened in 1884, without African representation, to resolve claims. It fuelled a scramble for land and influence. In a bid to formalize claims, the major European powers rushed to conquer and colonize.

In French-occupied North Africa, where proximity and cultivable land encouraged agricultural settlers, as well as in South Africa, where rich mineral resources lured the British, the arrival of hundreds of thousands of European migrants radically altered the population balance. In areas with fewer settlers, it was the balance of power that changed, with civil and military officials enforcing European control. Colonial rule displaced African people and, in areas such as Southwest Africa, resulted in their genocide.

Loss of land and liberty

Government-approved companies and government authorities seized land for private settlement and funded European migration. Commercial interests also snatched prime sites for large-scale plantations and mining operations. In many regions, Africans were forced to live on "reserves" – land, often of low agricultural value, allocated by the colonizers.

Small-scale farming became untenable, so Africans migrated to ports or mining towns to find work. This further impoverished rural districts, leading to famine and the decline of traditional villages, as few were left to help with local food production.

Europeans conscripted Africans to work on plantations, in mines, or building roads and railways for little pay and in poor conditions. Their workforce also included labourers brought from other colonies in South Asia, who established significant minorities in many African countries.

Administrative oppression

More Europeans came to work as colonial administrators and European influence grew as a result of new laws benefitting the colonizers and disenfranchising Africans. Missionaries reinforced this balance of power, promoting the myth of European superiority, and preaching submission in the face of European exploitation.

The enforcement of national boundaries based on European spheres of influence rather than ethnic composition created instability that lasted beyond the colonial period. Artificial borders brought together different ethnic groups, such as the Tutsi and the Hutu in Rwanda, to form countries with no sense of national unity while arbitrarily splitting others. The resulting inter-ethnic conflict decimated communities already weakened by colonial invasion.

By the end of 1914, 90 per cent of Africa was under European control. The restructuring of society and destruction of local communities continued to affect Africa long after decolonization (see pp.264–65).

△ **The colonization of Africa** by Europeans left only Liberia and Ethiopia as independent states by 1914.

▼ **Colonial texts** reinforced the ideological myth that Europeans were bringing enlightenment to "the dark continent" of Africa.

"The world had, perhaps, never witnessed a robbery on so large a scale. Africa is helpless to prevent it."

The *Lagos Observer*, 19 February 1885

6

Decolonization and Diasporas

1900 onwards

Decolonization and Diasporas

1900 onwards

Migrants in the 20th and 21st centuries moved for many of the same reasons humans always have, but the pace of technological change, the financial challenges, and scale of natural disasters and warfare meant that these movements were both larger and more rapid than ever before. Two world wars had created millions of migrants and refugees. Some, such as the Jewish people who moved to Israel, went to find a safe haven. Others, such as the Italians who moved to North America and Australia, did so to escape the economic ruin of their home countries.

Yet many left because border changes left them stranded under a government they found hostile – such as the Polish people who migrated west from the USSR, or the Germans who moved out of what became Polish territory in 1945.

The process of decolonization created problems, as new tensions erupted, such as those resulting from the Partition of India in 1947 – which led to 10 million refugees fleeing their homes and over a million deaths. Civil wars also plagued many newly independent countries, leading to huge displacements of people and resulting refugee crises.

The city of Smyrna burns as Greeks try to flee Turkey in 1922 (see pp.210–11)

Japanese refugees come out of hiding at the end of World War II (see pp.214–15)

"I marvel at the despair it would take me to put the people
I cherish most on a rickety boat to cross a vast sea..."

Khaled Hosseini, Afghan-American author, 2018

Economic motives have continued to drive migration – the farmers who fled the prairie states of the US when drought turned their fields to dustbowls in the 1930s; the Caribbean migrants who answered Britain's call for workers from the late 1940s; and the South and Central American migrants moving to the US all sought employment opportunities.

Technology has made movement across the globe easier than ever, making journeys that were once impossible or a matter of months achievable within a day, while contact with loved ones far away can be maintained cheaply by phone – and over the internet. Although opportunities for those that move are often greater than ever, far too many are still forced to move against their will, by war, famine, economic circumstances, or by people trafficking. There are now international conventions that protect migrants, refugees, and asylum seekers, but their implementation is uneven, and many experience resistance and prejudice in their new homes as immigration debates become increasingly bitter. For migrants, the move from home often still remains the greatest challenge of their lives.

A family awaits food and supplies during civil warfare in Peru (see pp. 250–51)

Afghan and Syrian refugees arrive at the island of Lesbos in 2015 (see pp. 270–73)

A world in motion

TRAVEL AT THE TURN OF THE 20TH CENTURY

▲ **The opening of new railways**, shipping lines, and canals made the world a more connected place.

▼ **Shipping lines** transported thousands of emigrants from Europe to the US. Railroad and shipping companies used new advertisements to attract passengers.

▶ **The 1900 Paris Exposition** brought together many different cultures at an event that showcased innovations and new technologies from countries around the world.

> "Sailing from Liverpool and New York every Wednesday, calling at Queenstown... second cabin and steerage passage at low rates."
>
> White Star Line advertisement, 1876

Global migration in the late 19th and early 20th centuries was greatly facilitated by advances in transport. Steam ships were large, fast, and comfortable, and shipping giants such as Cunard and the Hamburg-America Line expanded their routes and reduced fares as competition increased. In 1895, the price for a transatlantic crossing went as low as $10 (around £220 today), and tickets were often prepaid by family members already in the US. Migrants could also make use of new "boat trains"

that ran directly to harbours. The Suez Canal (opened in 1869) dramatically shortened the route between Europe and Asia, and reduced the journey to Australia to 35–40 days. Meanwhile, the Panama Canal (opened in 1914 and built with migrant labour) linked the Atlantic and Pacific Oceans, reducing journey times between the two.

Connecting the world

New railway networks expanded across Africa, Asia, and the Americas. They stimulated the growth of new industrial centres, and linked ports to inland regions, encouraging both permanent and seasonal migration. Completed in 1916, the Trans-Siberian Railway – the world's longest rail line, at more than 9,200 km (5,700 miles) – opened up vast regions of Russia to new settlement and industrialization.

The development of global telegraph networks in the late 19th century also had a profound impact on the movement of people and ideas. New submarine cable networks laid to India by 1870 and to Australia by 1872 allowed communication between continents, and by 1907, a transatlantic radio-telegraph service had been established. This aided communication in shipping and railways.

The spirit of this age of scientific breakthroughs, technological development, and burgeoning globalization was captured by events such as the 1900 Paris Exposition. Drawing 50 million visitors, this world fair showcased elaborate national pavilions from 40 countries and cutting-edge inventions, such as the diesel engine.

Migration booms

These significant technological and scientific developments triggered vast population shifts. Global migration exploded in the mid-1890s and almost doubled to over 3 million per year around 1910. Numbers peaked just before World War I (1914–18), with transatlantic migration reaching 2.1 million, and migration to Southeast and North Asia nearly 1.1 million in 1913.

Individual countries underwent seismic changes. For example, between 1880 and 1915, Italy experienced one of the largest voluntary emigrations in history, with around 13 million people leaving to escape poverty and seek new opportunities. Some 4 million Italians travelled to the US, and about 2 million to Argentina. Yet much of the global migration during this period was linked to restrictive, exploitative, and sometimes forced servitude (see pp.182–83). Between 1896 and 1901, for example, British colonial authorities sent around 35,000 indentured labourers from India to Africa to construct the Uganda-Kenya railway, and tens of thousands more to South Africa, to toil on plantations, in mines, and on railways.

▼ **A poster** advertises the Trans-Siberian Railway, which starts in Europe (Moscow) and ends in East Asia (Vladivostok, near the Chinese border).

The *Titanic*

When it set sail from the UK to the US in 1912, the *Titanic* carried 2,224 people, including hundreds of emigrants from the UK, Ireland, Russia, and Scandinavia. After striking an iceberg, the ship sank, and more than 1,500 people died.

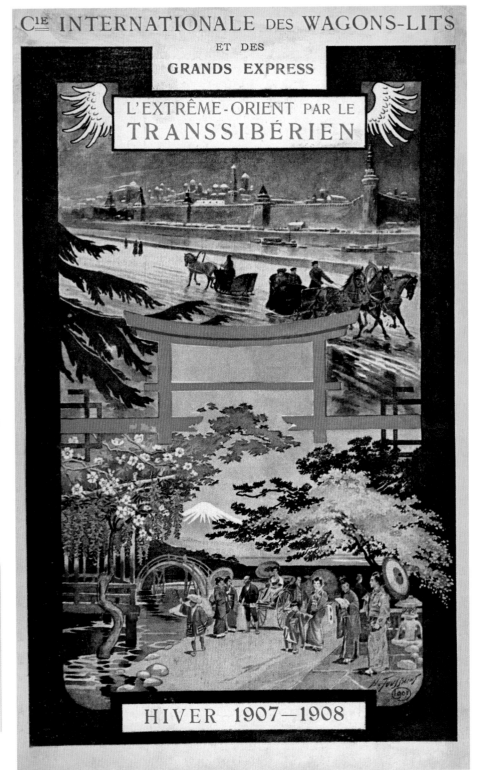

The war to end all wars

DISPLACEMENT BY WORLD WAR I

◀ Australian soldiers march through Melbourne before leaving for the battlefields in 1914. The Commonwealth of Australia pledged Britain its full support over the war and thousands of its soldiers fought with the Allied Powers.

The world's first modern global conflict claimed more lives and caused more destruction than any war that had gone before. Around 13 million civilians were killed and at least 10 million more were uprooted from their homes and displaced, either internally or across borders, creating a refugee crisis on a monumental scale.

Caught in the crossfire

More than 30 countries took part in the conflict that took place between 1914 and 1918, most joining on the side of the Allied Powers, whose main members were Britain, Russia, and France. Their opponents were the Central Powers: Germany, Austria-Hungary, Bulgaria, and the Ottoman Empire. Most of the fighting took place in Europe on the Western Front – in northern France and Belgium – and on the Eastern Front, to the east of Germany, which was more than twice the length of its Western counterpart.

As the armies advanced on and occupied enemy territory, huge numbers of civilians were displaced in an area that extended from Belgium to Armenia, taking in France, Italy, Austria-Hungary, the Russian Empire, and Serbia.

Many civilians living on the Western Front felt compelled to abandon their homes and property and leave with retreating troops. Both families and individuals fled to avoid atrocities – such as civilian executions and rape – at the

"One was left with nothing, ruined, and that's how people carried on talking about 'the refugee'. We weren't real people any more."

Belgian refugee

hands of enemy troops or to escape the oppressive occupation of their homeland. Many had to pack up and leave their lives behind in just a few hours.

Millions on the move

In 1914, Germany's invasion of Belgium and northern France, Poland, and Lithuania provoked an exodus of refugees. Of the 1.5 million Belgian civilians who fled, 600,000 sought shelter in France, Britain, and the Netherlands, where their arrival prompted unprecedented humanitarian action. In France, the refugees were given state financial support and charitable assistance for the duration of the war, saving the poorest from destitution. In Britain, more than 2,500 charitable committees helped resettle 250,000 Belgians, either with host families or in boarding houses created for this purpose. With the domestic workforce decimated, the refugees were soon used as a source of manpower – thousands were employed on farms and in munitions factories producing shells.

However, as the war raged on, public sympathy for refugees began to wane and their conduct was criticized. Typical of the complaints levelled at them was that they took charitable donations as their right and expected a higher standard of living than was justified, or that they were deserters who, lacking the courage to face the depredations of the enemy, had taken the easy way out.

Unlike the Western Front, where trench warfare dominated, fighting on the Eastern Front involved rapid movements, with large armies repeatedly

◀ **At the end of World War I**, the victorious Allied Powers redrew the maps of Eastern and Western Europe, the Middle East, and Africa. These new borders had political and geographic consequences that reverberate to this day.

▲ **Refugees from east Galicia** (now part of Ukraine) return to their villages with their horse-carts and cattle in 1915, following the defeat of Austria-Hungary by the Russians in the Battle of Galicia, one of the largest battles of World War I.

◀ **Belgian refugees** crowd aboard a train headed for the coast after the evacuation of the city of Antwerp ahead of advancing German troops during World War I.

crisscrossing the same massive swathes of territory. As Germany and Russia fought each other for dominance, millions of civilians fled for safety.

In the winter of 1915, Austro-Hungarian forces captured much of Serbia, prompting the flight of soldiers and civilians fearful of brutal treatment at the hands of the enemy. Half a million refugees retreated across Kosovo towards the Adriatic coast, moving on foot across snow-covered mountains. Around 200,000 died en route, but the survivors eventually reached Albania. While Serbian troops regrouped in Salonika in Greece in 1916, many civilians migrated to Corsica and France; others sought sanctuary in the French North African colonies of Tunisia, Morocco, and Algeria.

Wartime tactics

Various countries used the war as an excuse to expel huge numbers of their own citizens, targeting those suspected of undermining the war effort or siding with the enemy. Minority populations, such as the Christian Armenian community in the Ottoman Empire, were the most frequent targets.

In 1914, the Ottoman Empire was home to around 1.5 million Christian Armenians who had lived for generations alongside Muslim Turks and Kurds in Eastern Anatolia, although they were not treated equally. When Ottoman forces suffered military setbacks in the area, the Armenians were accused of colluding with the Russians to ensure an Ottoman defeat. In 1915, the government began to deport Armenians living near the combat zones, claiming their presence there was a national security threat.

Driven from their homes, Armenian men, women, and children had to trek on foot across valleys and mountains towards concentration camps in the barren desert regions in the southern empire. It is estimated that around 1 million Armenians perished during the conflict – either succumbing to dehydration, starvation, or disease on these death marches, or massacred. Those who escaped found refuge in the Middle East and Russia, where fellow Armenians gave them food and medicine, and cared for orphans.

Similar displacements occurred in the Russian Empire. By 1917, there were 6 million refugees in Russia (see pp.204–05), among them non-Russian minority communities such as Jews, Ukrainians, Latvians, and Poles. Russian commanders made them into scapegoats for military failures and deported them deep into the Russian interior.

Ravished Armenia
After the war, many Ottoman Armenians emigrated to North America. Among them was the teenager Aurora Mardiganian. Her account of being abducted during a death march and sold into slavery was made into a film, *Ravished Armenia* (1919), in which she played the leading role.

A new world order

The war and its aftermath brought about the collapse of the Russian, Austro-Hungarian, German, and Ottoman empires. The victorious Allied Powers divided these territories among themselves, founding in their place new nation states, such as Hungary, bound by common ethnicity. Many people who had been displaced by the war or expelled from the country in which they had lived suddenly found themselves stateless, unwanted in the country where they had taken refuge, or fearful of returning to a homeland now under different control.

The world order had been reorganized, but the refugee crisis remained. Affecting all European nations, it finally forced the development of the first international organizations and legislation to protect refugees (see pp.208–09), and a more coordinated approach to dealing with displaced populations.

◀ **Armenian refugees** gather in Baku, Azerbaijan, in 1918. Fleeing advancing Ottoman forces, many Armenians had escaped to the city from the surrounding region.

"A whole nation of people, although they come from many nations, wanders the world, homeless except for refuges which may at any moment prove to be temporary."

Dorothy Thompson, US journalist, 1938

KEY

▨ Southern states

New lives in the North

THE GREAT BLACK AMERICAN MIGRATION

The Great Migration refers to the mass movement of Black Americans from the rural South of the US to the urban North and West, from around 1910 to 1970. During this period, around 6 million Black Americans made the often long and arduous journey to seek a new life.

Following the end of the Civil War in 1865, many Black Americans sought to leave the South. Employment opportunities were scarce, and rampant racism, including racial violence, still had a hold over the South. This was institutionalized by the introduction of the Jim Crow laws from 1877 – a collection of statutes that legalized racial segregation and limited the rights of Black Americans. The emergence in 1865 of the Ku Klux Klan – a white supremacist terrorist group, which targeted Black Americans and carried out lynchings – also meant that life was dangerous for Black Americans in the South. The prospect of a safer life with fewer restrictions and better employment opportunities appealed to many Black Americans.

Heading to the cities

The first phase of the Great Migration ramped up with the outbreak of World War I in 1914. Industrial areas in the North and West faced a labour shortage, and recruiters began advertising in newspapers in the South to encourage Black Americans to migrate. In 1940, a second wave of migration began. This was a result of the increasing mechanization of agriculture, as well as a government act in 1938 that aimed to reduce crop surpluses by paying farmers not to plant on a portion of their land. Both reduced the demand for labour on farms in the South. The most popular destinations in the

1940s were often those that were easiest to access by train – Chicago, Cleveland, Detroit, New York, Pittsburgh, Philadelphia, and St Louis. Distances were frequently vast – as much as 1,600 km (1,000 miles) for those heading north and 3,200 km (2,000 miles) for those travelling to the West.

Once in the city, Black Americans continued to face injustices and hardship. Work opportunities and accommodation in overcrowded cities proved difficult to find. Those who did find jobs usually worked long hours in poor conditions, often in factories and slaughterhouses. And even though segregation was not legal, discrimination was still rife, and many Black people were denied housing and employment on the basis of their race.

A lasting legacy

Despite these challenges, many Black Americans succeeded in establishing their own businesses and infrastructures in cities in the North and West. Communities like Harlem in New York City gave birth to cultural movements, including the Harlem Renaissance – a blossoming of Black American creative arts and expression – and the New Negro Movement, which promoted racial pride. Black activist organizations and campaigns, such as the Civil Rights Movement and the Black Panther Movement, achieved major breakthroughs, chipping away at Jim Crow laws in the South.

By 1970, the demography of the US had changed dramatically. In 1900, around 90 per cent of Black Americans lived in the South, with 75 per cent living on farms. By 1970, about 47 per cent of Black Americans lived in the North and West; more than 80 per cent of these lived in cities.

▲ **Black Americans migrated** from the South of the US to the North and West between 1910 and 1970. Most migrants moved from rural areas to large cities.

▼ **A woman** brings her luggage out in preparation for a trip from Belcross, North Carolina, to a job in Onley, Virginia.

Ella Baker

Raised in the South, political activist Ella Baker (1903–86) moved to New York and became the highest-ranking woman in the National Association of the Advancement of Colored People (NAACP), encouraging Black Americans to fight for their rights.

▲ **A group of migrant farmers** from Florida are on their way to New Jersey, to pick potatoes. Black Americans moved north for work opportunities.

◀ **Black American migration** contributed to the Harlem Renaissance. Archibald J. Motley Jr.'s painting captures the thriving cultural scene of the 1920s and 1930s.

◀ **Early migrants** fled from southern Russia into Ukraine, Turkey, or to other Slavic countries. Many headed west to the Baltic states. In eastern Russia, refugees went to China.

▶ **The magazine** *Jar-Ptitza*, first published in 1921, was a monthly review of art and literature produced for Russian emigrants living in Berlin.

▼ **On arrival** at their destinations, many Russian emigrants had to take on new careers. Here, former Russian government officials work as toy makers in Germany.

KEY

➡ Emigration from Russia	▢ Siberia	1 Estonia	5 Turkmenistan
➡ Forced deportations	▢ Baltic states	2 Latvia	6 Tajikistan
▢ Russian boundary in 1922	▢ Central Asian Republics	3 Lithuania	7 Kyrgyzstan
		4 Uzbekistan	8 Kazakhstan

"We were happy that we were safe. This was the safety that was most important, and the optimism that things will get better."

Kyra Tatarinoff, "White Russian" in the Philippines, quoted in 2015

Russians in exile

FLEEING THE BOLSHEVIK REVOLUTION

The Russian Revolution in 1917 overturned the lives of every Russian, and it was to have a major impact on the balance of power around the world for decades to come. Russia was already in turmoil from World War I, in which millions died or lost their homes. Russians also endured a five-year Civil War (1917–22) as the Red Army fought to defend the new Bolshevik (Communist) government against its opponents. The execution of Tsar Nicholas II and his family by the Bolsheviks in 1918, which ended a 300-year-old imperial dynasty, struck at the heart of the Russian establishment.

Fleeing the regime

Between 1917 and 1922 some 2 million Russians fled the country. This first wave of emigrants following the revolution are often referred to as "White Russian émigrés", so named because many supported the "White" movement, which wanted to reinstate the Tsarist regime in Russia and opposed the Bolsheviks (or "Reds"). However, not all supported the "Whites", and they were in fact a disparate group that included aristocrats, business- and landowners, intellectuals, artists, members of the military, former officials, and more. Many emigrants remained wealthy and lived well in their new homes, while others had lost everything.

The destination countries for the refugees were varied. Many went to other Slavic countries in Europe, or to the Baltic states or Western Europe, especially Germany and France. Some went further, such as to the US. Several Russian artists became prominent in their new homes, including the composer Rachmaninov, the artist Chagall, the writer Nina Berberova, and the ballet impresario Diaghilev – bringing elements of Russian culture to the West.

Refugees from eastern Russia went to China, and large Russian communities emerged in cities such as Shanghai and Harbin. In Harbin, which became a sophisticated centre of Russian culture referred to as "the Moscow of China", business was often conducted in a pidgin language, *Moya-tvoya* (meaning "mine–yours") – a hybrid of Russian and Mandarin Chinese.

▲ **"White Russians"** who had emigrated to China found themselves displaced once again after the Chinese Communist Revolution in 1949. Over 6,000 refugees were evacuated to Tubabao Island in the Philippines, where they waited for their asylum to be granted by the international community.

Forced deportations

In the 1930s and 1940s, Soviet leader Josef Stalin conducted a mass deportation programme. This was part of Stalin's ethnic cleansing and collectivization policy, whereby smaller farms were merged to form larger, state-controlled farms. Stalin targeted the kulaks (wealthier peasants whom he viewed as "class enemies") and ethnic minorities, such as Crimean Tatars and Chechens, sending them to remote areas in the north, Siberia, or Central Asian republics, often to gulags (labour camps). Historians now believe that Soviet deportations killed at least 20 million people – some estimates of the death toll are considerably higher.

Crossing the Rio Grande

FROM MEXICO TO THE US

KEY
Origin states

Michoacan	Guanajuato
Sinaloa	San Luis Potosi
Chihuahua	Veracruz
Jalisco	Guerrero

After the Mexican–American War (1846–48), the US took more than half of Mexico's territory. The result was north to south migration, as many Mexicans in US-annexed areas moved to Mexican territory. This trend reversed in the late 19th century, when Mexicans migrated to work in the booming agricultural and mining industries in the southern US. The Mexican Revolution (1910–20), rural poverty, and the Cristero War (a Catholic anti-government uprising in 1926–29) boosted the flow.

In the 1920s, 50,000–100,000 Mexicans legally migrated to the US each year. Often regarded as temporary workers, they were vital to the economy and US farmers lobbied to exempt Mexico from immigration quotas. But the 1929 Wall Street Crash and subsequent depression saw industries collapse. Mexican migrants lost their jobs and faced hostility. Some voluntarily returned to Mexico; thousands more were forcibly repatriated by the US authorities.

Again short of labour during World War II, the US brought in 4.5 million Mexican men on short-term contracts under the 1942 Bracero programme. Braceros (manual labourers) were not allowed to bring their families and faced gruelling work, low wages, and discrimination. During the 22-year bracero period, many more Mexicans migrated illegally, and by 1947, there were 10 times more illegal than legal immigrants. They were desperate for work, and farmers learnt they could pay even less to undocumented workers.

A migrant corridor

In recent decades, thousands of Latin Americans have risked their lives to travel overland through Mexico to reach the US. Some are simply looking for better opportunities. Many more are fleeing violence, conflicts, and humanitarian disasters. The journey is incredibly dangerous: a 2017 survey of migrants and refugees from Guatemala, Honduras, and El Salvador by the NGO Doctors Without Borders found that 68 per cent were victims of violence while travelling in Mexico.

Risking death or detention

Many Latin American migrants using the Mexican corridor to the US take *La Bestia* ("The Beast"), a freight train that travels north from southern Mexico, to try to avoid police raids and highway checkpoints. As US immigration policy has become increasingly restrictive and border controls tighter, migrants and refugees have been forced to pay people smugglers known as "coyotes" to take them across the frontier. Many lose their lives.

Tens of thousands of those who make it over the border are held in detention centres for many days, often in poor conditions. For example, government authorities deliberately separated children from their parents in these facilities.

Immigration from Latin America remains a charged political topic in the US. Yet over 60 million people in the US have Latin American heritage and their diverse and vibrant communities have helped to shape the country's economy, culture, language, and cuisine.

▲ **Established migration** routes from various Mexican states to specific American cities can be worked out by following the flow of remittances sent by migrants to their families back home.

▼ **Adequate food**, shelter, and a minimum wage became legal obligations in the 1940s for migrants on the Bracero programme. However, many employers in the US failed to fulfil these basic requirements and exploitation of Mexican workers was common.

▼ **Mexican labourers** entered the US illegally in the 1940s, as Bracero programme quotas were limited. Here, migrants wade through the Rio Grande in 1948 to reach the US.

"... it was important to send my kids to school. That's what I was trying to do as a bracero. I wanted a real future."

Rigoberto Garcia Perez, a bracero in the 1950s

Southern Pacific company trains transported braceros across the border in the 1940s to work on farms in the US. On arrival, the labourers were sent to processing centres, where they underwent health checks and fumigation before starting work.

▲ **Fridtjof Nansen** (second from right) poses with Greek refugees in Rodosto, Greece (now Tekirdağ, Turkey), forced to leave Turkey at the end of the Greco-Turkish war in 1922.

◄ **Polish refugee children** attend a language class at the United Nations Relief and Rehabilitation Administration camp at Indersdorf, Germany, in 1945.

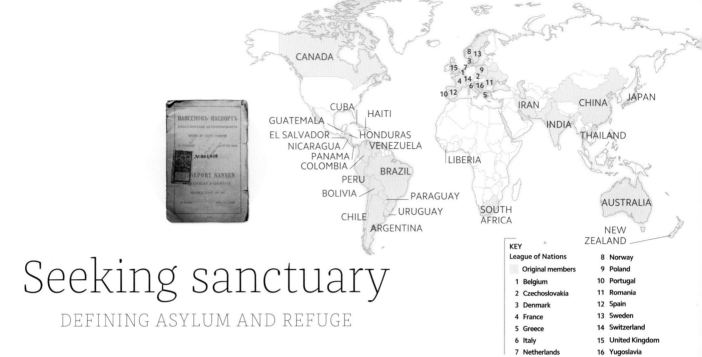

Seeking sanctuary

DEFINING ASYLUM AND REFUGE

Modern ideas about the treatment of those seeking asylum and refuge date from the late 1910s. This was when the turmoil of World War I and the Russian Revolution, along with the collapse of the Ottoman Empire, resulted in mass movements of displaced people across Europe and parts of the Middle East. Millions were made stateless, having been held as prisoners of war, expelled from their countries, forcibly repatriated, caught up in population exchanges, or displaced in other ways. It was now urgent to plan how to provide support for these people.

Nansen passports

In 1921, the League of Nations – an international organization founded in 1920 that aimed to peacefully solve conflicts between countries – appointed Fridtjof Nansen (see box, right) as its first High Commissioner for Refugees. His agency was the first international body to provide refugees with support and protection. It initially focused on helping the approximately 1.5 million Russian refugees scattered throughout Europe following the Russian Revolution (see pp.204–05), but went on to assist Armenian, Assyrian, Turkish, Greek, and Spanish people, and Jewish people from Austria and Germany, among others. Between 1922 and 1938, 450,000 refugees were given "Nansen passports" – internationally recognized identification papers – to help them move through Europe.

The League of Nations had expected these passports, and its refugee efforts more generally, to be a temporary measure. Instead, more people became stateless during the 1920s and 1930s. Nations began to close their borders to refugees in the build-up to World War II, leaving many Nansen passport holders trapped in camps around Europe, uncertain of their futures. One such person was the singer Alide Heller. Born in 1891 in Tsarist Russia, in what is now Jelgava, Latvia, she was forced to flee her home as a result of the Russian Revolution and lived as a stateless person in Milan, then Berlin, while training to be a singer. Her Nansen passport allowed her to perform for audiences in Paris, Berlin, Milan, and Rome, but when World War II broke out she became trapped in Berlin and turned to a local camp for displaced people for assistance. The records suggest that Heller was forced to remain in Germany until at least 1968.

The United Nations

In 1947, after World War II had displaced tens of millions of people in Europe alone, the League of Nations was replaced by the United Nations (UN), which expanded its predecessor's support for refugees beyond Europe. The following year, representatives from the 51 nations in this organization came together under the leadership of the chair of the United Nations Human Rights Commission, Eleanor Roosevelt, to create the 1948 Universal Declaration of Human Rights. This milestone document included some key rights for refugees and asylum seekers, stating in Article 14 that everyone has a right to "seek and to enjoy in other countries asylum from persecution".

In 1951, the UN put together the landmark Convention Relating to the Status of Refugees. This defined the term "refugee" and outlined the rights to which refugees are entitled. It remains the foundation of international refugee law.

▲**This map** shows the original members of the League of Nations in 1920. Today there are 193 members.

▼**Nansen passports** were identity papers issued to European refugees by the League of Nations between 1922 and 1938 to facilitate travel across Europe.

Fridtjof Nansen

Born in 1861, Fridtjof Nansen was an Arctic explorer, scientist, statesman, and humanitarian from Norway. He received the Nobel Peace Prize in 1922 for his role in repatriating prisoners of war in Europe and his international relief work on behalf of the League of Nations.

Forced expulsions

THE GREECE-TURKEY POPULATION EXCHANGE

KEY

Turkey before the Greco-Turkish war

Annexed by Turkey, 1921

Restored to Turkey after Treaty of Lausanne, 1923

Following the collapse of the Ottoman Empire after World War I, Greece tried to annex parts of Turkish Anatolia to reclaim what they saw as their ancient homeland. However, the invasion was a disaster. The Greco-Turkish war that ensued (1919–22) led to massacres on both sides and resulted in the first internationally ratified compulsory population exchange in history. Agreed in January 1923, in Lausanne, Switzerland, this exchange involved the expulsion of over 1 million Greek-Orthodox Christians from the newly formed Republic of Turkey and the expulsion of about 350,000 Muslims from Greece. The League of Nations (see pp.208–09) was tasked with overseeing the operation.

Migrations, evacuations, and expulsions

Prior to the forced population exchange, hundreds of thousands of Christians (mainly Greeks and Armenians) had already fled Anatolia as a result of the Greco-Turkish war. By 1922, more than 250,000 Christian refugees had arrived in Greece, seeking refuge from Turks retaking territory in Anatolia. Many more arrived after Smyrna, which the Greeks had occupied since 1919, was destroyed by fire in September 1922 (see box, right). Christian refugees crowded onto the dockside in Smyrna, where they waited to be evacuated by Greek naval vessels, merchant ships, and small fishing boats that would take them across the Aegean to Greece.

In brokering the expulsion of Christians from Turkey and Muslims from Greece, the Greek and Turkish governments hoped to formalize their borders and create stable, homogeneous states. However, the population exchange, based on

religious lines, took no account of the complex linguistic or ethnic identities of the peoples involved. Orthodox Christians and Muslims had lived side by side in the disputed areas for centuries, resulting in a blurring of traditions and cultures. Many of the Christian refugees arriving in Greece could not speak the language and were ostracized by their new neighbours; similarly, Muslims arriving in Turkey identified as Greeks and were regarded as outsiders.

Forced resettlement

All those who were forcibly resettled lost the nationality of the country they left behind, their property, and their livelihoods. Many of the Christian refugees were successful professionals and business owners who had created comfortable lives in Turkey. They arrived in Greece destitute and with few prospects. Greece was impoverished by war and, since its population had increased by 20 per cent in just a few months, struggled to house and support the influx of refugees.

In Turkey, Muslim refugees faced only marginally better conditions. Most had been peasant farmers in Greece, and while the flight, genocide, and final expulsion of Orthodox Christians in Turkey had left land vacant, many homes were destroyed or occupied by locals before the refugees' arrival, leaving them without shelter.

By 1926, the exchange was largely complete. However, for the refugees the attempt to rebuild their lives was only just beginning. Promises of compensation for possessions left behind in their countries of origin were rarely honoured, and many refugees faced an ongoing struggle with poverty and discrimination.

▲ **Refugee movements**, which began during the Greco-Turkish war (1919–22), were finalized and formalized by the 1923 exchange of populations.

▼ **The Lausanne Treaty**, signed in 1923, resolved land claims in the Balkan area, and agreed the exchange of Christians, Muslims, and prisoners of war between Greece and Turkey.

Smyrna burns

In September 1922, Turkish forces retook the port city of Smyrna in Anatolia (modern Izmir, Turkey), from the Greeks. Four days later, terrible fires broke out. Raging for nine days, the fires destroyed the Greek and Armenian quarters of the city. Thousands were killed, and many more fled to Greece by boat, arriving as refugees.

▲ **Muslim refugees**, taking only what they could carry, boarded boats in northern Greece to make the perilous sea journey to Turkey.

▶ **Refugee camps and soup kitchens** were set up in cities such as Athens and Thessaloniki to care for the thousands of Christian refugees waiting for permanent homes in Greece.

"When they need us they call us migrants, and when we've picked their crop, we're bums and we got to get out."

Dust Bowl migrant boy, interviewed in 1936

The 1936 photograph of Florence Thompson and her children, taken at a Californian pea-pickers camp by Dorothea Lange, came to symbolize the desperate plight of Dust Bowl migrants.

The Dust Bowl

FROM THE GREAT PLAINS TO THE WEST COAST

The plight of the Dust Bowl migrants began in the 1930s when around 2.5 million people, mostly poor farming families, left states in the southern Great Plains region. They came largely from Oklahoma, Nebraska, Arkansas, Missouri, and Texas, and most travelled to California, especially to Los Angeles and the San Joaquin area.

The Plains' problems began with a massive influx of inexperienced farmers between 1862 and 1910. Some of these settlers believed in Manifest Destiny (see pp.168–69) and were given land grants by the government. Crop production started well with a series of wet years, and farmers were able to benefit from the rising demand for wheat in Europe. Eager to catch the boom, settlers stripped away the prairie grass to cultivate ever more marginal lands.

From boom to dust

When the Great Depression hit the US in the late 1920s, wheat prices began to collapse. Desperate to sustain their income, farmers pushed even further into marginal lands. Then in 1931, the rains stopped and a prolonged drought set in. It was clear that the fragile Plains soil could not cope with the level of cropping. Without deep-rooted prairie grass to bind it, the soil quickly turned to dust. Severe dust storms or "black blizzards" swept across the region – known as the Dust Bowl – choking the air, burying homesteads, and carrying soil particles as far as New York. Crops and livestock were destroyed. Over 35 million acres of farmland were rendered useless and another 125 million were on the brink.

Farming families clung on until they had almost nothing, but were eventually forced to migrate in search of work to avoid starvation. Packing their few belongings into old cars and trucks, families headed west, many along Highway 66. Most hoped to reach California, attracted by good reports from friends and family, and by the mild climate, which promised the kind of growing conditions that would make farming easy.

Unwelcome arrivals

Many migrants could not afford food or petrol on the journey west and were forced to beg at farms for work or supplies. On reaching California, migrants found they were not welcome after all. In the Plains, they had been a tight-knit community, but they were seen by many Californians as disruptive outsiders who posed a threat to local jobs. Barred from businesses, and often forced to camp on the outskirts of towns, migrants were derided as "Okies" (a large proportion came from Oklahoma). But they kept coming, and soon made up the majority of California's residents in rural areas.

The dearth of jobs only ended for the Dust Bowl refugees after 1941, when the US joined World War II. Okies signed up to fight, and met the need for workers in West Coast shipyards and aircraft factories. At the same time, new migrants stopped coming as the drought broke and rains fell.

▲ **Dust Bowl refugees** came from a broad area, including states such as Missouri and Arkansas, which were suffering from drought and the effects of the Depression.

▼ **Fears in California** that migrants would take local jobs and drain public resources led to a "bum blockade" in 1936, which attempted to deter new settlers in the state.

▼ **"Riding the rails"**, by jumping on trains without paying, became a popular method of travel for homeless migrants desperately searching for work.

A hellish world

SEEKING REFUGE DURING WORLD WAR II

World War II (1939–45) directly involved tens of millions of men and women in fighting, and devastated the lives of ordinary people around the world. Many millions across Europe and Asia were forced from their homes through expulsion, deportation, and mass evacuation, or trying to escape hostilities. A few could pack their bags and leave quietly, but others were held at gunpoint, herded on to closed trains, and taken to unknown destinations with just the clothes on their backs.

Mass movements

There were population displacements on both sides during the war, but the most cataclysmic were those in Central and Eastern Europe, enforced by the Nazis and the Soviet Union. This included the eradication of most of Europe's Jewish population. Even before the war, Jews were fleeing increasing persecution in Germany, and had hastily organized *Kindertransport* ("Children's transport", see pp.216–17) trains to send children to safety in countries such as Britain. During the war, the Nazis deported Jews trapped in Europe – as well as POWs, Romani, gay men, physically and mentally disabled people, and others they deemed inferior or threatening to the Aryan race – sending them by train to internment and then death camps.

When the Nazis invaded Poland, their plan was not just to eliminate Jews, but to remove Poles altogether and replace them with a German population. Up to 2 million Poles were driven out of Poland, and millions more were transported as forced labourers to work in German factories and fields. Meanwhile, half a million *Volksdeutsche* ("ethnic Germans") from all over Eastern Europe were moved into the emptied region by the German government's "resettlement department", taking over homes vacated by the Poles.

In the Soviet Union, Volga Germans, Crimean Tatars, Kalmyks, Chechens, Ingush, Koreans, and other ethnic peoples were massacred, or deported as forced labour to Central Asia and Siberia. One survivor of the Ingush expulsion, Isa Khashiyev, aged 10 at the time, recalled in 2014 how the men were taken off separately, and likely killed, while women, children, and the elderly were herded into cattle trucks for a 15-day journey to Kazakhstan without water and food. Many millions died on the way.

Following the US bombings of Hiroshima and Nagasaki, the Japanese government advised survivors to leave the cities. Many had nowhere to go, so built makeshift huts on the city outskirts or slept in train stations. A large number developed symptoms of radiation poisoning.

In the aftermath

When the war ended, 20 million people were left displaced in Europe alone. The United Nations Relief Rehabilitation Administration was set up in 1943 to help get them home. Among the displaced were millions of ethnic Poles and Germans, uprooted by changes to the borders of the USSR and Poland.

"In two days, we travelled 70 km [43 miles] on foot... We were part of this colossal stream of evacuees."

Jacques Desbonnet describes fleeing France as a teenage refugee in 1940

▶ Forced migrations
during and after WWII were predominantly to the west, apart from Russians returning to their homeland from Austria and Germany.

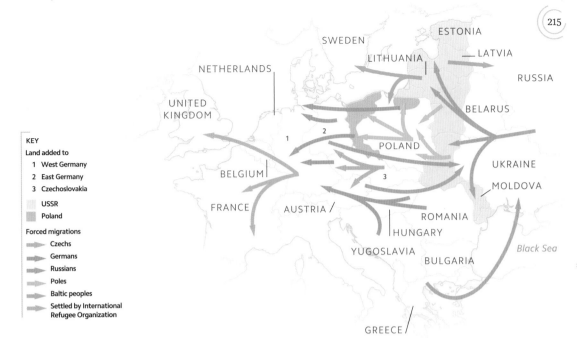

KEY

Land added to
1 West Germany
2 East Germany
3 Czechoslovakia

USSR

Poland

Forced migrations

Czechs

Germans

Russians

Poles

Baltic peoples

Settled by International Refugee Organization

◀ A handful of survivors of the 150 German refugees who left Lodz, Poland, two months earlier in October 1945, follow railway lines in their bid to reach Berlin and find shelter.

◀ Refugees leave Paris in June 1940 in anticipation of the German invasion. Two million Parisians fled in just a few days, joining a further 8 million French refugees already on the road heading southwards. The image has been colourized.

▼ Japanese refugees return from hiding places in the hills to the lowlands of Okinawa, in the Ryukyu Islands, following Japan's surrender to US forces in September 1945.

"We were 1,000 children; it was already the second Kindertransport to England. My mother said, 'Don't go to England. Go to Holland. Then you can come back on foot. Take a little wagon, a farmer will drive you for a bit, or you'll walk home. You won't be able to get back over water.'

... At first we lived on the coast in Dovercourt in a summer camp, with bunk beds on each side... It was a cold winter... the first time it had snowed in 20 years.

Every day people arrived who wanted to take children. They wanted to adopt little blond boys up to two years old.

... One day Mrs. Jacobs from Manchester came seeking 10 girls from age 14. I said to Ilse, 'Come, let's go to the dog selection, maybe she'll take us.'"

Kitty Suschny, an Austrian Jew who signed up for the Kindertransport with her friend Ilse after *Kristallnacht* in November 1938, when Nazis attacked Jewish people and property (including businesses and synagogues). Suschny ended up doing office work in Manchester, UK, before returning to Vienna in 1946. Her mother was killed in the Nazi death camp at Maly Trostinec (in Belarus) in 1943.

Jewish children arrive in London in February 1939 in what is known as the Kindertransport. From December 1938 to May 1940, around 10,000 Jewish children were sent to safety in the UK from Germany, Austria, Czechoslovakia, Poland, and the Netherlands.

Severing the subcontinent
THE PARTITION OF INDIA

At midnight on 14 August 1947, India gained independence after 200 years of British colonial rule on the subcontinent. "On the stroke of the midnight hour," announced Nehru, India's first prime minister, "when the world sleeps, India will awake to life and freedom." This "Tryst with Destiny" speech followed a long, tumultuous period of tension between British rulers – whose governing style has been described as negligent, inept, and based on an inflammatory system of divide and rule – and the Indian people, who had been campaigning for self-determination for almost 100 years. The campaign gathered momentum after World War I, when Britain made some concessions to share power with India, and after World War II became unstoppable, as Britain was nearly bankrupt.

The division of a nation
The All-India Muslim League, founded in 1906, began demanding independence from Britain around 1913. Initially, the plan was for Hindus and Muslims to live side by side in India, but in 1940 the group's leader, Muhammad Ali Jinnah, started campaigning for a separate Muslim-majority state, fearing that Muslim rights would come under attack. Meanwhile, Gandhi – a practicing Hindu and leader of the nationalist movement against British rule of India – called for Hindu–Muslim unity and spoke out against Partition.

In the 1940s, violence escalated between Hindus and Muslims, largely triggered by the prospect of independence, with each group having very different ideas regarding the future shape of the subcontinent. In response, the British took the hasty, controversial decision to partition India into two independent nation states: a Hindu-majority India and a Muslim-majority Pakistan, which in 1956 became the world's first Islamic republic. Lord Mountbatten, the last viceroy of India, announced the plan in June 1947, and a British judge, Cyril Radcliffe, who had never been to India, was brought in to draw up the border, which divided two of India's most powerful provinces – Punjab and Bengal – splitting them across the borders of India and the newly created West and East Pakistan respectively. For political reasons, the precise location of the border lines were not revealed until 17 August – two days after independence.

The partition of India had a catastrophic effect on the subcontinent, leaving a bloody legacy that endures to this day. Families and neighbours were divided and millions displaced, and the division resulted in the largest forced migration of people (except as a result of war or famine) in history. In highly populated and majority-Muslim border provinces, where mixed communities had co-existed peacefully for centuries, Muslim and non-Muslim districts were quickly established. Violence ensued on a vast and unprecedented scale.

Mass migrations
In the months immediately following Partition, the population exchanges between India and Pakistan initiated an urgent refugee crisis. Tides of people flowed in and out of India and Pakistan, travelling in a variety of ways – by train, ship, or car, in bullock carts or on foot, in large groups known as caravans, which often extended for 80 km (50 miles). The journey was long and fraught with the

KEY
- Movements of Hindu and Sikh refugees
- Movements of Muslim refugees
- Union of India
- Pakistan (1948)
- Large princely states not acceding to either country upon independence
- British Indian Empire before partition

▲ **The regions of West and East Pakistan** were the destination for Muslims, while Hindus and Sikhs headed for India. Jammu and Kashmir were left unresolved and have remained flashpoints for unrest.

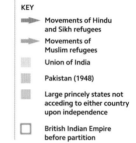

▼ **Muslim refugees** fleeing India arrived in their thousands in the newly created country of Pakistan, in 1947.

Trains crammed with people, heading either to Pakistan or India, became the target of mobs looking to attack individuals of another faith. These images became enduring symbols of the chaos of Partition.

A convoy of migrants cross Punjab province after Partition, travelling in bullock carts or on foot, and seeking safety in numbers. These Muslims are crossing the Sikh-majority state of Faridkot, India.

danger of disease and violence. It is estimated that up to 1 million women, routinely targeted as symbols of family honour, were kidnapped and raped. Mob violence was common, and transit camps were often under armed guard, as were the trains, which in the first three weeks following independence transported 700,000 passengers across the subcontinent. Often, the trains arrived at their destination full of corpses. In October 1947, the first Indo-Pakistani war began over the disputed territories of Jammu and Kashmir, and yet more people emigrated to flee the fighting. By 1948, around 15 million people had been displaced and up to 2 million had died as a result of Partition.

The aftermath of Partition

The subcontinent continued to change inexorably, and its cities were radically transformed by migration on an historic scale. In India, Calcutta (now Kolkata) and Delhi turned into sprawling urban settlements. The refugee population of Delhi, for example, doubled in four years, from 1 million refugees in 1947 to just under 2 million in 1951. In Pakistan, the provincial towns of Karachi, Hyderabad, and Sukkur were reconfigured into major industrial centres.

With the influx of migrants came a wholesale change in the diversity, culture, and demographic makeup of urban communities. When refugees arrived in the cities they stayed in camps, schools, barracks, temples, gurdwaras (Sikh places of worship), and in parks and on pavements. Refugee camps formed new neighbourhoods. Agricultural land and forests around cities were swiftly bought by the government to be used for resettlement.

In Delhi alone, the rapid influx of half a million refugees pouring into the city from West Punjab, Sindh, and the North-West Frontier caused an entire satellite city, Faridabad, to be built on its outskirts to accommodate them.

Enduring legacy

Migration between India and Pakistan continued throughout the 1950s and 1960s, fuelled on both sides by religious persecution and discrimination. In 1965, the second war over the disputed territories of Jammu and Kashmir followed a series of clashes along the Line of Control (the military border), leading to further Muslim migration to Pakistan. Today, the subcontinent still suffers from tensions between Muslims and Hindus.

In 2019, Indian prime minister Narendra Modi's nationalist government allowed some refugees fleeing religious persecution in neighbouring countries to apply for citizenship, but made no mention of Muslims. He also formally revoked Kashmir's special status and split it into two Union Territories. In 2021, a crackdown on India's 40,000 Rohingya Muslims (from Myanmar) led to around 170 Rohingya refugees being put into detention centres and threatened with deportation.

Partition, the defining event of the 20th century in South Asia, caused terrible wounds. However, it also gave birth to new identities. In India and Pakistan's ever-expanding metropolises, the migrant population led to an explosion of retail and small-scale industry. In independent India's capital, New Delhi, the new arrivals stamped their cultural and political mark on the city, transforming it from the stately, slow-paced place it was in 1947 into the enterprising, cosmopolitan centre it is today.

▲ *Indian Households* (2008–11) by M. F. Husain depicts urban families from the three main faiths in India: Islam, Hinduism, and Sikhism. Prior to Partition, 25 per cent of India's population was Muslim; this dropped to about 15 per cent by 2011.

◄ A young victim of the upheaval sits on the walls of a refugee camp in Delhi after Partition. Conditions were poor in the camps where many refugees stayed for months or even years.

Bangladesh war

In March 1971, Pakistani forces began a violent campaign to suppress the Bengali mass uprising in East Pakistan. The Bengalis were fighting to retain their cultural identity and language, as West Pakistan wanted them to adopt Urdu. In December 1971, East Pakistan gained independence and was renamed Bangladesh. About 10 million Bengalis fled to India to escape the war.

Shifting ties
POSTCOLONIAL MIGRATIONS

KEY

→ South Asian migrants
→ Indonesian migrants
→ East African migrants
→ Algerian migrants
→ Portuguese returnees
→ Caribbean migrants

The middle of the 20th century saw the world start to move slowly and unevenly into the postcolonial era. In the aftermath of World War II, countries across Asia and Africa claimed their independence from European colonial rule – through negotiation, force, or a combination of the two. Even so, ties between many ex-colonies and their colonizers were not completely severed. In some cases ex-colonies opted to become self-governing overseas territories as opposed to independent states, and migration from ex-colonies to their colonizer was not uncommon. This is one way that the legacy of colonialism continues to exert a powerful economic, political, and cultural influence.

Wars of independence
Postcolonial forces shaped global migration – both voluntary and enforced – for decades to come. Wars of independence sparked major population movements, as did hastily drawn borders. When India gained independence from the UK in 1947, the country was split in two: Hindu-majority India and Muslim-majority Pakistan (see pp.218–21).

Two years later, Indonesia won its independence following a war with the Netherlands, which had ruled the country, in one form or another, for almost 350 years. In response, around 300,000 Dutch and Indo-Dutch people migrated from Indonesia to the Netherlands. This number included 12,500 inhabitants of the Molucca Islands, part of Indonesia. Mostly former soldiers, and their families, they had chosen to fight alongside the Dutch in the conflict. Over the following decades, most of the rest of Indonesia's Dutch population followed suit and left for the Netherlands.

In 1962, Algeria won its war of independence against France after a bitter conflict that had lasted eight years and was marked by atrocities on both sides. In the aftermath, 60,000 Harkis – Algerians who had fought on behalf of the French – were allowed to travel to France. However, the Harkis were not French citizens and the authorities viewed them as refugees and forced them to live in internment camps. The racism, marginalization, and poverty they endured has lasted for decades. Controversially, France left tens of thousands of Harkis to their fate in Algeria, where their fellow Algerians widely saw them as traitors. They and their families faced violent reprisals and many were killed. Around 800,000 French and European settlers in Algeria also left for France. The latter, known as *pieds noirs* ("black feet"), had emigrated to Algeria during French rule, often as labourers and farmers, and held French citizenship, even though many of them had never been to France. Like the Harkis, these settlers were, for the most part, unwelcome in France, although they did receive limited government benefits and housing.

Encouraged migration
Conflict was not the only force driving postcolonial migration. After the devastation of World War II, European countries faced major rebuilding projects and severe labour shortages. They turned to their colonies (or former colonies) for help, often easing

▲ **Many countries gained their independence** in the 1950s and 1960s, though they retained links with their former colonial rulers. Residents of former colonies often migrated to the colonizing country to work, study, or seek greater opportunities.

▼ **An Algerian Harki child** in the Rivesaltes refugee camp in southern France in 1962, having fled newly independent Algeria with her family.

▼ **Moluccan Islanders**, who had fought with the Dutch against Indonesian nationalists, arrive as refugees in the Netherlands in 1951.

"We are here
because you
were there."

Ambalavaner Sivanandan,
director of the Institute of
Race Relations, London, 2008

◀**Migrants from South Asia**
find work in a foundry near
Bradford, having been invited
to the UK to help overcome
labour shortages in the 1960s.

▲ **Sikh children**, descendants of Indian migrants, celebrate Vaisakhi, the start of the Sikh New Year, on 13 April 1983 in Toronto. The day also commemorates the Amritsar Massacre of 1919, when British troops killed hundreds of unarmed nationalists, a defining moment in India's fight for independence from the UK.

indentured labourers and later in waves as traders, merchants, and administrators. They occupied a middle role in the colonial system in the region. After gaining their independence in the early 1960s, countries such as Kenya and Tanzania launched "Africanization" policies, prompting many residents of Asian heritage to leave, predominantly for the UK. In 1972, the dictator Idi Amin ordered the expulsion of Asians from Uganda (see pp.244–45). Tens of thousands fled but they were unable to take much with them. Roughly half had British passports and were eventually able to settle in the UK, but often in poor-quality housing and working in low-paid jobs.

Many of the migrants who settled in Europe sought to bring their spouses, children, and parents from former colonies to join them. Family-based migration, sometimes referred to as "chain migration", allowed this, though opposition increased over the decades and, in the UK and France, for example, the governments passed laws restricting immigration from their former colonies in 1971 and 1974, respectively.

immigration restrictions and, in some cases, expanding access to citizenship. The UK encouraged migrants from the Caribbean, South Asia, Africa, Hong Kong, and Cyprus, among others. Seeking greater opportunities and the chance to work and study, the migrants fulfilled vital roles in the National Health Service, public transport, the textiles industries, and many other areas of society. But they also faced inflammatory political rhetoric, racial discrimination, and violence. Many politicians and members of the public demanded tighter immigration controls, even though the number of Britons emigrating during this period exceeded that of immigrants entering the UK.

In the face of prejudice and hostility, people of Black and Asian heritages campaigned for their rights. High-profile protests such as the 1963 Bristol bus boycott played a key role in the passing of the 1965 Race Relations Act, the first piece of legislation to address racial discrimination in the UK. The first outdoor Notting Hill Carnival – now one of the world's largest street festivals – took place in 1966, following a series of racially motivated attacks against the Black population in west London. The carnival was a display of defiance but also an attempt to unite the local community and celebrate Caribbean culture and traditions.

Other forms of migration

In the late 19th and early 20th centuries, thousands of people migrated from British-controlled India to British colonies in East Africa, initially as

Effects on Europe

Postcolonial migration reshaped the countries of Europe, creating multicultural and cosmopolitan societies that are evident today in cities such as London (see pp.146–47), Paris, Amsterdam (see pp.226–27), and Lisbon (see pp.116–17). However, the descendants of migrants often experience prejudice, disadvantage, and discrimination, and in some areas their situation is worsening.

Portugal's returnees

In 1975, after long-running wars of independence, Angola and Mozambique ended Portuguese colonial rule. An estimated 500,000 people, the majority Portuguese settlers, then fled the violence of the ensuing civil wars. Known as *retornados*, most flew back to Portugal, but many found it difficult to settle and build new lives.

With the Kenyan government making it increasingly difficult for people of Asian descent to run businesses and work, there was a mass exodus of Asian families to the UK in 1968. As a result, a bill was rushed through Parliament restricting annual arrivals to 1,500 permit holders and their dependants.

CULTURAL INFLUENCES

Armenian merchants

Amsterdam's Armenian community dates back to the textile and spice traders of the 14th century. Their numbers remained small until they were boosted by those fleeing persecution in the Ottoman Empire in the 1920s. Immigrants became successful in trading carpets, tobacco, and diamonds. Armenian merchants can be seen here in Dam Square.

Lutheran church

The Ronde Lutherse Kerk on the Singel Canal served the city's Lutherans from 1671. As Calvinism was the main form of Protestantism that became established in the Netherlands, the Lutheran community was always small and composed mainly of migrants from Germany and Scandinavia, where the church was more dominant.

Jewish refugees

From the 16th and 17th centuries, Jewish refugees came to Amsterdam, having been denied residence in other Dutch cities such as Middleburg. The first migrants were Sephardim Jews from Spain and Portugal, who founded the Portuguese Synagogue (shown) in 1675. Later, Ashkenazim Jews arrived from Germany and Poland, and soon dominated the diamond trade.

Amsterdam

THE VENICE OF THE NORTH

Amsterdam's history has been shaped by water – its network of canals and prosperity as a port making it a destination for migrants since its 13th-century beginnings as a fishing village. Working together, locals built a dam to control the waterways and under the jurisdiction of the counts of Holland, it was granted a charter in 1306. Ships from here sailed for the Baltic Sea and established a successful trading network. Its cooperative and liberal atmosphere also offered a haven for those seeking refuge from political and religious turmoil: the Protestants who escaped Spanish oppression in the southern Netherlands in the 1560s; the Sephardic Jews who fled intolerance in Spain and Portugal in the 1630s; and the Protestant Huguenots who left France in the 1680s (see pp.134–35).

Colonial and labour migration

At its peak in the 17th and 18th centuries, the Dutch Empire (see pp.136–37) brought new migrants to Amsterdam. When it collapsed following World War II, thousands of people of mixed Indonesian Dutch descent left the former Dutch East Indies for the Netherlands. Their numbers were increased by migrants from the Dutch Antilles and Suriname, from where many "Hindustanis" – Indians who had migrated there in the late 19th century to work on plantations – came to Amsterdam.

The city was heavily damaged during World War II and reconstruction brought thousands of guest workers, from Southern Europe, Turkey, North Africa, and Morocco. The Dutch Family Reunification Law in 1974 spurred a second wave of migration from these countries, adding to the city's diversity. From the 1980s, Amsterdam has also welcomed refugees from regions such as Syria (see pp.270–73) and Afghanistan (see pp.256–57). Today, almost a third of Amsterdammers have a non-European heritage.

▲▲ **Amsterdam's Moroccan community** celebrate their heritage by taking part in the Canal Parade at the city's annual LGBTQ+ Pride event.

▲ **The mural in Amsterdam's Central Station** is inspired by the tin-tile glazing skills brought to the city by Flemish artisans in the 16th century.

◀ **Amsterdam's famous narrow canal houses**, shown here in a 2008 painting by Faisal Khouja, were built for merchants during the 16th and 17th centuries. The links these merchants made with trading ports brought many more migrants to the city.

> "I am lucky to have made it to Amsterdam... now I have to make up for lost time."
>
> Mohammed Al Masri, Syrian migrant and Amsterdam tour guide, 2017

Chinese migrant workers

Amsterdam's Chinese community dates back to around 1910, when seamen serving on ships that traded with Dutch colonies in East Asia settled around the Binnen Bantammerstraat. Soon restaurants, apothecaries, and markets sprang up to serve them in a Chinatown that also includes temples such as the Fo Guang Shan Hue He.

Indonesian rice tables

Migrants from Indonesia came in large numbers after the country secured independence from the Netherlands in 1949, including 30,000 Moluccans who had fought for the Dutch during the Indonesian National Revolution (1945–49). Their legacy includes *rijstaffel* (rice table), an Indo-Dutch buffet served with a large number of side dishes.

Surinamese celebrations

Migrants from Suriname wear carnival finery, a sign of the mixed Indigenous American, Caribbean, and Indian culture which migrants brought to Amsterdam after their country became independent in 1975. The Netherlands has more than 400,000 Surinamese residents.

Children of the *kibbutz* in Palestine were cared for collectively. People lived together in agricultural settlements, sharing all income and duties. By the early 21st century, there were more than 250 of these settlements in Palestine.

"Israel is our unforgettable historic homeland."

Theodor Herschel, Austo-Hungarian Zionist, in *The Jewish State*, 1896

A Jewish homeland

MIGRATION TO ISRAEL

Only small communities of Jews had survived in Palestine through the Middle Ages. However, the 19th century Zionist movement, dedicated to the establishment of a Jewish state, led increasing numbers to migrate there. The establishment of Israel in 1948, and the forced displacement of Palestinians, transformed the region's demography.

Zionist *Aliyah*

While earlier arrivals had founded small settlements such as Rishon Le Zion in 1882, there were comparatively few Jewish settlers in Palestine until the founder of modern Zionism, Theodor Herzl, issued a call in 1897 to create a home for Jewish people in *Eretz Israel* ("the Land of Israel"). The first *Aliyah* ("ascent"), or wave of emigration to Palestine, saw an influx of thousands of Jewish migrants as Jewish benefactors abroad purchased land for agricultural settlements. Thousands more arrived during the second *Aliyah* from 1904, as many fled persecution in Eastern Europe and the Russian Empire. The first *kibbutz* ("gathering") – agricultural communal settlements founded by socialist Zionists – was established in 1909 in Degania, and that same year, Tel Aviv was founded close to Jaffa, growing into a major commercial centre in the 1920s with Jewish newspapers, businesses, and an emerging sense of community.

The influx into Palestine was accelerated both by growing antisemitism in Europe and by hopes created by the British Balfour Declaration of 1917, which promised the Zionist movement support for "a national home for the Jewish people" in Palestine. The Jewish population in Palestine, some 60,000–100,000 in 1914 (10–15 per cent of the total), increased during British Mandate rule to over 400,000 (around 30 per cent of the total) by 1939. Many were refugees from Nazi Germany.

Migration and the Holocaust

While Palestinian Arab communities resisted Zionist settlement, the British crushed any uprisings. Conflict also emerged between the British and the Zionists over immigration, with the British interning tens of thousands of refugees upon their arrival in Palestine. In February 1942, the steamer *Struma*, carrying almost 800 Jews escaping the Holocaust, was sunk by a Soviet-fired torpedo off the coast of Istanbul after the British refused to admit the refugees. Yet more than 100,000 Jews entered "illegally" from 1933–48, many seeing a Jewish state as their only safe haven.

In May 1948, following the United Nations' 1947 proposal to partition Palestine, the Zionist leadership declared the establishment of the State of Israel. Over the next decades, Middle Eastern countries such as Morocco, Iraq, and Yemen, became the main source of Jewish migration to Israel, followed in the 1990s by immigrants from the former Soviet Union. Zionism continues to motivate Jewish migration to Israel, even as tensions with the Palestinians remain unresolved.

▲**This map** shows the proposed United Nations' partition of 1947, with separate Jewish and Arab states and Jerusalem as an international zone.

▼**Jewish immigrants** arriving in Haifa, Israel, waving the future flag of the State of Israel. Thousands arrived by boat from 1947 onwards.

▼**Ethiopian Jewish women** pray during the Sigd holiday on a hill overlooking Jerusalem. Zionists helped Ethiopian Jews to migrate to Israel from the early 20th century.

LEBANON

Haifa — Acre ■ Safad — SYRIA

■ Tiberias

Nazareth ■

Jenin ■

Tulkarem —

■ Nablus

Jaffa ■

Ramla ■ Ramallah

Jerusalem ■

Gaza ■ Hebron — JORDAN

Beersheba ■

EGYPT

KEY

Israel (1948)

Regional boundaries

A people in exile

PALESTINIAN MIGRATION

The Palestinians are an Arab group of more than 13 million people, around half of whom live outside their original homeland (now Israel and the occupied Palestinian territory). Since 1948, when 700,000–800,000 were expelled or fled from what became Israel, Palestinians have spread around the globe. Many live in Syria, Jordan, and Lebanon. Jewish migration to Palestine in the 1920s and 1930s (see pp. 228–29) had shifted the demographic balance. Following the 1947 United Nations (UN) proposal to partition Palestine, violence escalated. Zionist armed groups seized territory to establish a state, and in May 1948, neighbouring Arab states sent in troops to stop them.

Long-term refugee camps

Over 80 per cent of Palestinians living in what became Israeli territory were forcibly displaced, with more than 400 villages destroyed in what is known as the *Nakba* ("Catastrophe") of 1948. The majority went to the West Bank of the River Jordan; the Gaza Strip (bordering Egypt); or Lebanon. Hundreds of thousands more refugees were displaced in the 1967 war between Israel and its Arab neighbours. In refugee camps, temporary tents soon gave way to more long-term shelters as Israel refused to allow refugees home. Three generations have now lived in the camps, under the auspices of the UN Relief and Works Agency (UNRWA), set up in 1948 to provide immediate relief. In 2020, the UNRWA had 5.7 million Palestinian refugees on its books.

In countries such as Lebanon, Palestinians were denied citizenship to avoid upsetting the balance between its religious groups. In Jordan, most have citizenship and only a minority live in camps.

Following the *Nakba*, some Palestinians took up armed resistance, and later formed groups such as the Palestine Liberation Organisation (PLO). Today there remains widespread support amongst Palestinians for the right of return, pointing to UN resolution 194 (which defines principles for that very outcome). Agreements reached by Israel and the PLO in the 1990s established limited Palestinian autonomy in parts of the West Bank and in the Gaza Strip, but the territories remain under Israeli occupation and broader political progress remains a distant prospect – including a solution to the Palestinian refugees' plight.

The Palestinian diaspora

Those Palestinian refugees who were able to seek better lives abroad were among the best educated population in the Arab world, and some found jobs in the Gulf states that had grown rich through oil. Others have engaged in secondary migrations, moving on from the countries they first sought refuge in, so that there are now more than 250,000 people of Palestinian descent in the United States, around 60,000 in Brazil, and more than 80,000 in Germany. The ripples of the *Nakba* have carried them far, but the dream of, and demand for, return remains.

△ **The *Nakba*** caused mass displacements of Palestinians. Some fled west, towards Gaza, others east towards the River Jordan. Many fled to nearby Arab states such as Lebanon.

▽ **Refugee Kamleh Kadada**, aged 76, shows the key to her former home in 2008 while living at the al-Shati refugee camp in Gaza City. Hundreds of thousands of Palestinians were displaced in 1948 as a result of the Arab-Israeli War.

▽ **During the Lebanese Civil War** (1975–90), Beirut's Bourj el-Barajneh camp was partially destroyed, exacerbating the poor living conditions of Palestinian refugees there.

"We didn't have time to pack, all we had were the clothes we were wearing, and all around us was the sound of women wailing and the explosions of Israeli mortar fire."

Zarifa Atwan, Palestinian refugee, 2012

Women and children leave their village for the West Bank, with as much as they can carry, during a truce between Israeli and Arab forces in June 1948.

***Windrush* passengers John Hazel, Harold Wilmot, and John Richards** (seen in this colourized image from Tilbury Docks in June 1958) were among the first of more than 500,000 Commonwealth citizens to arrive in Britain.

"They tell you it is the mother country... when you come here you realize you're a foreigner and that's all there is to it."

John Richards (above right), *Windrush* passenger, in a 1998 interview

The Windrush generation

FROM THE CARIBBEAN TO THE UK

▲ **Hopeful migrants** were collected from Trinidad, Jamaica, Mexico, and Bermuda, and taken to the UK.

Between 1948 and 1973, almost half a million people from the West Indies left their homes to live in Britain. Facing major labour shortages after World War II, the British government had invited its Commonwealth citizens to help rebuild the nation, promising secure jobs and better prospects for their children. Many of the first migrants were from Jamaica, which had recently been devastated by a hurricane. Some migrants intended to work for a while, save some money and then return home. Others wanted to rejoin the armed forces, while some simply wanted an adventure.

Over the next thirty years, more than 500,000 Caribbean people migrated to the UK, settling across the country, from Manchester and Birmingham to Bristol and Plymouth. They built organizations and created events, such as the Notting Hill carnival, to bring their communities together. Some arrivals opened cafes and clubs in the cities, bringing their cultures to these areas. However, in 1971, the Immigration Act was passed which restricted the number of people entering Britain. As a result, the large-scale migration of Caribbean people ended the following year.

▼ **HMT *Empire Windrush*** transported passengers from the Caribbean. When the ship docked in Kingston, Jamaica, to collect servicemen, many others decided to make the journey too, drawn by the prospect of a better life.

The Windrush generation

The first migrants – around 1,000 people – arrived on the HMT *Empire Windrush* ship from Jamaica, which docked in Essex in 1948, after a 22-day trip. Many arrivals made the journey alone, their families having pooled their earnings to buy one ticket – a journey cost between £28–£48 (£1,044–£1,790 today). These, and the migrants who followed until 1973, were called the Windrush generation, and they came from Jamaica, Barbados, and Trinidad.

Though some migrants succeeded in finding places to live and work, others endured difficulties. British landlords often refused accommodation to Caribbean people. The migrants faced racism and discrimination and were often relegated to low-level, low-paid work. Despite being highly qualified, skilled workers in their countries of origin, migrants could often only obtain unskilled positions in iron, steel, and coal industries, or in factories. However, others joined the newly formed National Health Service and London Transport network, becoming a key part of these institutions.

Scandal and amends

In 2018, Windrush generation migrants were brought into the public eye when a report found that the UK government had denied many Caribbean migrants their legal rights, with many threatened with deportation and some actually deported. In 2020, some received compensation, but others are still fighting for their rights. Windrush Day, on 22 June, is now celebrated annually to pay homage to this generation and their contributions to Britain.

▼ **A Caribbean bus driver** and conductor at a south London bus garage. London Transport began a direct recruitment drive in the Caribbean in 1956.

"Jamaicans are a proud people. They tend to call a spade a spade. We do not think that anyone is superior to us. We were then largely law-abiding, churchgoers who respected others, honoured queen and country, and were 'more British than the English' in many ways. Britain was a real culture shock for many of us, who were mainly secondary school leavers that had come to work and/or further our education.

... A lot of us women made very unsuitable marriages, started a family, were forced to take low-paying jobs, separated from our husbands, and found ourselves trapped for decades."

Verona Franceta Pettigrew (née Bennett), a Jamaican woman who migrated to the UK in 1956, from her memoir, *The Daybook of Mrs Pettigrew*.

West Indian fans queue outside the Oval cricket ground in South London, to watch the final Test Match in the series between England and the West Indies in August 1963. Cricket became important to Caribbean communities in the UK, as they established their own cricket clubs, which became major social hubs.

ORIENT LINE
to AUSTRALIA

New lives "Down Under"

THE "WHITE AUSTRALIA" POLICY

▼ **A 1940s poster** advertises the SS *Orcades*, one of the Orient Line's fast and stylish new ships purpose-built to carry migrants from Britain to Australia.

In 1901, 78 per cent of migrants to Australia came from Britain. By 2001, Britons accounted for around 25 per cent of settlers, with the rest coming from a range of European and Asian countries, including China, the Philippines, and India. This change over the course of a century transformed Australia from a cultural outpost of Britain into a truly multicultural nation, and was the result of new immigration policies after World War II driven by economics, politics, and world affairs.

White Australia policy

In the first half of the 20th century, immigration was shaped by laws enacted by the first Australian government following federation in 1901, when the different colonies of Australia joined together. This legislation, which included the 1901 Immigration Restriction Act, sought to limit non-European migrants – especially those from Asia – amid fears that Chinese workers lured by the Australian gold rush were driving down wages and taking local jobs. The acts reflected a desire to keep Australia predominantly British, and formed the basis of what came to be known as the White Australia policy. They prohibited entry to certain ethnicities and created assessment systems that prevented almost all non-European immigration. One of the methods they used was a dictation test that required migrants to write down 50 words in a European language chosen at will by the presiding customs officer; almost all migrants failed.

It was only after World War II that attitudes to migrants began to change. Keen to solve post-war labour shortages and gain more people to defend Australia from potential attacks, the government launched a programme to increase the country's population. British migrants were still favoured,

▼ **Planning to emigrate**, a British family are given details about Australia at the High Commission, London, in 1953. More than 1 million took advantage of the assisted passage scheme on offer.

> "… Australia should be open to any nationality. We make Australia. We are all Australian."
>
> Nick Kalogeropoulos, emigrated from Greece in 1976

with assisted passage schemes attracting many "Ten Pound Poms" (nicknamed after the cost of the subsidized ticket); but more migrants were needed.

A new multiculturalism

In 1947, the Australian government agreed to resettle at least 12,000 refugees a year from camps housing Europeans displaced by World War II. These refugees – mostly from Eastern European countries such as Poland and Yugoslavia – were joined in the 1950s and 60s by migrants from the Middle East and increasing numbers from Southern Europe. Attracted by government-subsidized travel to Australia and the prospect of a better life, Italian and Greek migrants in particular established large communities in cities such as Melbourne.

The pattern of immigration changed again in the 1970s, when the White Australia policy was officially abandoned, and new criteria that evaluated skills rather than race and ethnicity were introduced. For the first time, migrants from Asia were welcomed, and tens of thousands arrived – especially from Vietnam, Laos, and Cambodia, fleeing poverty and persecution in the aftermath of the Vietnam War. The number of migrants arriving in Australia from Asia has continued to increase, with China and India being the main countries of origin today. No longer reliant on migration from Britain, Australia has become a truly diverse, multicultural society, where immigrants from all over the world participate in the labour force and add value to the economy.

▲ **Vietnamese refugees** at the Westbridge Migrant Hostel, Sydney, in 1984. The Vietnam War led to the arrival of more than 50,000 asylum seekers between 1975 and the 1980s.

▶ **Immigration to Australia** after World War II broadened from mainly British arrivals to include migrants from Eastern and Southern Europe and, later, Southeast Asia, China, and India.

Across the archipelago
INDONESIA'S TRANSMIGRATION PROGRAMME

 Oil palm plantations have replaced rainforest in large parts of Sumatra, farmed by transmigrants from Java who have been settled on the island since the 1980s. Here, young palm plants are being sprayed with pesticide.

Indonesia is the world's largest archipelago, made up of more than 17,000 islands. However, around 60 per cent of the country's population lives on the island of Java. In 1905, when the country was under Dutch colonial rule, the *transmigrasi*, or the transmigration programme, was set up, and continued by the Indonesian government after the country gained independence in 1949. Many people on the overpopulated inner islands lived in poverty; the scheme aimed to change this by developing rural areas and moving people to the more sparsely populated outer islands.

The programme was at its height in the 1970s and 1980s, under President Suharto's regime. More than 3.5 million Indonesians transmigrated between the mid-1970s and 1990, moving from the

central islands of Java, Madura, Bali, and Lombok to the outer islands, including Sumatra, Sulawesi, Kalimantan, Papua, and East Timor. These people were mostly landless farmers lured by the promise of a better life in a new part of the country.

The Indonesian government encouraged people to sign up for transmigration, offering each migrating family a house, land (typically around 2 hectares (5 acres) of newly cleared forest), money, and tools to start a small farm. In reality, however, this so-called farmland on the outer islands was often unsuitable for farming and irrigation systems were inadequate. Many transmigrants turned to other work to provide an income, and though some found lucrative jobs such as rubber cultivation, most remained poor.

Culture clashes
The programme caused problems both for the transmigrants and the Indigenous populations of the outer islands. Many transmigrants from Java, for example, ended up in South Sumatra. There, they often maintained their own language, culture, and religious practices, and did not integrate with the Indigenous communities, who viewed the transmigrants as a threat to their way of life. This was also the case in other regions that received transmigrants. Typically, Indigenous populations affected by new developments for transmigrants were not consulted or compensated, and as more people moved, resentment towards the migrants grew – sometimes with violent consequences.

◄ **Land cleared for farmland** and housing in Sumatra is destroying the rainforest and endangering native species. The land is also hard to farm, with inadequate water supplies.

In 1996 and 1997, then in 2001, thousands of migrants from the island of Madura were brutally murdered by the Dayaks, the Indigenous people of West and Central Kalimantan. Those who survived were left displaced after fleeing their homes.

Has transmigration worked?

The transmigration scheme was a failure. It had little impact on the overpopulation in the central islands, and caused environmental and social problems in the outer islands. Huge areas of rainforest were cleared to create farmland, and Indigenous land rights were often ignored in the process. The programme slowed down after President Suharto's resignation in 1998, but, despite criticism of past efforts, Indonesia reintroduced *transmigrasi* in 2019 with a plan to develop 52 transmigration sites into new cities.

▲ **Jakarta's poorest residents** live dangerously close to the water, which is polluted with rubbish. Indonesia's capital, on the island of Java, is sinking, and about 40 per cent of its land now sits below sea level.

▼ **Indonesia's large islands** are heavily populated while its many small islands remain undeveloped. Government policies have relocated inhabitants away from Java to the smaller islands.

KEY
➤ Transmigration route
Population density per sq km
■ Above 1,000
■ 116–1,000
□ 0–115

A South Vietnamese helicopter pilot and his family are evacuated during Operation Frequent Wind in April 1975. Over two days, the US evacuated more than 7,000 people from Saigon by helicopter.

"... the strength and determination to move on... is stronger than the pain and hardships that they have been through."

Tony Le Nguyen, refugee from Vietnam in 1979

THAILAND

to Japan

PHILIPPINES

to Europe

to USA and Canada

to New Zealand

to Australia

MALAYSIA

SINGAPORE

INDONESIA

Escaping war and genocide

THE INDOCHINA REFUGEE CRISIS

KEY

Vietnam

Number of Vietnamese refugees

0–50,000

50,000–100,000

more than 100,000

In 1954, following the end of the First Indochina War between the French colonial rulers and the Viet Minh (the communist independence movement), Vietnam was divided into the Democratic Republic of Vietnam (DRV), in the north, and the Republic of Vietnam (RVN) in the south. With the Viet Minh in control of the North, around 800,000 people, mostly Catholics, fled to join the non-communist South.

Although the division was intended to be temporary, war broke out between the US-backed RVN and the communist DRV. By 1965, US involvement had escalated, and by the late 1960s, 10 million South Vietnamese people had lost their homes, migrating within and outside of Vietnam.

Chaotic evacuations

In April 1975, with the RVN on the brink of defeat, US forces began to withdraw from Vietnam. The US evacuated American personnel and Vietnamese civilians from the RVN in Operation Frequent Wind, a mass helicopter evacuation.

A series of chaotic exoduses followed. Operation New Life saw around 140,000 Vietnamese evacuees move to Guam to live in temporary housing before resettling in the US and other parts of the world. In Operation Babylift, the US evacuated thousands of Vietnamese children – some fathered by US GIs – from the RVN. They were adopted by families in the US and other Western countries. Thousands of other refugees fled in small boats to nearby countries.

In the same year, communists took control of Cambodia and Laos. Between 1975 and 1979, around 2 million people were killed in the Cambodian genocide led by Pol Pot and the Khmer

Rouge (the Communist Party of Kampuchea). Around 50,000 Cambodians fled to Thailand, and 150,000 to Vietnam. Thousands more refugees followed after the Khmer Rouge regime collapsed.

Vietnamese boat people

Numbers of refugees fleeing Vietnam by sea, known as the "Vietnamese boat people", continued to rise. Travelling in small, overcrowded boats, up to 400,000 people fell victim to starvation, disease, and storms. Pirates in the Gulf of Thailand increasingly attacked boats in the 1980s, abducting, raping, and killing hundreds of people at sea. Of those who did make it, many settled in nearby Malaysia, Singapore, Thailand, and Hong Kong.

The boat people continued to migrate for two decades from 1975 to 1995, resulting in a refugee crisis and intervention from the United Nations. The Orderly Departure Programme of 1979 allowed Vietnamese people to safely migrate to other countries, reducing the numbers leaving by boat. New anti-piracy and rescue-at-sea measures also enhanced refugee protection.

At the end of the crisis, 2.5 million people are thought to have found new homes across the world from Canada and the US to the UK and Australia. Vietnamese people brought their culture with them and continue to observe *Tet* and other Vietnamese holidays.

▲ **Vietnamese refugees** were firstly moved to camps in Guam, Hong Kong, Thailand, and Malaysia. They were then resettled in Australia, New Zealand, the US, Canada, and parts of Western Europe.

▼ **A mother carries two** of her children and their belongings in baskets as she travels during an evacuation from Vietnam in 1967. Around 10,000 people made this journey.

▼ **Vietnamese boat people** arrive in Hong Kong. An estimated 200,000 refugees fled to Hong Kong in the late 1970s and 1980s.

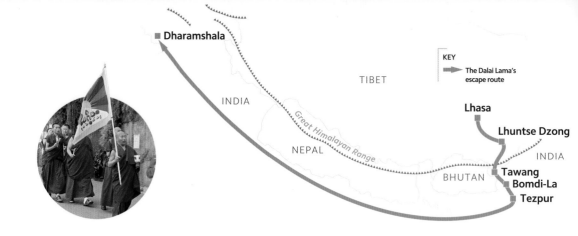

Leaving the "roof of the world"

TIBETANS IN EXILE

The people of Tibet had little contact with the rest of the world until the Chinese invasion of their country in 1950. Up to that point, Tibet had been an independent Buddhist nation with a distinct culture and way of life. Years of turmoil followed after the communist Chinese government took control, suppressing Buddhism and restricting other freedoms. In 1959, tensions and anti-Chinese sentiment culminated in a major Tibetan uprising, triggered by rumours that the Chinese government planned to abduct, arrest, or kill the 14th Dalai Lama – the spiritual and then-political leader of Tibet. The State Oracle, the Dalai Lama's advisor, urged him to flee. Indian prime minister Jawaharlal Nehru granted the Dalai Lama refugee status and permitted him to establish a government-in-exile – known as the Central Tibetan Administration (CTA) – in Dharamshala, in northern India.

Escape through the Himalayas

Between 1959 and 1970, 80,000 Tibetan refugees crossed the Himalayas to join their leader in India. The initial Tibetan immigrants were generally welcomed in India, whose government granted Tibetans land to build settlements in and around Dharamshala. They were permitted to practise their religion as well as other cultural traditions. Tibetans were also given resident permits, which allowed them to work. In 1962, the Indian army created the Special Frontier Force, which consisted mainly of Tibetan refugees, to protect the Himalayan border from China.

Meanwhile, in Tibet, the Chinese continued to suppress Tibetan Buddhism, destroying most of the 6,000 Tibetan monasteries during the Cultural Revolution that took place between 1966 and 1976. During this period, thousands of monks and nuns were imprisoned and executed.

Another wave of immigrants from Tibet arrived in India in the 1980s, when the Chinese introduced a more liberal policy, allowing more free movement. Then in 1994, the Chinese authorities reimposed restrictions on Tibetan culture and religious activities, prompting another surge of refugees, including monks and nuns escaping persecution.

Life in exile

Tibetans arriving in India in the 1980s and 1990s did not receive the same level of hospitality as the earlier immigrants, and many were denied residence permits. Moreover, the settled Tibetans in India did not wish to integrate with the new generation of arrivals, considering them "contaminated" by the Chinese; as a result, the early refugees and relatively new migrants tend to live in separate communities.

Following a crackdown by China in 2008, and more restrictions on the movement of Tibetans in recent years, the number of refugees has decreased dramatically. In India, limitations on Tibetans' rights to travel, find jobs, and own property remain controversial. However, in 2014, India introduced the Tibetan Rehabilitation Policy, which gave Tibetan refugees access to the same welfare schemes and benefits as Indian citizens.

▲ **This map shows the escape route** the Dalai Lama took from Tibet to India in 1959. Many refugees have followed in his footsteps.

▼ **Tibetan monks** living in exile in McLeod Ganj, where the Dalai Lama resides in India, march in protest against Chinese human rights abuses in Tibet.

▼ **Tibetan rebels** file out of Potala Palace, Lhasa, in 1959, forced to surrender to the Chinese after a hard-fought uprising. The palace had been the winter home of the Dalai Lama since the 7th century.

"If we go back now, though much has been preserved, it will be a new Tibet. Shangri-la is finished and gone."

Ngawang Tsultrim, member of the Council for Tibetan Education, 1985

◄ **Fleeing her country** after the Chinese occupation in 1950, a Tibetan refugee makes the long, dangerous journey on foot over the Himalayas to India, to escape religious and cultural persecution.

▲ **Ugandan Asians wait with Black Ugandans** at a bus stop outside a shopping centre in Kampala in 1972, just months before Amin's expulsion.

◄ **Ugandan Asians arrive** in the UK. They arrived with little money, granted a cash allowance of only £55 (£635 today).

"Anything we couldn't carry we had to leave. There was no question of selling our house or our business. You just had to go."

Ugandan Indian refugee Zebun Hirji

A sudden expulsion

UGANDA FORCES OUT SOUTH ASIANS

In 1972, around 50,000 people of South Asian heritage were forced to leave Uganda, accused by its new leader, Idi Amin, of "milking Uganda's money". These people, who had worked hard to establish successful businesses, were left with nothing.

Following the Scramble for Africa (see pp.190–91), the Uganda Protectorate was set up between 1894 and 1896, as part of the British Empire. Work began on the Uganda Railway, linking Mombasa (modern-day Kenya) with Uganda in 1896; the British recruited indentured workers (see pp.182–83), mostly from South Asia, to build it. Labourers were bound to work for a set length of time, but on completion of the railway in 1901, many remained in Uganda.

More South Asians migrated to work as colonial administrators and traders. Many set up businesses, having been supported by the British in securing employment, resulting in much of the Ugandan Asian population forming an urban middle class, while much of the African majority remained in lower-class roles in traditional, agricultural settings.

Migrant workers

Uganda claimed its independence from Britain in 1962, and in the years that followed, the rise of "Africanization" policies meant that Black Ugandans gained more control over economic and political infrastructure. At the same time, anti-Asian sentiment grew with the government accusing the community of disloyalty and a lack of integration. Though Ugandan Asians made up around 1 per cent of the population, they owned up to 90 per cent of Ugandan businesses. When former army commander Idi Amin overthrew Uganda's president in a military coup in 1971, he swiftly ordered the expulsion of Ugandan Asians in a bid to "transfer the economic control of Uganda into the hands of Ugandans".

Starting again

About 27,000 Ugandan Asians migrated to the UK, having received British citizenship after Uganda's independence. Others migrated to nearby nations such as Kenya, moved to India, or went further afield to Canada. In the UK, many initially struggled to find work, despite their qualifications. It was not easy – families had to seek work and get their children into schools while often facing language barriers and a cultural divide. They received a frosty reception from some British people, with warnings that there was no space for them in the crowded country. Yet through hard work many built businesses and rose to top positions in politics and the media.

In 1986, Yoweri Museveni took power in Uganda and invited exiled Ugandan Asians to return. Today, they make up less than 1 per cent of the population, but play a leading role in the country's economy once again.

▼ **This 1972 British cartoon**, entitled "Departheid", depicts Idi Amin "booting" Asians out of Uganda – from prosperity to joblessness and homelessness.

▼ **Around 50,000 Asians left Uganda** in 1972, most bound for the UK, Canada, India, and Kenya. Pakistan, Malawi, the US, and Germany each received 1,000 migrants. Only those who were Ugandan citizens were allowed to stay.

KEY

▢ Uganda

South Asian migration

➡ 0–1,000

➡ 1,000–10,000

➡ 10,000–30,000

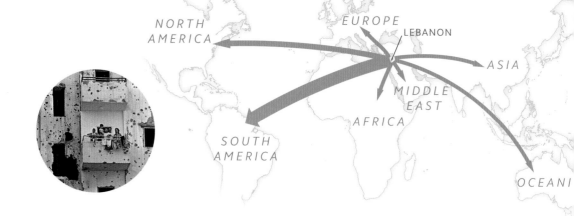

NORTH AMERICA

EUROPE

LEBANON

ASIA

MIDDLE EAST

AFRICA

SOUTH AMERICA

OCEANIA

A far-flung people

THE LEBANESE DIASPORA

The Lebanese Civil War between 1975 and 1990 resulted in the emigration of nearly 1 million people – around 40 per cent of the total pre-war population of Lebanon. Fleeing the fighting that destroyed hundreds of thousands of homes and businesses, as well as massacres by sectarian militias, refugees escaped to countries around the world, with many joining the already established Lebanese diaspora that had been growing since the mid-19th century.

Waves of emigration

Lebanon has a unique and complex cultural and religious mix. Muslims form the majority, but over one-third of the population is Christian (by far the largest Christian population in the Middle East); in both cases, the populations are split across many denominations. The small but powerful religious group, the Druze, began as a movement within Islam but became a religion in its own right. Such divisions have been a frequent source of tension over the centuries, and Lebanon's location puts it in the middle of many conflicts in the Middle East.

The first main wave of emigration from Lebanon began 1860–80, after fighting between Christians and Druze. Economic factors were also a major driver of emigration at this time, with many seeking prosperity in the expanding economies of North and South America. Emigration halted in World War I (1914–18), but resumed after the war ended. This second emigration wave included new destinations, such as Australia and West Africa.

After World War I, the Ottoman Empire broke up and the French obtained a mandate to govern Lebanon, which many Lebanese, especially

Muslims, resented. The situation improved in 1943, when Lebanon finally gained its independence and experienced a brief period of cosmopolitan prosperity. However, political unrest soon returned following the Suez Crisis (1956), the Arab–Israeli War (1967), the Lebanese Civil War, and the Israeli invasion of Lebanon (1982). Many headed to the Gulf states, where there was a rising demand for labour due to the "oil boom", or to the US, Canada, and Europe to seek better education.

Home and homeland

By the 1980s, the Lebanese diaspora was a well-established global network significantly influencing life in Lebanon, as well as overseas. Continuing ties to the homeland helped keep Lebanese culture alive in cities such as São Paulo, Brazil, while financial support flowed in the opposite direction. However, as Lebanon's governmental collapse has seen Beirut descend into civil crisis, its population left without basic necessities of power and medicine, it seems that few émigrés are likely to return.

△ **Lebanese emigration** to every continent, especially to North and South America (particularly Brazil), has resulted in a diaspora population much larger than the population in Lebanon.

▽ **Families in Lebanon's capital Beirut** besieged by Israeli forces in 1982 were already living in a city destroyed by years of continual bombing. Many fled the country to escape the conflict.

Arabic Detroit

Dearborn, near Detroit, is a Lebanese home from home, with signs in Arabic and many Lebanese restaurants and cultural institutes. Lebanese immigrants first arrived in the 1880s. More came in the 1920s to work in Detroit's motor industry, and to escape the civil war in the 1970s. People from other Arab countries live here too, forming the largest Muslim community in the US.

▲ **Inhabitants flee** from a Christian invasion of a Muslim enclave in Beirut during the civil war. The city became split along religious and ethnic lines as militia groups asserted control over different areas.

◄ **Refugees from the civil war** disembark from a US naval ship in Piraeus, Greece, in 1976. As the fighting intensified, more countries around the world admitted Lebanese migrants on humanitarian grounds.

Chongqing has a population of 16 million that is set to grow as the Chinese government's Go West campaign continues to attract more businesses to western China.

"Farmers from converted areas do not change as quickly, ... holding... to the threads that tether them to yesterday."

Maciej Leszczynski, *Life inside China's megacity Chongqing*, The Spaces, 2018

Into the cities
THE URBANIZATION OF CHINA

Once a country whose economy was based mainly on agriculture, China's rapid transformation from rural to urban began in 1958 with the Great Leap Forward campaign. It was launched by Chairman Mao Zedong, with the aim of surpassing the world's largest economies by increasing agricultural and industrial output using human labour rather than investing in factories and machinery.

In the same year the government formalized the *hukou* system, whereby they classified every resident as "agricultural" or "non-agricultural" and assigned them a living location in either a rural area or urban area. Those with non-agricultural *hukou* received more favourable benefits, such as better access to healthcare, education, and subsidized housing. It was almost impossible to move from the countryside to the city.

The Chinese government forced millions with agricultural *hukou* to move to rural communes across the country, and assigned former farmers the task of melting down scrap metal in small backyard furnaces to produce steel. The goods were poor quality, and the large-scale diversion of farm labour into small-scale industry was catastrophic. Lack of food production led to a mass famine, killing at least 20 million people.

The Open Door policy
China had long been closed to the global economy, but in 1978 the new leader Deng Xiaoping began economic reforms, opening up China to foreign businesses. He created four Special Economic Zones, with the first being Shenzhen, to attract investment from neighbouring Hong Kong's many manufacturers. The government removed workers from the fields to accommodate the city's rapid development and relaxed the *hukou* system. Throughout the 1980s millions of rural migrants from all over China poured into Shenzhen, which had been a fishing village of 30,000 inhabitants, to work in the expanding factories and construction sites. As Deng opened up further cities in the 1990s, China's urban population continued to grow.

Inequality in the cities
While large cities offered a wealth of work opportunities, many migrants from rural areas faced poor living conditions due to overpopulation and the environmental impact of industrialization. In addition, they still had agricultural *hukou* so did not have the same benefits as permanent city-dwellers. Migrant children were not given the same education as urban children, resulting in many parents leaving their children in the countryside, where the education was better. Older generations who lost farmland to cities also had difficulties adapting to urban life.

Since 1980, almost 500 million Chinese from rural areas have moved to cities, and the percentage of those living in urban areas has increased significantly, from 19 to 63 per cent. At least 15 cities in China have a population of over 10 million. Further mass movements from rural to urban areas are very likely. In 2014, China launched its New Urbanization Plan, setting out its goals for optimizing urbanization, and in 2019 it relaxed *hukou* restrictions to tackle inequality and encourage further rural to urban migration.

▲**The coastal cities** of Shenzhen, Zhuhai, Shantou, and Xiamen were designated Special Economic Zones by the Chinese government, and opened up to migrant workers in the 1980s and 1990s.

▼**A passport and temporary residence permit** are essential for all migrant workers with agricultural *hukou* planning to work in cities in China.

▼**Many migrant workers** lived in crowded dormitories like this one in Shenzhen in the 1980s. People flocked to the cities for greater work opportunities.

Searching for safety

REFUGEE CRISES IN CENTRAL AND SOUTH AMERICA

Economic factors have traditionally driven migrants from Central and South American countries to wealthier nations such as the US and Spain, whose economies have offered more jobs and opportunities. But particularly since the 1980s, a search for nearby safety has taken priority, as migrants have become refugees fleeing civil war, political upheaval, drug-related violence, natural disasters, and climate crises (see pp.260–61).

Instability and war

Civil wars and revolution between the 1960s and 1990s in El Salvador, Guatemala, and Nicaragua initiated a period of extreme violence and political and economic upheaval. The ongoing legacies of these conflicts – and the continued US "war on drugs" – are systemic corruption, poverty, and the proliferation of guns and gangs, which have allowed organized crime and the drug trade to flourish. In this climate of violence, hundreds of thousands of refugees from northern Central America leave each year to escape gang warfare, threats, and human rights abuses such as arbitrary arrests, censorship, sexual violence, and intimidation by the authorities. Natural disasters, such as Hurricane Mitch, which devastated the region in 1998, and the intensifying impact of the climate crisis have increased this flow.

Flight and displacement

Many refugees have fled north to Mexico, often contending with kidnappers and drug cartels in the hope of eventually gaining asylum in the US.

Approximately 500,000 others have sought safety in neighbouring Latin American countries, especially Panama, Belize, and Costa Rica, hoping to start new lives in places with a shared culture and language.

Internal displacement has also reached crisis level, especially in Colombia. Here, conflict between government forces, paramilitaries, guerrillas, and drug cartels has displaced more than 4.9 million, with Indigenous and Black communities particularly affected – being forced off their land to make way for lucrative crops and receiving little protection once displaced. And yet Colombia is also a destination for immigrants. With conditions worsening in neighbouring Venezuela, more than 5.6 million Venezuelans have fled violence, repression, hyper-inflation, and shortages of basic supplies – a third of whom have headed to Colombia.

Further opportunities

In other Latin American countries, such as Belize, Panama, and Costa Rica, migrants have access to emergency healthcare, basic education, and help finding housing. However, their credentials are often not recognized and many struggle to secure work that matches their skills. Many also have difficulty getting permanent legal status. Overall, however, Latin American countries have shown solidarity in accommodating such large-scale migration over a short period of time and continue to tackle the ongoing crises.

▲ **Refugees are fleeing** many Central and South American countries, with the majority seeking asylum in nearby countries.

▼ **A border crossing reopens** in 2016 between Venezuela and Colombia and thousands of Venezuelans cross to buy food and medicine.

▶ **Nicaraguan civilians flee** their neighbourhood in June 1979, as the national airforce threatens retaliation against opposition rebels in the area.

> **Peruvian villagers gather** to receive food and medical supplies in an area affected by civil warfare instigated by the Shining Path terrorist group.

"We left Venezuela because of hunger. My baby and I were both malnourished, and I was trying to breastfeed."

Mariangel Blanco, Venezuelan migrant, 2019

"We are now living in a new world."

Soviet president Mikhail Gorbachev resigns, 25 December 1991

▲Thousands queue to obtain an exit visa and a passport. The USSR finally passed a law in May 1991 granting citizens the right to travel and emigrate freely, after decades of restrictions on foreign travel.

◄Since the collapse of the USSR, Russia has seen an influx of hundreds of thousands of immigrants from countries in Asia, such as Vietnam. Rising migration is not only from former Soviet states.

A superpower collapses

MIGRATION AFTER THE FALL OF THE SOVIET UNION

KEY

- ☐ USSR
- Baltic states
- Central Asian Republics

Former Soviet States

1 Estonia	8 Armenia
2 Latvia	9 Azerbaijan
3 Lithuania	10 Uzbekistan
4 Belarus	11 Turkmenistan
5 Ukraine	12 Tajikistan
6 Moldova	13 Kyrgyzstan
7 Georgia	14 Kazakhstan

When the Soviet Union (USSR) collapsed in 1991, about 60 million people, which amounted to 20 per cent of the former USSR's population, were living outside their home countries – for example, ethnic Kazakhs living outside of Kazakhstan. They were spread out over more than 20 separate nations, from Latvia, Estonia, and Lithuania in the northwest to Kazakhstan and Kyrgyzstan in Central Asia. Over 25 million were ethnic Russians.

Population transfer and resettlement

During the Soviet era (1922–91), the authorities had moved people around the country to promote development, increase control, and "Russify" the ethnic minorities, pressing them to adopt the Russian language and culture. For example, in 1954, the USSR's premier Khrushchev launched his "Virgin Lands" Scheme, to send hundreds of thousands of ethnic Russian "volunteers" to settle and cultivate so-called "idle" areas of Kazakhstan, even though livestock breeding had been a key economic activity in Kazakhstan for centuries. By 1959, Kazakhs had become a minority in their own region, reduced to less than one-third of the population. Similar movements happened in other areas, such as Ukraine. To prevent non-Russians from forming a critical mass, the authorities moved the boundaries of many autonomous republics.

When the break up of the USSR came, the millions living in their home country were jubilant to have independence. However, for many who were far from home the future was uncertain. The forced deportations had left millions of internally displaced persons, refugees, and migrants, many desperate to be reunited with friends, families, and their former homes. Yet there were now borders and many other obstacles in their way. Despite this, migrants flowed into Russia from former Soviet states, many pushed by armed conflicts and ethnic tensions.

Post-Soviet republics

The collapse of governing structures in the former USSR initially left a power vacuum, opening the way for crime, corruption, and conflict. Border disputes still rage between Armenia and Azerbaijan over Nagorno-Karabakh, and Russia's takeover of Crimea from Ukraine has caused turmoil. There are also large differences in wealth, resulting in people from Central Asia and Siberia migrating to Moscow to seek work. However, many nations formerly under Soviet rule are beginning to thrive. Central and Eastern Europe have witnessed one of the most dramatic economic growth spurts of any region of the world, although many former USSR republics are losing a generation of young people to opportunities in the West (see pp.254–55).

▲ **The USSR** split into 15 new individual states in 1991. The creation of these new borders led to migration within the former USSR and outside it.

▼ **In August 1991**, tanks rolled into Moscow's Red Square to suppress a coup staged by Communist hardliners to oust President Gorbachev. By the end of the year, Gorbachev had resigned and the USSR had collapsed, triggering migration from former Soviet states.

Soviet aliyah

In 1989, President Gorbachev allowed Jewish people to emigrate. From 1989–2006, 1.6 million Soviet Jews and their non-Jewish family members emigrated from the former Soviet Union, mostly to Israel, but also to the US and Germany.

Freedom of movement

MIGRATION IN THE EUROPEAN UNION

In 1993, the Maastricht Treaty established the European Union (EU), joining an initial 12 nations in economic partnership. A key principle of the union was freedom of movement – the idea that people should be able to move without visas between EU countries. This became a reality in 1995 under the Schengen Agreement, a deal between Belgium, France, Germany, Luxembourg, the Netherlands, Spain, and Portugal that abolished borders between the countries and harmonized visas.

The Schengen Area has continued to expand, covering many EU member states, as well as others such as Norway, Iceland, and Switzerland. More than 400 million citizens can now travel, live, and work without visas in an area that stretches from Portugal in the southwest to Estonia in the northeast.

Balancing benefits

For a small percentage of Europeans, the abolition of internal borders has been liberating. Two million people work in a Schengen country other than their homeland, and more than 3.5 million people cross Schengen borders daily for work. Students have also benefitted from European integration, able to study in other EU nations under the Erasmus scheme. For those choosing to stay in their home country, freedom of movement may seem to have little impact, aside from easing holiday travel. Yet the blending of cultures created by open borders and the movement of so many people is powerful and growing.

The positive aspects of removing border controls are balanced by whether free movement facilitates free passage into EU countries for criminals and potential terrorists. More recently, the movement of refugees and asylum seekers has also been

brought into debate. The benefits of free movement for all are also not equal, with some countries gaining economically and demographically, and others losing out.

Push and pull

Inequalities within the EU have meant that larger, richer countries, such as Germany, have often acted as magnets for talent, while smaller countries to the east of the zone, such as Latvia and Bulgaria, have seen an exodus of both young and highly skilled people to the west. Baltic countries are now working hard to bring their diaspora home again. Some, such as Latvia, have started government programmes to attract young people back. Meanwhile Estonia has extended the concept of European identity by pioneering e-residency – a form of digital citizenship allowing non-residents to start Estonian-registered businesses from anywhere in the world. Whether in person or digitally, the efforts of these European countries continue to encourage migration and the survival of the principle of free movement.

▲ **Net migration rates** indicate which EU and Schengen countries are gaining migrants, and which are losing them. This map uses data from 2017 and therefore includes the UK.

▼ **Brussels, Belgium, the EU's "capital"**, has one of the highest populations of EU migrants, and is where the European Commission is based.

Brexit

After the UK voted to leave the EU in 2016, large numbers of Britons took to the streets. Fearing new restrictions on the flow of people, trade, and goods, protestors demanded a review of the decision. But the withdrawal was ratified, and the UK officially left the EU on 31 January 2020.

"The plan was to work for two years then go back and buy a house."

Marcin Poltorak, a Polish migrant who arrived in the UK in 2004. He was still living there in 2021.

▲ **A migrant worker** from Eastern Europe harvests broccoli in Scotland. Many farmers rely on seasonal workers travelling across the EU to help process their crops.

◀ **The city of Talinn**, in Estonia, has fostered a growing digital technology sector, hoping to lure expats home, and attract new migrants and investment from across the EU.

A family flees the village of Khanabad in northern Afghanistan in 2001, after the US launches airstrikes on Taliban positions nearby.

Fleeing the Taliban

THE AFGHAN REFUGEE CRISIS

For more than 40 years, Afghans have been forced from their homes, often never to return. Today, more than 2.6 million registered refugees – one in 10 of the world's refugees – are from Afghanistan. The Afghanistan refugee crisis began in the late 1970s as people fled over the border into Pakistan to escape the violence of the hardline communist Taraki and Amin governments. After the Soviet Union invaded in 1979, in an attempt to prolong communist rule in the country, the number of refugees escalated.

In 1989, the withdrawal of Soviet forces from Afghanistan saw some refugees return, but soon sparked a civil war that forced many into exile once more. The conflict ended in 1995 with the capture of Kabul by the Taliban, an Islamic fundamentalist regime, which imposed a harsh interpretation of sharia law, brutally stifling opposition and limiting women's rights, causing many more Afghans to flee.

Life as a refugee

By 2000, more than 6 million Afghans had migrated to neighbouring Pakistan and Iran. Any welcome they received there soon evaporated. In Pakistan, many still live in refugee camps, and as the country is not a signatory to refugee-related international agreements, their legal status is precarious. They have limited access to education, healthcare, and other basic rights, and work is hard to come by.

The situation in Pakistan reached a low point in 2014 when 132 schoolchildren were massacred in Peshawar by a Taliban cell that included two Afghans. In response, Pakistan and Iran began to repatriate refugees, with 365,000 forced to leave Pakistan in 2016. Most returnees, including the half a million assisted by the United Nations (UN)

refugee agency to go back, have found themselves in a dangerous situation. Although a US-led coalition ousted the Taliban from power in 2001, its fighters regrouped and, in August 2021, captured Kabul, toppling the US-backed government and triggering a new wave of refugees.

A state of uncertainty

The UN estimates that by 2018 more than half of Afghanistan's population had been forcibly displaced by violence at least twice. After the fall of Kabul in 2021, Western governments scrambled to evacuate Afghans who had worked for them or foreign aid organizations, while other refugees had to find their own way out. Around 9,000 fled to Pakistan in the next month, even as Pakistan's government claimed it could not accept any more. Iran, meanwhile, closed its borders to Afghans. Other nations have since stepped in to help – including the UK and Canada, each pledging to resettle 20,000, and Uganda, which agreed to host 2,000 Afghans temporarily. But for Afghans in exile and at home, the future remains uncertain.

▲ **Since the late 1970s**, large numbers of Afghans displaced by violence and war have taken shelter in the neighbouring countries of Pakistan and Iran or further afield in Europe and North America.

▼ **Afghan refugees** pile into a van headed for Pakistan in 1982, as the Soviet–Afghan War continued to take its toll on rural communities.

◀ **Some Afghan children**, like these in Peshawar, Pakistan, in 2001, have never known life outside the refugee camp in which they were born.

KEY

Number of international migrants

- 10,000,000 or over
- 5,000,000–10,000,000
- 2,500,000–5,000,000
- 1,000,000–2,500,000
- 500,000–1,000,000
- 100,000–500,000
- Less than 100,000
- No data

A world of migrants

GLOBALIZATION AND MODERN INFRASTRUCTURE

People have been exchanging goods and ideas across national boundaries for centuries, and by the 17th century, it had become possible to do business on a global scale. The late 20th century heralded a new age of globalization, brought about by innovations in digital technology, freer movement of goods and services, and the rise of transnational mega-corporations that operate across multiple countries – transcending the power of any one nation to regulate them. This rapid growth in global connectivity has been mirrored in migration.

Record migration

Since the 1980s, more and more people have moved countries, attracted by economic opportunities or driven by war or natural disasters. Revolutions in transport and information technology have made both reaching a new country and retaining links with the old one far easier. By 2020, 272 million people were living outside their birth country – an increase of more than 100 million since 2000 and the greatest surge in migration in human history.

Two-thirds of migrants live in high-income countries, where ageing populations and gaps in job markets, especially for lower-skilled jobs, create a constant demand for labour. Europe and the US together are home to 141 million migrants. Critical sectors, such as the UK's National Health Service (with one-seventh of its 1.3 million workers foreign-born) now depend on migrants. Migrants' home countries, too, rely on their labour. For example, more than 85 per cent of Filipino nurses end up working abroad, and they, along with migrant domestic servants, sent £22.5 billion in remittances in 2020, supporting families and economically fragile communities back in the Philippines. Skilled overseas workers, in particular, have benefitted from the opportunities provided by better links between markets and enhanced communications, while established migrant networks in receiving countries have made it easier for others to follow them.

Barriers and opportunities

Yet the rising number and diversity of migrants have also caused tensions: for example, German chancellor Angela Merkel's decision to welcome hundreds of thousands of Syrian refugees in 2015 helped fuel the rise of anti-immigrant parties such as the Alternative für Deutschland (AfD). And even highly skilled migrants, frequently favoured by points-based government migration schemes, often face negative public attitudes.

Globalization has not helped those displaced by war or natural disasters (which meant that in 2020 there were more than 26 million refugees), or resolved the vulnerabilities of migrant workers in informal sectors who may be exploited, but it has provided new opportunities. Education is one of these: since the 1970s, the number of people studying at institutions outside their country of birth has tripled to 2.7 million, bringing a greater familiarity with other cultures and languages, and bestowing valuable skills that can be employed to help students' home economies.

▲ **This world map** shows the percentage of each country that is made up of migrants according to a 2019 UN study.

▼ **Dean Ellis's 1960 illustration** celebrates the evolution of transport over the centuries, which has enabled people and goods to travel around the world at speed.

Digital nomads

Ever-improving mobile technology is allowing people in the digital sector, like "Chris the Freelancer" – who set up a blog giving advice on remote working – to do their jobs from anywhere in the world, rather than being tied to one location.

▲ **Protesters in London, UK**, attempt to persuade the British government to relax its anti-immigration stance and accept more refugees during the 2016 European migrant crisis.

◄ **Filipino migrant workers**, pictured enjoying their day off, now form the largest ethnic minority in Hong Kong. Many are domestic helpers, who work long hours and send most of their earnings home.

When disaster strikes

CLIMATE MIGRATION

The climate crisis is set to become the biggest cause of global migration. Human activity is causing rising temperatures – the 10 hottest years on record have all been since 2005 – which in turn fuels more extreme weather, natural disasters, and food and water shortages, and this global crisis is prompting the movement of people. So far, most migration is internal, with people typically moving from flooded coastal or rural areas to towns and cities within the same country, and often staying only temporarily. But this is likely to change in the future as the crisis intensifies.

Coastal flooding

Rising sea levels, coastal erosion, and flooding are among the most serious issues and are already forcing huge numbers of people to move. Around 10 per cent of the world's population – more than 600 million people – live in coastal areas that are less than 10 metres above sea level, putting them at risk of flooding. Densely populated, low-lying, and flood-prone, Bangladesh is one of the most vulnerable countries. It is estimated that sea level rises could trigger waves of migration from coastal areas that could affect 1.3 million Bangladeshis by 2050. Low-lying Pacific island nations such as Kiribati and Tuvalu face being at least partially submerged. Many countries have drawn up plans to relocate their most-threatened communities, and to cope with the loss of agricultural land.

A global crisis

In other parts of the world, droughts and water shortages exacerbated by climate change are driving wider population movements. Millions of people in the Dry Corridor of Central America (an arid zone that stretches from southern Mexico through Guatemala, El Salvador, Honduras, and Nicaragua) have suffered major crop failures due to droughts and erratic rainfall. This is one of the key drivers of migration from the region to the US. Prolonged droughts in the Horn of Africa – which encompasses Somalia, Ethiopia, Eritrea, and Djibouti – have forced around 1.8 million people from their homes in recent years. Most now live in overcrowded camps with little access to even the most basic services.

The climate crisis has also been linked to more frequent and powerful storms. For example, two tropical cyclones – Idai and Kenneth – struck Mozambique in quick succession in 2019, causing a humanitarian disaster that displaced around 2.2 million people. Many others around the world are likely to experience similar situations over the decades to come.

The 1951 Refugee Convention does not class people who are forced to leave their homes because of extreme weather as refugees. However, in 2020, the UN ruled it unlawful for governments to return people who are seeking asylum from countries where the climate crisis threatens their lives, setting an important precedent.

▲ **Different climate disasters** are a threat to people around the world. This map shows some major areas of concern.

▼ **The melting of ice caps** leads to rising sea levels, causing flooding and erosion of coastal areas, and making hurricanes more frequent.

▼ **Migrants**, mostly from Honduras, have been driven from their homes by hurricanes and flooding. This picture shows them headed to the US.

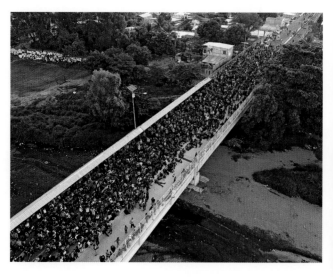

A dust storm rages at a refugee camp in Dadaab, Kenya, in 2011. Somalian refugees fled here following a terrible drought affecting the Horn of Africa. It is estimated that the lives of 12 million people were threatened.

"We were farmers before but then we had drought... In the end we had nothing left."

Hadija Kiona, farmer in the Tana River region, Kenya, 2011

"I left [Tuvalu] in 2010. When I came back I immediately noticed the difference. The heat is sometimes unbearable now, and the erosion is also dramatic. Some of my favourite spots have disappeared.

I feel like [Tuvalu] is a part of who I am and I shouldn't just run away from it, even though it's disappearing. To just abandon it at such a time as this, when it is hurting – I don't feel comfortable. I don't feel like I can do that."

Tapua Pasuna, a native of Tuvalu, a Pacific Island country, and Miss Tuvalu 2019. Pasuna is also an ambassador working to protect the ocean and raise awareness about climate change.

People swim through the water that has flooded parts of the Pacific island of Kiribati. Like Tuvalu, Kiribati's residents face the prospect of rising sea levels destroying their homes. The governments of these "drowning" islands have encouraged their people to "migrate with dignity", but many are reluctant to leave, choosing instead to turn to measures such as temporary sea walls to keep the island afloat.

Independent Africa

INTRA-AFRICAN MIGRATIONS

▼**Lagos, Nigeria**, is one of Africa's few "megacities". With a steady influx of migrants from all over Nigeria and nearby states, it is one of the world's fastest-growing cities.

Since the 1960s, following the independence of many African nations, migration within and from the continent has increased significantly, influenced by a range of economic, social, and environmental factors. Although poverty, drought, and violent conflict have been driving forces in some cases, studies indicate that most Africans move for aspirational reasons, such as higher education and employment. The notion that African migration is essentially driven by poverty is further contradicted by the fact that most migrants originate from the relatively wealthier countries in North Africa and coastal West Africa, while the poorer sub-Saharan states have lower levels of emigration.

Migration within Africa

Intra-African migration has grown steadily since African countries gained independence from colonial rule. Six million people migrated within Africa in 1960; by 2017, this number had grown to around 19.5 million. Studies in 2019 showed that 53 per cent of African-born migrants were living elsewhere within the African continent. Economic and social developments on the continent have led to improvements in education, material resources, and access to media and online networks, while better infrastructure and transportation have made travel easier and safer than ever before.

►**Gibe III dam** in Ethiopia has doubled the country's output of electricity. But Indigenous groups, who relied on the river's seasonal flooding to grow crops, have had to move to survive.

One major "pull factor" of internal African migration is the development of industries in particular countries, resulting in demand for labour. South Africa, with its agriculture, financial services, telecommunications, mining, and construction industries, is a key destination for African migrants. Other African countries with the highest influx of intra-continental migration include Nigeria, Africa's main oil producer, and Côte d'Ivoire, whose lucrative cash-crop industry attracts seasonal migrants.

One of the most transformative types of intra-African migration has been the movement from rural to urban areas, resulting in rapid African urbanization and growth. Several African cities are among the world's largest and fastest growing.

The Rwandan genocide in 1994 led to the mass exodus of more than 2 million Rwandans to neighbouring countries. These refugees are waiting to cross the border into the Democratic Republic of Congo (formerly Zaire).

New destinations

Since the late 1980s, African migration patterns have shown signs of change. Although intra-African migration remains high, the migration intensity (its rate based on the total population) has decreased, possibly as a result of rising nationalism and the demarcation of borders, restricting free movement.

There has also been a marked rise in emigration from Africa to other continents. While in previous decades Africans tended to emigrate to European destinations (usually former colonizers such as the UK and France), increasingly restrictive immigration policies in these countries have led many migrants to look elsewhere. Today, migration is growing rapidly towards new destinations, including the US and Canada, where visa applications depend on skills and education, and fast-growing economies in Asia, where the demand for labour is high.

Johannesburg
THE CITY OF GOLD

Johannesburg is a young city in an area with a long history. Some of the earliest hominin skeletons ever discovered – including one dating back 3.67 million years – came from the Sterkfontein cave system, northwest of the city. From the Stone Age onwards, the region was inhabited by San hunter-gatherers, and by around 1100 CE, Bantu-speaking peoples had settled in the area, founding villages and engaging in mining.

In the 1830s, Dutch-speaking settlers known as Boers arrived during the Great Trek (see pp.162–63), seizing land and forcibly displacing Indigenous peoples. Johannesburg was founded in 1886 after gold was discovered on a farm in the region, then known as the South African Republic or Transvaal. The world's biggest gold rush was soon underway, drawing people from far and wide. Within a decade, Johannesburg had a population of more than 100,000 and was nicknamed the "City of Gold".

Overcoming segregation

After victory in the Boer War (1899–1902), the British brought thousands of Chinese indentured workers to fill labour shortages in the mines. Racist white policies later forced the Chinese to return, and they were replaced by Black migrant workers. Racial segregation, oppression, and white minority rule – already deeply rooted – were further entrenched in Johannesburg during apartheid (1948–94), when racial groups were kept apart by law.

Johannesburg has continued to grow, partly due to the arrival of migrants from African countries, including Zimbabwe, Nigeria, Malawi, and Tanzania. Despite enduring bouts of xenophobic violence, migrants make up an estimated 6.7 per cent of the city's population, and have played a large part in the growth and social dynamism of Johannesburg today.

▲▲ **Beads are made and sold** at the Lesedi Cultural Village just outside the city, giving visitors an insight into the Pedi, Zulu, Xhosa, Basotho, and Ndebele cultures.

▲ **South Africa's Hindu community** celebrate Diwali at a Johannesburg temple. Many of their ancestors were indentured workers brought over in the 19th century.

▶ **Murals on a power station** in Soweto were created by South African artists to celebrate the country's diverse culture. This one marks local Black history and includes the Soweto String Quartet, a typical Black township, and former president Nelson Mandela.

> "All roads lead to Johannesburg. If you are white or if you are Black, they lead to Johannesburg. If the crops fail, there is work in Johannesburg..."
>
> Alan Paton, *Cry, the Beloved Country*, 1948

CULTURAL INFLUENCES

Sotho-Tswana pastoralists

The fields of the Sotho-Tswana pastoralists of the 11th century are depicted here, with their traditional farming methods. These Bantu-speaking peoples moved west from 1100–1300 CE into what is now Gauteng, the province surrounding Johannesburg. They built large settlements encircled by stone walls, many of which were excavated in the 19th century.

Voortrekker settlements

Dutch-speaking settlers migrated into the interior of South Africa in the 1830s following tensions with the British in the Cape Colony. Known as the Great Trek, it led to the founding of several Boer republics, including Transvaal. Constitution Hill (below) is the site of an old prison fort built by Boer settlers in 1892.

South African miners

Migrant workers took to the mines of Transvaal following the discovery of vast gold reserves in Witwatersrand in the 1880s. Coming from across the south of the continent, all faced low wages, racism, and segregation. Mines are still in existence around Johannesburg today, and many facing poverty have resorted to illegal mining in dangerous conditions.

British colonizers

The Supreme Court building is an example of Beaux-Arts architecture, using symmetry and Greek and Roman decorative elements such as columns. This grand building was constructed under British colonial rule. Such monumental structures marked the city's new status as an outpost of the British Empire, following the British victory in the Boer War in 1902.

Zimbabwean migrants

During the 1980s, many Ndebele people arrived in the city from Zimbabwe after fleeing the Gukurahundi, a series of ethnically-based massacres. Economic and political crises from 2000 prompted many more Zimbabweans to cross the border. Here, a Zimbabwean refugee artist, Lovemore Kupeta, hangs his work on a fence in the suburb of Sandton, Johannesburg.

Ethiopian Christians

A Christmas mass held at the Tewahedo Holy Trinity church in Johannesburg is attended by Ethiopian Orthodox Christians. Escaping conflict, asylum seekers and migrants have built a community in the city, with Ethiopian shops and restaurants in the Jeppestown neighbourhood, which has been nicknamed "Little Ethiopia".

A Gulf of opportunities

SOUTH ASIAN MIGRANT WORKERS

The oil-rich Gulf states in the Middle East are home to a large proportion of the world's migrant workers. When oil prices skyrocketed during the 1970s, wealth poured into the region. Gulf countries began improving infrastructure and building schools, hospitals, and houses, and the demand for labour increased dramatically.

Limited by their small populations, Gulf states looked to attract both qualified experts and construction workers to execute these huge projects. Enticed by the lucrative salaries on offer, men from southern Asia began to flock to the Middle East, firstly from India and Pakistan, and then from Sri Lanka, Nepal, and Bangladesh. Many were driven by poverty at home, with the struggling economies of their countries unable to generate enough jobs for their expanding populations. Work in the Gulf was often seen as an insurance policy against crop failure, or a fast way to pay off family debt. By the 1980s, Gulf households had become wealthier and wanted live-in helpers, which led many Asian women, too, to move for work.

A road well travelled

Today, workers from southern Asia make up 15 million of the 35 million migrants living in the Gulf, Lebanon, and Jordan. To get there, many pay exorbitant fees to recruitment agencies, which often offer very different jobs from those the migrants end up with. Yet, the promise of higher wages continues to appeal. In Saudi Arabia and the UAE, low-skilled Indian labourers can expect to earn 50 per cent more than they would at home. Migrant workers tend to send most of their salary home to their families, enabling them, for example,

to build a house or pay school fees. In 2018 alone, remittances (money sent) from the Gulf to South Asia totalled more than $78 billion (£58.5 billion).

Poor working conditions

Salaries may be higher in the Middle East, but the work is often difficult, dangerous, and in some cases, deadly. During a decade of preparations for the 2022 World Cup in Qatar, more than 6,500 migrant workers died. Working hours are long, and living conditions, poor. Unpaid wages are commonplace, as are violence and sexual abuse by employers who are rarely prosecuted.

Many blame poor conditions and the high death toll on the *kafala* (sponsorship) system, which exists in the Gulf, Jordan, and Lebanon. Under the system, a migrant worker's residency is bound to an employer or sponsor. Workers typically have their passports confiscated and cannot change jobs or leave the country without their sponsor's permission, leading some to equate the system with modern slavery. The situation is particularly bad for migrant domestic workers, usually women, who are isolated in homes.

Jordan and Lebanon also restrict foreign workers' career options, barring them from professions such as engineering and medicine, to ensure that they fill lower-skilled jobs that the locals do not want to do. These rules apply not only to South Asian workers but to the populations of displaced refugees from elsewhere in the Middle East.

▲ **Since the 1970s**, a steady stream of workers have left southern Asian countries, including India and Nepal, for the Middle East. The origins and destinations of these migrants can be worked out by tracing the flow of remittances.

▼ **Working high above the ground** in intense heat, these migrants are constructing the steel framework of a building in Dubai's finance district.

▼ **Purpose-built labour camps** such as this one in Dubai, UAE, typically house migrant workers. Most are from poor backgrounds and work long hours as unskilled labourers.

"I regret coming here but what to do? We were compelled to come just to make a living..."

Nepalese migrant worker, Qatar, 2013

▲ **Many of the Gulf's iconic skyscrapers** have been built by foreign construction workers, who often cannot afford to return home once their contracts have ended.

Nepalese migrants

Many of the Gulf's migrants come from Nepal. Mostly men, Nepali migrants often end up working in the construction industry. They send much of what they earn back to their families in Nepal, boosting the Nepalese economy. The few women that migrate from Nepal tend to work as domestic helpers. However, in 2017, Nepal banned its citizens from travelling to the Gulf for domestic work in an attempt to guard against abuse and exploitation.

"We felt maybe it's our turn to die. But we didn't want to die. So we made up our minds to leave."

Sahar, a Syrian refugee in Lebanon, 2021

A Syrian boy tries to cool off at a refugee camp in Idlib, Syria. Temperatures can reach up to 43°C (109°F) in the day.

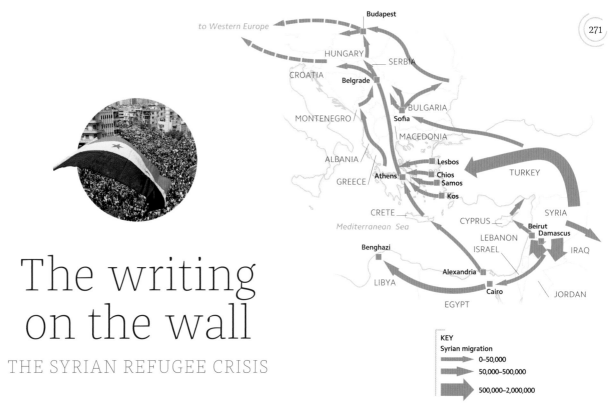

to Western Europe

KEY
Syrian migration

→ 0–50,000

⇒ 50,000–500,000

➡ 500,000–2,000,000

The writing on the wall

THE SYRIAN REFUGEE CRISIS

From 2010, a series of pro-democracy protests, known as the Arab Spring, swept across the Middle East and North Africa. A year later, inspired by regime changes in Tunisia and Egypt, a Syrian teenager scrawled, "It's your turn, Doctor" across a wall in the city of Deraa, Syria. The graffiti, which challenged Syria's President Bashar al-Assad, landed the teenager and his friends in jail, where they were tortured. When peaceful protestors spilled onto Deraa's streets, security forces opened fire.

Civil war and displacement

Huge demonstrations across Syria followed. Assad's response was to kill hundreds of demonstrators and imprison many more. Meanwhile, defectors from the military formed the Free Syrian Army in a bid to overthrow the government. The violence escalated, resulting in civil war.

The conflict enflamed existing divisions, with members of different sects of Islam (Sunni, Shia, and Alawite), as well as Kurds and jihadists, all vying for political power. The US called for Assad to step down, while Russia and China vetoed UN resolutions that would have condemned his actions. To date, the civil war (which officially began in March 2011) has killed around 500,000 people, 55,000 of them children.

The war has also forced record numbers of people from their homes. Some 6.7 million have been displaced within Syria, and those who remain face desperate conditions: around 95 per cent lack adequate healthcare, and 70 per cent have no regular access to clean water. With the economy in tatters, 80 per cent of Syrians now live in poverty.

A further 6.6 million have fled the country. Of those, approximately 5.6 million have remained in the Middle East or gone to nearby countries in North Africa. There are about 3.6 million in Turkey, almost 1 million in Lebanon, over 600,000 in Jordan, and 250,000 in Iraq. Over 150,000 settled in North African countries, including Egypt and Libya. In total, over half the Syrian population has been displaced.

Movement to Europe

Many Syrian refugees in the Middle East longed to return home but lost hope as violence continued to tear their country apart. Seeking a fresh start, over 1 million Syrian refugees migrated to Europe. Some of them arrived by land, crossing Turkey's border with Bulgaria, but most went by boat, either sailing across the Aegean Sea from Turkey to Greece, or across the Mediterranean Sea from Libya to Italy.

With few legal routes open, many refugees had no choice but to turn to smuggler gangs. The journey is costly and perilous, with large

▲ **In 2011, Syrian refugees** made their way to the nearby countries of Turkey, Lebanon, Jordan, Iraq, Egypt, and Libya. From there, thousands moved on to Europe, many to Greece, Italy, and Bulgaria.

▼ **Thousands of Syrians** gather in the capital Damascus to show support for President Bashar al-Assad, who faced a wave of dissent in 2011.

▼ **Syrian Kurds** cross the border into Turkey to escape attacks by the Islamic State (IS) group in 2014.

groups crammed into small rubber dinghies and flimsy wooden boats: in April 2015, 800 people died in the largest refugee shipwreck on record. Many refugees suffered abuse and exploitation by the smugglers, while some were taken hostage and released only if their families paid huge ransoms. In addition, both Turkish and Greek forces killed Syrian refugees on their borders.

By 2021, over 70 per cent of Syrian refugees in Europe had settled in just two countries: Germany (almost 600,000) and Sweden (115,000). A further 100,000 went beyond Europe, to Canada and the US.

Refugee camps

In 2021, about 8 per cent of Syrian refugees lived in camps, many of which are run by the United Nations (UN) and are often vast and underfunded. The largest camp for Syrian refugees is Zaatari in north Jordan, just 12 km (7½ miles) from the Syrian border. With war continuing to rage, return seems unlikely for most residents – what began as a temporary fix is becoming a permanent settlement. At the peak of the conflict, Zaatari was home to 150,000 Syrians, making it Jordan's fourth-largest city. Since then, its population has fallen, but in 2021, some 80,000 Syrians still lived there. However, less than 20 per cent of Zaatari's residents have work permits, so many are forced to work illegally or survive on limited aid. One such resident was Bassam Alhamden, who fled to Jordan with his family in 2013 to escape the airstrikes, which left them without electricity, water, and food. However, life in the camp was not much easier: there was no electricity, fruit, or vegetables, and no schooling.

Meanwhile, the EU's migration policy, which restricts refugee intake into the EU, has left many Syrians stuck in refugee camps in Europe. One such camp was Moria, on the Greek island of Lesbos. Before it burnt down in 2020, Moria was Europe's largest camp, and the living conditions were atrocious. About 20,000 people lived under tarpaulins strung between olive trees, the muddy ground was strewn with rubbish, and there was no electricity and little water.

Life outside the camps

For those refugees living outside the camps, life is also frequently challenging and precarious. Families often have to share cramped accommodation, sometimes in non-residential structures, such as garages, shops, or farm buildings. Many live in

extreme poverty and lack basic amenities. Although many of the refugees are highly educated (38 per cent of Syrian refugees in Europe have a university degree), many experience difficulties finding work.

Despite facing great hardship, Syrian refugees have generally held on to their culture, which is helping many to get back on their feet. Syrian restaurants, for example, now feature in a number of European cities. Imad Alarnab is just one example of a successful refugee restaurateur. After fleeing Damascus in 2015, he made his way to Calais, where he cooked for fellow refugees. He then moved to London, was granted asylum, and in time opened his own restaurant: Imad's Syrian Kitchen, in the West End.

▲ **Refugees arrive safely** on the island of Lesbos in October 2015, having sailed across the Aegean Sea from Turkey. While more than 400,000 refugees, mostly Syrians and Afghans, fled to Greece in 2015, dozens drowned as they attempted the crossing.

BMW trains refugees

A Syrian refugee (right), shown here with his mentor, joined BMW's "Work Here!" programme in 2015. BMW saw the migrants' arrival as a chance to fill vacant positions at a time of low unemployment, and devised the programme to help 500 qualified refugees integrate into the German workplace.

Around 1 million Syrian refugees have migrated to Lebanon. One-third are in camps in the Bekaa Valley, along the country's border with Syria. Living conditions are basic, and winters are extremely cold.

"The brutality of the civil war forced my family to leave [our] house and to start the journey to be refugees."

Shafaq, refugee in Lebanon's Bekaa camp, 2017

▲ **Kazakh nomads use golden eagles** to hunt foxes, wild cats, hares, and wolves for their fur during the harsh winters in Western Mongolia. The ancient art of falconry is passed down through the generations.

◄ **Roma people in Turkey** celebrate the arrival of spring with the festival of Kakava, which includes horse races, dancing, and music. Revellers leap over a bonfire to gain protection from the "evil eye".

Life on the move

MODERN NOMADIC COMMUNITIES

For some cultures, such as the Bedouin, migration is a way of life and always has been. For others, including many Gypsy, Roma, and Traveller (GRT) communities, moving from place to place is a matter of survival in the face of discrimination, hostility, and often violence from society at large. Yet despite the prospect of being marginalized, more and more people are now choosing a life on the move.

Since humans formed the first farming settlements about 10,000 years ago, only a few cultures have sustained a nomadic lifestyle. Of these, the Roma – who include Romani people, who arrived in Britain in the 16th century – make up the largest nomadic ethnic minority group in Europe. Descended from people who migrated from northern India as far back as the 6th century (see pp.92–93), they speak one language, though each subgroup has its own dialect. Irish Travellers, who originated in Ireland around the 12th century and later migrated to Britain and the US, also speak their own language, known as Shelta.

For GRT communities, life revolves around the extended family and its hierarchy, and they tend to marry young. They traditionally travelled around, and some still do, but government policies and years of oppression have led many to live in settled communities. Even so, forced evictions remain common, as with the Dale Farm evictions in Essex, UK, in 2011, when 80 Traveller families were made to leave their homes for breaching planning laws.

Life on the edge

In the Middle East and North Africa, Bedouin (from the Arabic for "desert dweller") have lived a nomadic existence for thousands of years. Like GRT people, many Bedouin now live in villages, towns, and cities, but others retain the pastoral way of life, herding camels and goats across desert areas in search of grazing land. Meanwhile, in remote Western Mongolia, Kazakh nomads move their herds up to six times a year, building temporary camps each time they relocate. But these nomadic communities are increasingly threatened by extreme weather and livestock diseases, and many have moved to cities.

New nomads

The nomadic lifestyle may not be easy, but many people are now choosing to adopt it. Technological developments, along with freedom of movement in some regions, have enabled many to become "digital nomads", people who work remotely, anywhere in the world.

Others are being forced into a nomadic existence. Unaffordable housing, insecure work, insufficient pensions, high medical bills, and lack of social care provision have pushed many Americans out of their homes and into cars, camper vans, and mobile homes. Often in their sixties and seventies, they have become a nomadic workforce, travelling across the US to provide low-wage, seasonal labour for multinational companies, as depicted in the Oscar-winning film *Nomadland*, 2020.

▲ **Only a handful of nomadic cultures** exist today. GRT communities are distributed around the world, whereas Bedouin and Kazakh nomads have kept to their traditional heartlands.

▼ **Bedouin women cross the road** on donkeys in the city of Be'er Sheva, Israel. Many nomads have been displaced since the Israeli government brought in new laws restricting Bedouin settlements in the Negev Desert.

> "Becoming a nomad is about, for many of us, going through the darkness of the tunnel, looking for the light at the other end."
>
> Bob Wells, American nomad, 2021

INDEX

ACKNOWLEDGMENTS

DK would like to thank Anna Fischel for editorial assistance; Katie Cavanagh for design assistance; Alexandra Beeden for proofreading; Helen Peters for indexing; Subhashree Bharati for cartography; Mrinmoy Mazumdar for technical assistance. This title was created with support from the DK Diversity, Equity & Inclusion community. In particular, special thanks goes to Pamela Afram and Abigail Mitchell for originating this title.

The publisher would also like to thank the following for their kind permission to reproduce their photographs:

Key: a-above; b-below/bottom; c-centre; f-far; l-left; r-right; t-top

2 Sanna Dullaway: FPG / Hulton Archive / Getty Images. **4 Alamy Stock Photo:** Album (tr). **5 Alamy Stock Photo:** Art Collection 2 (tr). **Getty Images:** De Agostini / DEA / G. Nimatallah (tl). **6 Alamy Stock Photo:** Heritage Image Partnership Ltd / The Print Collector (tl). **Photo Scala, Florence:** Smithsonian American Art Museum / Art Resource / Newell, James Michael (tr). **7 Getty Images:** Hulton Archive / Fred Ramage (t). **8 Alamy Stock Photo:** American Photo Archive. **10 Alamy Stock Photo:** World History Archive. **12 Alamy Stock Photo:** DU Photography (br); Natural History Museum, London (bl). **13 Alamy Stock Photo:** Heritage Image Partnership Ltd / Werner Forman Archive (br). **Shutterstock.com:** chrisdaviez (bl). **14 Alamy Stock Photo:** World History Archive (tc). **Science Photo Library:** Richard Bizley (br). **15 Science Photo Library:** John Bavaro Fine Art. **16 Dreamstime.com:** Neil Harrisonf (tc). **16–17 Alamy Stock Photo:** Album (b). **17 Alamy Stock Photo:** Natural History Museum, London (t). **18–19 Alamy Stock Photo:** DU Photography. **18 Alamy Stock Photo:** Dawn Black (tl). **19 Getty Images:** Lisa Maree Williams (br). **20–21 Shutterstock.com:** chrisdaviez. **22 Alamy Stock Photo:** Sabena Jane Blackbird (bl). **Shutterstock.com:** W. Scott McGill (tc). **23 LookatSciences:** Reconstruction: Elisabeth Daynes / Photo: Sylvain Entressangle,. **24 Kenneth Geiger. 25 Getty Images:** De Agostini Picture Library (br); Chris Gorman (tc). **26 Alamy Stock Photo:** Heritage Image Partnership Ltd / Werner Forman Archive (br); World History Archive (tc). **27 Alamy Stock Photo:** Falkensteinfoto (bl); INTERFOTO / Personalities (bc). **© The Metropolitan Museum of Art:** Fletcher Fund, 1947 (br). **Museum of Fine Arts, Boston:** Gift of Landon T. and Lavinia Clay in honor of Malcolm Rogers (cl). **28 Alamy Stock Photo:** IanDagnall Computing (bc); Chris Wood (t); Science History Images / Photo Researchers (bl). **Getty Images:** De Agostini / DEA / G. Dagli Orti (br). **29 4Corners:** Stefano Torrione (br). **Alamy Stock Photo:** Melvyn Longhurst (bl); Xinhua / Meng Tao (tl). **Dreamstime.com:** Evren Kalinbacak (cla). **TopFoto:** Roger Viollet (bc). **30 Alamy Stock Photo:** Chris Hellier. **32 Getty Images:** De Agostini / DEA / G. Nimatallah (bl). **© The Metropolitan Museum of Art:** Rogers Fund, 1930 (br). **33 Alamy Stock Photo:** The Picture Art Collection (bl). **Science Photo Library:** Sheila Terry (br). **34–35 Getty Images:** De Agostini / DEA / G. Nimatallah (b). **34 Alamy Stock Photo:** Azoor Photo (tc). **35 Getty Images:** Universal Images Group / Universal History Archive (tc). **36 Alamy Stock Photo:** Inge Johnsson. **37 Alamy Stock Photo:** Chris Hellier (tr); Ferdinando Piezzi (br). **38 Alamy Stock Photo:** Danita Delimont / Russ Bishop (br). **Wikimedia:** Yanajin33 / National Museum of Ethnology, Osaka (tc). **39 Alamy Stock Photo:** Album (cl); Douglas Peebles Photography (bc); Craig Ellenwood (br). **The University Of Auckland:** (bl). **40 Bridgeman Images:** © Look and Learn / Illustration for Geologische Bilder der Vorwelt und der Jetztwelt by Ferdinand von Hochstetter (J F Schreiber, 1873) (tl). **Getty Images:** Hulton Archive / Heritage Images / Fine Art Images (br). **41 Dreamstime.com:** Daboost. **42 Getty Images:** De Agostini / DEA / A. Dagli Orti (tc). **42–43 Dreamstime.com:** Beibaoke1 (b). **43 Getty Images:** Hulton Archive / Print Collector / Ann Ronan Pictures (br). **44 Alamy Stock Photo:** Classic Image (b); Lanmas (t). **45 Alamy Stock Photo:** Peter Horree (tc); Prisma Archivo (br). **46 Alamy Stock Photo:** David Levenson. **47 Alamy Stock Photo:** CPA Media Pte Ltd / Pictures From History (tc); Heritage Image Partnership Ltd / Sites & Photos / Samuel Magal (br). **48–49 Alamy Stock Photo:** agefotostock / Javier Larrea. **50–51 © The Metropolitan Museum of Art:** Rogers Fund, 1930 (b). **50 © The Metropolitan Museum of Art:** Gift of Norbert Schimmel Trust, 1989 (tc). **51 Dreamstime.com:** Maurice Brand (tr). **52 Alamy Stock Photo:** Christopher Scott (bl). **© The Metropolitan Museum of Art:** The Michael C. Rockefeller Memorial Collection, Gift of Nelson A. Rockefeller, 1965 (tc). **53 Alamy Stock Photo:** Artokoloro (bc); Ian Shaw (cl). **Getty Images:** De Agostini Picture Library (br). **54 NARA National Museum:** Tanzan-jinja. **55 Alamy Stock Photo:** Malcolm Fairman (br). **© The Metropolitan Museum of Art:** The Harry G. C. Packard Collection of Asian Art, Gift of Harry G. C. Packard, and Purchase, Fletcher, Rogers, Harris Brisbane Dick, and Louis V. Bell Funds, Joseph Pulitzer Bequest, and The Annenberg Fund Inc. Gift, 1975 (tc). **56 Alamy Stock Photo:** Pictures Now (bc). **Getty Images:** De Agostini / DEA / A. De Gregorio (tc). **57 Alamy Stock Photo:** Granger Historical Picture Archive, NYC (t). **58 Alamy Stock Photo:** The Picture Art Collection (bl). **Dreamstime.com:** Chuyu (br). **Getty Images:** De Agostini / DEA / G. Dagli Orti (bc); The Image Bank Unreleased / Tuul & Bruno Morandi (t). **59 Alamy Stock Photo:** Imaginechina-Tuchong (tl); Peter Treanor (bc). **Dreamstime.com:** Presse750 (bl). **Getty Images:** China Photos (cla); Moment / Weiming Chen (br). **60 Alamy Stock Photo:** Peter Horree (bc); The Picture Art Collection (br). **Bridgeman Images:** (tr); © Museum of London (bl). **Getty Images:** Hulton Archive / Heritage Images (cr). **61 Getty Images:** Universal Images Group / Prisma by Dukas (br). **62–63 Science Photo Library:** Sheila Terry (t). **62 Getty Images:** De Agostini / DEA / A. De Gregorio (b). **63 Alamy Stock Photo:** The Print Collector / Heritage Images / CM Dixon (br). **64 Alamy Stock Photo:** CPA Media Pte Ltd / Pictures From History. **66 Alamy Stock Photo:** www.BibleLandPictures.com / Zev Radovan (bl). **Getty Images:** Hulton Fine Art Collection / Art Images (br). **67 Getty Images:** Hulton Archive / Heritage Images / Fine Art Images (br). **Photo Scala, Florence:** The Morgan Library & Museum / Art Resource, NY (bl). **68 Dreamstime.com:** Heritage Pictures (tc). **69 akg-images:** (b). **Alamy Stock Photo:** North Wind Picture Archives (t). **70 Alamy Stock Photo:** www.BibleLandPictures.com / Zev Radovan. **71 Alamy Stock Photo:** imageBROKER / BAO (bl). **Getty Images:** De Agostini / DEA / A. Dagli Orti (tr). **72–73 Bridgeman Images:** © Edinburgh University Library / Rashid al-Din (1247–1318); 'History of the World'; attributed to the Luhrasp Master and perhaps another hand (b). **72 National Commission for Museums and Monuments, Lagos, Nigeri:** (tc). **73 Bridgeman Images:** © Dirk Bakker (cra). **74–75 Getty Images:** Hulton Fine Art Collection / Art Images. **75 Alamy Stock Photo:** Neil Bowman (tr); Peter Horree (br). **76–77 Alamy Stock Photo:** John Warburton-Lee Photography / Nigel Pavitt. **78 Alamy Stock Photo:** Heritage Image Partnership Ltd / Werner Forman Archive / National Maritime Museum,Greenwich (tc); The History Collection (br). **79 akg-images:** Roland and Sabrina Michaud. **80 Alamy Stock Photo:** Dallet-Alba (bl). **Bridgeman Images:** © Brooklyn Museum of Art / Gift of Beatrice Riese (tr). **81 Alamy Stock Photo:** Heritage Image Partnership Ltd / © Fine Art Images. **82 Alamy Stock Photo:** Historic Collection (bc); Xinhua / Khalil Dawood (cla); The Print Collector (bl); Volgi archive (br). **Getty Images:** Moment / Rasoul Ali (tl). **83 Alamy Stock Photo:** arabianEye FZ LLC / Rasoul Ali (br); Images & Stories (t); Science History Images (bl). **Getty Images:** Hulton Archive / Fox Photos / J A Freakley (bc). **84 Alamy Stock Photo:** Tatiana Morozova (br). **© The Trustees of the British Museum. All rights reserved:** (bl). **© The Metropolitan Museum of Art:** Gift of J. Pierpont Morgan, 1917 (cra). **Peabody Museum of Archaeology & Ethnology Harvard University:** Gift of the Estate of Dr. Lloyd Cabot Briggs, 1975, 975-32-50 / 1192 (bc). **85 Alamy Stock Photo:** Hemis.fr / Franck Charton (tc). **Getty Images:** Corbis Historical / Photo Josse / Leemage (br). **86 Alamy Stock Photo:** Heritage Image Partnership Ltd / Index. **87 Alamy Stock Photo:** Science History Images / Photo Researchers (br). **Getty Images:** Universal Images Group / Godong (tc). **88 Dorling Kindersley:** Universitets Oldsaksamling, Oslo / Peter Anderson (tc). **Photo Scala, Florence:** The Morgan Library & Museum / Art Resource, NY (br). **89 © The Trustees of the British Museum. All rights reserved. Getty Images:** LightRocket / Wolfgang Kaehler (clb); LightRocket / Roberto Machado Noa (br). **90 Alamy Stock Photo:** The Picture Art Collection. **91 Alamy Stock Photo:** Michael Brooks (tc). **Wikimedia:** Michel Wolgemut, Wilhelm Pleydenwurf (br). **92 Alamy Stock Photo:** The History Collection (tc). **Getty Images:** Universal Images Group / Sepia Times (bl). **93 Burgerbibliothek of Bern. 94 Alamy Stock Photo:** Album (br). **Getty Images:** Hulton Archive / Heritage Images / Fine Art Images (tc). **95 Photo Scala, Florence:** The Jewish Museum / Art Resource / Szyk, Arthur. **96 Berlin, Staatsbibliothek zu Berlin - Pressischer Kulturbesitz - Handschriftenabteilung. 97 Alamy Stock Photo:** CPA Media Pte Ltd / Pictures From History (tc, br). **98–99 Alamy Stock Photo:** Art Collection 2 (b). **99 Alamy Stock Photo:** CPA Media Pte Ltd / Pictures From History (tr). **100 Alamy Stock Photo:** Art Collection 3. **101 123RF.com:** petervick167 (tc). **Getty Images:** Universal Images Group / Photo 12 (br). **102 Getty Images:** De Agostini. **103 © The Trustees of the British Museum. All rights reserved. Dreamstime.com:** Anna Om (br). **104–105 Alamy Stock Photo:** imageBROKER / Harald von Radebrecht. **106 Alamy Stock Photo:** agefotostock / Tolo Balaguer (bl); imageBROKER / Horst Mahr (t). **Getty Images / iStock:** E+ / stockcam (br). **Getty Images:** Universal Images Group / PHAS (bc). **107 akg-images. Alamy Stock Photo:** Reuters / Henry Romero (bl). **Getty Images:** Michael Ochs Archives / Earl Leaf (bc); NurPhoto / Eyepix (cla). **Francis McKee:** (br). **108 AF Fotografie. 110 Alamy Stock Photo:** North Wind Picture Archives (br). **Bridgeman Images:** © Brooklyn Museum of Art / Bequest of Mary T. Cockcroft (bl). **111 Alamy Stock Photo:** World History Archive (bl). **Instituto Moreira Salles:** (br). **112 Alamy Stock Photo:** Terry Allen (bl). **Powerhouse Museum / Museum of Applied Arts & Sciences:** Gift of The Asian Arts Society of Australia in memory of Mayo Harriss, 200 (tc). **113 Alamy Stock Photo:** Sabena Jane Blackbird. **114 Bridgeman Images:** © Brooklyn Museum of Art / Bequest of Mary T. Cockcroft. **115 Bridgeman Images. 116 Alamy Stock Photo:** Endless Travel (bl). **Dreamstime.com:** Viktor Bondar (br); Stevanzz (t); Nikolay Tsuguliev (bc). **117 Alamy Stock Photo:** Amani A (bc); UtCon Collection (bl). **Dreamstime.com:** Coplandj (tl). **Getty Images:** AFP / Patricia De Melo Moreira (cla). **Shutterstock.com:** Sipa / Jean Luc Petit (br). **118 Alamy Stock Photo:** Heritage Image Partnership Ltd / Ashmolean Museum of Art and Archaeology (tc); North Wind Picture Archives (br). **119 Courtesy National Gallery of Art, Washington. 120 Alamy Stock Photo:** Everett Collection Historical (tr); North Wind Picture Archives (bc). **121 Bridgeman Images:** © Archives Charmet. **122 Alamy Stock Photo:** Science History Images / Photo Researchers (bl). **Concordia University Records Management and Archives:** Jack Marlo (br). **Jody Freeman:** Cedar Eve. **Getty Images:** Universal Images Group / Universal History Archive (bc). **123 Bibliothèque et Archives nationales du Québec:** (cla); BAnQ Vieux-Montréal (bl). **Dreamstime.com:** Ronniechua (tl). **Festival du Monde Arabe:** Yakimo Bohio (br). **Getty Images:** George Rose (bc). **124 Alamy Stock Photo:** Sabena Jane Blackbird (br). **Dreamstime.com:** Derejeb (tc). **125 Leibniz-Institut für Länderkunde (IfL):** Collection Alphons Stübel / Alberto Henschel. **126 Bridgeman Images:** © Christie's Images / Agostino Brunias(Artist) (tr); © Royal Albert

Memorial Museum / Allan Ramsay(Artist) (br). **127 Instituto Moreira Salles:** Gilberto Ferrez Collection / Marc Ferez. **128–129 National Museum Of Denmark Besøg Nationalmuseets hjemmeside. 130 Alamy Stock Photo:** Album (bc); Frederic Reglain (t). **Colecao Museu Nacional de Belas Artes/PHAN/MinC:** (bl). **Getty Images:** Royal Geographical Society / F. Tuckett (br). **131 Alamy Stock Photo:** Realy Easy Star (bl); robertharding / Alex Robinson (tl). **Getty Images:** AFP / Vanderlei Almeida (br); LightRocket / Brazil Photos / Ricardo Beliel (cla). **New York State Archives:** (bc). **132–133 Alamy Stock Photo:** Album (b). **132 Alamy Stock Photo:** World History Archive (tc). **133 Alamy Stock Photo:** World History Archive (t). **134 Alamy Stock Photo:** Robertharding / Stuart Forster (tc). **135 Alamy Stock Photo:** Granger Historical Picture Archive, NYC (t); Signal Photos (b). **136 Alamy Stock Photo:** Heritage Image Partnership Ltd / The Print Collector (br); Peter Horree (tc). **137 Alamy Stock Photo:** BTEU / RKMLGE (t); CPA Media Pte Ltd / Pictures From History (bc). **138 Alamy Stock Photo:** V&A Images. **139 Los Angeles County Museum of Art:** Gift of Diandra and Michael Douglas (br). **140 Alamy Stock Photo:** North Wind Picture Archives (tc). **140–141 akg-images. 141 Bridgeman Images:** © CCI (tc). **142 Getty Images:** Oxford Science Archive / Hulton Archive / Print Collector (tc). **142–143 Getty Images:** Corbis Historical / Hulton Deutsch (b). **143 The J. Paul Getty Museum, Los Angeles:** Thomas Annan (t). **144–145 Alamy Stock Photo:** MeijiShowa. **146 Alamy Stock Photo:** Jon Arnold Images Ltd / Jane Sweeney (cla). **Bridgeman Images:** © London Metropolitan Archives (bc). **Getty Images:** Corbis Historical / Hulton Deutsch (tl); Science & Society Picture Library (bl); Hulton Archive / Fox Photos / Woolnough (br). **147 4Corners:** Lisa Linder (bl). **Alamy Stock Photo:** Nathaniel Noir (br). **Getty Images:** Anadolu Agency / Tolga Akmen (t); Mirrorpix / Daily Mirror (bc). **148 Rare Books and Special Collections, University of Sydney Library. 150 Alamy Stock Photo:** Chronicle (bl). **Getty Images:** Universal Images Group / Universal History Archive (br). **151 Nueva Vision Co. Ltd:** Francisco Hsu Chung Mao (br). **State Library of New South Wales:** (bl). **152 Alamy Stock Photo:** PWB Images (tc); SuperStock (br). **153 Getty Images:** Universal Images Group / Universal History Archive (t); Universal Images Group / Photo 12 (b). **154–155 State Library of New South Wales. 154 Sydney Living Museums:** (tc). **155 State Library of New South Wales. 156 Rare Books and Special Collections, University of Sydney Library. 157 Alamy Stock Photo:** Design Pics Inc / Hawaiian Legacy Archive / Pacific Stock (bc). **The New York Public Library:** The Miriam and Ira D. Wallach Division of Art, Prints and Photographs / Frank Coxhea (tr). **158 Alamy Stock Photo:** MediaServicesAP / Hugh Peterswald (cra); The Print Collector (bl). **Getty Images:** Mondadori Portfolio / Mario De Biasi (br). **Shutterstock.com:** marcobrivio.photo (bc); Michael Xiaos (tr). **159 Getty Images:** Fairfax Media Archives / Steve Christo (bc); Brook Mitchell (bl); Lisa Maree Williams (br). **Unsplash:** Photoholgic / @photoholgic (t). **160 Alamy Stock Photo:** Art Collection 3 (bl); Lebrecht Music & Arts (tc). **161 Getty Images:** Universal Images Group / Universal History Archive. **162 akg-images:** Africa Media Online / Iziko Museum (bl). **Alamy Stock Photo:** Chronicle (tc). **163 Alamy Stock Photo:** Chronicle. **164 Getty Images:** Anadolu Agency / Suryanto (tc); Corbis Historical / Hulton Deutsch (bl). **165 Nueva Vision Co. Ltd:** Francisco Hsu Chung Mao. **166 Chris Wolf Edmonds:** (tc). **167 Johnnie Diacon:** (t). **Oklahoma Historical Society:** (b). **168 Alamy Stock Photo:** Everett Collection Inc. **169 Alamy Stock Photo:** North Wind Picture Archives (br). **Getty Images:** Archive Photos / Nawrocki / ClassicStock (tc); Hulton Archive / General Photographic Agency (cl). **170–171 Alamy Stock Photo:** Granger Historical Picture Archive, NYC. **172 Museum of Fine Arts, Houston:** Museum purchase funded by the Buddy Taub Foundation, Dennis A. Roach and Jill Roach, Director (tc). **Photo Scala, Florence:** Smithsonian American Art Museum / Art Resource / William H. Johnson (br). **173 Getty Images:** Archive Photos / Cincinnati Museum Center (b). **Photo Scala, Florence:** Smithsonian American Art Museum / Art Resource / Newell, James Michael (t). **174 Alamy Stock Photo:** Contraband Collection (tc). **Getty Images:** Hulton Archive / Francis Guy / Sean Sexton (br). **175 Getty Images:** Hulton Archive / Edwin Levick. **176–177 Getty Images:** Universal Images Group / Universal History Archive. **176 Library and Archives Canada:** George F. Ridsdale collection / a12265 (bl). **177 Library of Congress, Washington, D.C.:** LC-DIG-nclc-04146 / Hine, Lewis Wickes (tc). **178–179 Getty Images:** Bettmann. **180 Alamy Stock Photo:** The Granger Collection (bl). **Sanna Dullaway:** Library of Congress (bc). **The New York Public Library:** The Miriam and Ira D. Wallach Division of Art, Prints and Photographs / Berenice Abbot (br). **Shutterstock.com:** NurPhoto / Deccio Serrano (t). **181 Alamy Stock Photo:** Artepics (tl). **Da Ping Luo:** (cla). **Getty Images:** Hulton Archive / BIPS (bc); Michael Ochs Archives (bl); LightRocket / Erik McGregor (br). **182–183 Getty Images:** Popperfoto / Paul Popper (b). **182 AF Fotografie. 183 Getty Images:** Hulton Archive / Archive Farms (cr). **184 Alamy Stock Photo:** Everett Collection Inc. **185 Alamy Stock Photo:** David Grossman (tc). **Getty Images:** Bettmann (br). **186 Alamy Stock Photo:** Historic Images (tc). **187 Dreamstime.com:** Pablo Hidalgo (tr). **Shutterstock.com:** The LIFE Picture Collection / John Phillips (b). **188 Alamy Stock Photo:** CPA Media Pte Ltd / Pictures From History (tc). **188–189 Alamy Stock Photo:** Everett Collection Historical (t). **189 Getty Images:** Bettmann (bc). **190 Alamy Stock Photo:** Chronicle (b); World History Archive (t). **191 Alamy Stock Photo:** CPA Media Pte Ltd / Pictures From History (tc). **192 Getty Images:** LightRocket / Gerhard Joren. **194 Bridgeman Images:** © Look and Learn (bl). **Getty Images:** Hulton Archive / Central Press (br). **195 Getty Images:** AFP / Dimitar Dilkoff (br); Corbis Historical / Gregory Smith (bl). **196 Alamy Stock Photo:** Shawshots (tc). **Getty Images:** Archive Photos / Buyenlarge (c). **197 Alamy Stock Photo:** North Wind Picture Archives (bc). **Bridgeman Images:** © Archives Charmet (r). **198 Getty Images:** Archive Photos / FPG / Paul Thompson (tc). **199 Alamy Stock Photo:** Scherl / Süddeutsche Zeitung Photo (tr). **Shutterstock.com:** The LIFE Picture Collection (b). **200–201 Getty Images:** Universal Images Group / Windmill Books / Robert Hunt. **201 Alamy Stock Photo:** CPA Media Pte Ltd / Pictures From History (tr). **202 Getty Images:** Archive Photos / Afro Newspaper / Gado (br). **Library of Congress, Washington, D.C.:** LC-USF33-020600-M3 / Delano, Jack (tc). **203 Bridgeman Images:** © Chicago History Museum / © Estate of Archibald John Motley Jr. All reserved rights 2021 (b). **Library of Congress, Washington, D.C.:** LC-DIG-fsa-8c02701 / Delano, Jack (t). **204 Getty Images:** Corbis Historical / Hulton Deutsch. **205 Bridgeman Images:** © Archives Charmet (tc). **The President Elpido Quirino Foundation:** (cr). **206 Getty Images:** Bettmann (tc); Bettmann (br). **207 Shutterstock.com:** The LIFE Picture Collection / J R Eyerman. **208 Bridgeman Images:** © Usis-Dite (b). **Getty Images:** Gamma-Keystone / Keystone-France (t). **209 Getty Images:** Corbis Historical / Library of Congress / Underwood & Underwood (br); Hulton Archive / Heritage Images / Fine Art Images (tc). **210 Bridgeman Images:** © Look and Learn (br). **Getty Images:** Gamma-Keystone / Keystone-France (tc). **211 Benaki Museum Athens:** Stephanos Xouzaios (b). **ICRC ARCHIVES (ARR) / International Committee of the Red Cross:** V-P-HIST-02493-14 (t). **212 Library of Congress, Washington, D.C.:** LC-DIG-fsa-8b29516 / Lange, Dorothea. **213 John Aster Archive:** (tc). **Getty Images:** ullstein bild Dtl. (br). **214 Getty Images:** Hulton Archive / Fred Ramage (tc). **214–215 Sanna Dullaway:** FPG / Hulton Archive / Getty Images (bc). **215 Getty Images:** Hulton Archive / Central Press (br). **216–217 Getty Images:** Gamma-Keystone / Keystone-France. **218 Getty Images:** Popperfoto (tc). **219 Bridgeman Images:** © Look and Learn (t). **Shutterstock.com:** The LIFE Picture Collection / Margaret Bourke-White (b). **220–221 Getty Images:** Universal Images Group / Photo 12. **221 Alamy Stock Photo:** Dinodia Photos (br). **V&A Images / Victoria and Albert Museum, London:** Image Copyright of the MF Husain Estate (t). **222 Getty Images:** STF / AFP (tc). **Shutterstock.com:** The LIFE Picture Collection / Cornell Capa (br). **223 Shutterstock.com:** The LIFE Picture Collection / Terence Spencer. **224 Getty Images:** Paris Match Archive / Jean-Claude Deutsch (br); Toronto Star / Colin McConnell (t). **225 Getty Images:** Hulton Archive / Ted West. **226 Alamy Stock Photo:** www.BibleLandPictures.com / Zev rad (br). **Amsterdam Museum:** (bl). **Bridgeman Images:** © Faisal Khouja (t). **Getty Images:** De Agostini / DEA / Biblioteca Ambrosiana (bc). **227 Alamy Stock Photo:** Jussi Puikkonen (bc); Reuters / Michael Kooren (tl). **Dreamstime.com:** Dennis Van De Water (cla). **Getty Images / iStock:** Sjo (bl). **Shutterstock.com:** Dutchmen Photography (br). **228 Getty Images:** Gamma-Keystone / Keystone-France. **229 Alamy Stock Photo:** UPI / Debbie Hill (br). **Shutterstock.com:** The LIFE Picture Collection / Dmitri Kessel (tc). **230 Getty Images:** AFP / Mohammed Abed (tc); Hulton Archive / Tom Stoddart Archive (br). **231 Getty Images:** Bettmann. **232 www.mediadrumworld.com:** Tom Marshall. **233 Getty Images:** Hulton Archive / Central Press (br); SSPL / Daily Herald Archive (tc). **234–235 Getty Images:** Hulton Archive / Fox Photos / William Vanderson. **236 Alamy Stock Photo:** Shawshots (tc). **Getty Images:** Corbis Historical / Hulton Deutsch (b). **237 Getty Images:** Fairfax Media Archives / Peter Kevin Solness (tr). **238 Getty Images:** UniversalImagesGroup (tc); UniversalImagesGroup (bl). **239 Getty Images:** LightRocket / Jonas Gratzer. **240 Getty Images:** Archive Photos / PhotoQuest. **241 Getty Images:** LightRocket / Gerhard Joren (br). **Shutterstock.com:** AP / Henri Huet (tc). **242 Getty Images:** Bettmann (br); Universal Images Group / Education Images (tc). **243 Getty Images:** Corbis Historical / Hulton Deutsch. **244 Getty Images:** Hulton Archive / Daily Express / P. Felix (b); Popperfoto / Rolls Press (t). **245 Getty Images:** Mirrorpix / Daily Mirror (tc). **246 Getty Images:** Anthony Lanzilote (br); Sygma / Alain Nogues (tc). **247 Getty Images:** Hulton Archive / Keystone (b); Sygma / Claude Salhani (t). **248 Dreamstime.com:** Sean Pavone. **249 Alamy Stock Photo:** Lou Linwei (tc); Top Photo Corporation (br). **250 Getty Images:** AFP / George Castellanos (tc). **251 Getty Images:** Corbis Historical / Gregory Smith (t); Sygma / John Giannini (b). **252 Alamy Stock Photo:** Chuck Nacke (t). **Getty Images:** Hulton Archive / Laski Diffusion (b). **253 Getty Images:** AFP / Dima Tanin (tc); AFP / Sven Nackstrand (bc). **254 Alamy Stock Photo:** Paul Brown (br). **Getty Images:** Stone / Buena Vista Images (tc). **255 Alamy Stock Photo:** Iain Masterton (t). **Getty Images:** Cavan Images (b). **256 Getty Images:** Sion Touhig. **257 Getty Images:** AFP / Marwan Naamani (bc); Gamma-Rapho / Michel Baret (tc). **258 Getty Images:** Hulton Archive / GraphicaArtis (tc); julief514 (br). **259 Alamy Stock Photo:** Steve Vidler (b); ZEN - Zaneta Razaite (t). **260 Getty Images:** AFP / Carlos Alonzo (br); TCYuen (tc). **261 Getty Images:** Oli Scarff. **262–263 Getty Images:** LightRocket / Jonas Gratzer. **264 Getty Images / iStock:** E+ / peeterv (tc). **264–265 Getty Images:** AFP / Jenny Vaughan (b). **265 Getty Images:** Corbis Historical / Howard Davies (tr). **266 Alamy Stock Photo:** Jeffrey Isaac Greenberg 20+ (tl). **Bridgeman Images:** © Look and Learn (bl). **Dreamstime.com:** Richtphoto Smile (bc). **Getty Images:** Anadolu Agency / Ihsaan Haffejee (cla); Royal Geographical Society (br). **267 Alamy Stock Photo:** Hemis.fr / Bertrand Rieger (t); imageBROKER / Peter Schickert (bl). **Getty Images:** Anadolu Agency / Ihsaan Haffejee (br). **Shutterstock.com:** EPA / Jon Hrusa (bc). **268 Alamy Stock Photo:** Reuters / Anwar Mirza (br). **Getty Images:** Hulton Archive / Construction Photography / Avalon / Adrian Greeman (tc). **269 Getty Images:** AFP / Karim Sahib (t); AFP / Prakash Mathema (bc). **270 Getty Images:** Anadolu Agency / Muhammed Said. **271 Getty Images:** AFP / Anwar Amro (tc); AFP / Bulent Kilic (br). **272 Getty Images:** AFP / Dimitar Dilkoff (tr); Joerg Koch (br). **273 Alamy Stock Photo:** Reuters / Thaier Al-Sudani. **274 Alamy Stock Photo:** Pacific Press Media Production Corp. / Piero Castellano (b). **Getty Images:** Barcroft Media / Joel Santos (t). **275 Getty Images:** Uriel Sinai (tc). **288 Shutterstock.com:** AP / Henri Huet (c).

All other images © Dorling Kindersley